# Aggressive Volleyball

# Aggressive Volleyball

## Pete Waite

Human Kinetics

**Library of Congress Cataloging-in-Publication Data**

Waite, Pete.
  Aggressive volleyball / Pete Waite.
    p. cm.
  Includes index.
  ISBN-13: 978-0-7360-7441-4 (soft cover)
  ISBN-10: 0-7360-7441-4 (soft cover)
  1. Volleyball--Training. 2. Volleyball--Coaching. 3. Volleyball--Psychological aspects.
4. Aggressiveness. I. Title.
  GV1015.5.T73W35 2009
  796.325--dc22

                                         2009004387

ISBN-10: 0-7360-7441-4 (print)          ISBN-10: 0-7360-8631-5 (Adobe PDF)
ISBN-13: 978-0-7360-7441-4 (print)      ISBN-13: 978-0-7360-8631-8 (Adobe PDF)

This publication is written and published to provide accurate and authoritative information relevant to the subject matter presented. It is published and sold with the understanding that the author and publisher are not engaged in rendering legal, medical, or other professional services by reason of their authorship or publication of this work. If medical or other expert assistance is required, the services of a competent professional person should be sought.

**Acquisitions Editor:** Laurel Plotzke; **Developmental Editor:** Amanda Eastin-Allen; **Assistant Editor:** Laura Podeschi; **Copyeditor:** Tom Tiller; **Proofreader:** Kathy Bennett; **Indexer:** Betty Frizzéll; **Graphic Designer:** Nancy Rasmus; **Graphic Artist:** Kim McFarland; **Cover Designer:** Keith Blomberg; **Photographer (cover):** ALEXANDER JOE/AFP/Getty Images; **Photographer (interior):** Neil Bernstein, unless otherwise noted; **Photo Asset Manager:** Laura Fitch; **Visual Production Assistant:** Joyce Brumfield; **Photo Production Manager:** Jason Allen; **Art Manager:** Kelly Hendren; **Associate Art Manager:** Alan L. Wilborn; **Illustrator:** Lineworks, Inc.; **Printer:** United Graphics

We thank the University of Wisconsin in Madison, Wisconsin, for assistance in providing the location for the photo shoot for this book.

Human Kinetics books are available at special discounts for bulk purchase. Special editions or book excerpts can also be created to specification. For details, contact the Special Sales Manager at Human Kinetics.

Printed in the United States of America          10  9  8  7  6  5  4  3  2  1

The paper in this book is certified under a sustainable forestry program.

**Human Kinetics**
Web site: www.HumanKinetics.com

*United States:* Human Kinetics
P.O. Box 5076
Champaign, IL 61825-5076
800-747-4457
e-mail: humank@hkusa.com

*Canada:* Human Kinetics
475 Devonshire Road Unit 100
Windsor, ON N8Y 2L5
800-465-7301 (in Canada only)
e-mail: info@hkcanada.com

*Europe:* Human Kinetics
107 Bradford Road
Stanningley
Leeds LS28 6AT, United Kingdom
+44 (0) 113 255 5665
e-mail: hk@hkeurope.com

*Australia:* Human Kinetics
57A Price Avenue
Lower Mitcham, South Australia 5062
08 8372 0999
e-mail: info@hkaustralia.com

*New Zealand:* Human Kinetics
Division of Sports Distributors NZ Ltd.
P.O. Box 300 226 Albany
North Shore City
Auckland
0064 9 448 1207
e-mail: info@humankinetics.co.nz

*Margie Fitzpatrick and Steve Lowe both coached at the University of Wisconsin before me. Both battled cancer and were taken from us too early. Their passion for the game and for their players continues to inspire me. They remind me to work hard but also to enjoy life.*

# Contents

# Preface

I wrote this book with the understanding that there are generally two types of volleyball. There is recreational volleyball, in which people are playing but not really training, either as individuals or as a team; good examples include pickup games in the backyard or swimming pool. Then there is competitive volleyball—what most people would consider "serious" volleyball. Those who play competitive volleyball include high school teams, club teams, college teams, and adult open teams. People who play recreational volleyball do it for the social benefits that the game has to offer. They play for fun and may not follow all of the rules or employ much strategy. Some folks may play aggressively in a pickup game, but they probably won't be very popular with the rest of the crowd. In contrast, people who play competitively love playing aggressive volleyball. They thrive on the intensity and emotion of the game, and they are usually training and practicing to raise the level of their game. In this arena, the most aggressive players are often the most successful, and in this book I focus on what it really means to play aggressive volleyball. Whether you are a player or a coach, this book offers you insight into how playing aggressive volleyball can take you and your team to the highest possible level.

Many teams practice with the aim of being champions. So what separates the teams at the top from those in the middle of the pack? How can some teams do the same drills yet be so different? All coaches and players want their team to play aggressive volleyball, but only a select few coaches have the vision and ability to make it happen. After 35 years of enjoying this sport as a player and coach in the high school, club, junior college, and Division I ranks, it's time to share what I've learned. I believe that this book—the first full volume I've written—will be helpful to people who coach volleyball players ranging from 13 years old to college age. In fact, anyone who plays volleyball will be able to absorb the concepts featured in *Aggressive Volleyball* and apply them directly to his or her own game.

As a teacher and coach, I know that people learn in various ways, and we have included a great variety of photos and diagrams to help you understand everything I'm talking about. If you are reading this book, it means that you are open to learning, and there is nothing more important for a player or a coach than the ability to expand one's base of knowledge. If you want to grow, you must be willing to step outside of your comfort zone and try new things. You have to be flexible and creative in order to be prepared for every challenge your team or your opponents may throw at you. While I've enjoyed every game I've won in my career, I know that I usually learn more from the losses. Whether you're a player or a coach, you have to reevaluate everything after a loss. You have to be open to changes and work hard to eliminate the weaknesses that your opponent was able to expose.

One of the most exciting aspects of writing this book has been the opportunity to realize how much I've learned from others. The players who create new shots amaze me. The coaches who squeeze the most out of their teams impress me. The teams and coaches who meet the stiff challenge of staying at the top of their conference year after year intrigue me. I enjoy analyzing players and teams to find the little things that give them the edge. Now it's time for me to pass on what I've come to know—that playing aggressive volleyball is at the core of building championship teams.

# Acknowledgments

I want to thank a number of people for helping get me to this point in my career. They have contributed to who I am, what I know, and how I coach. My parents, Gloria and Bill, have been phenomenally supportive all along the way. They helped me attend Ball State University so that I could play the game I love, and they often drove the 7 hours to watch me play. When I was coaching in Illinois, they drove 2 hours to watch most of the matches, no matter what the weather, and I was amazed by their support. I'm happy that I was able to come back home to work at the University of Wisconsin–Madison, where they have only a 15-minute drive to come watch my teams. It's nice to know they're close, and they've been there while I've gone full circle. My given name is William Peter Waite, yet I was called Peter from birth. My dad, like my grandfather, is named Bill (William), and my mom always told me, "William Peter Waite would look great when you write your first book." I never imagined writing a book, but, as always, Mom was right.

My wife Carrie and sons Ryan and Eric have been wonderful, and they have sacrificed the most for me. Carrie and I moved seven times in my first 8 years after college. Each move took me to a higher level of coaching and gave me the experience to earn the next job. Carrie was always supportive, even though she sometimes had to move away from very good friends. Ryan was born when I was coaching club volleyball in Chicago, and Eric was born when I was an assistant coach at Illinois State. Now Ryan is 25 and has graduated from the University of Wisconsin–Madison, and Eric, 21, is a junior at the University of Wisconsin–Oshkosh. During 23 years of college coaching, the boys have gone from sitting on my players' laps on the bus as toddlers to socializing with them as fellow college students. While the life of a coach can be fun, I have spent a lot of time in the gym and on the road. I really need to thank Carrie for doing so much while I was gone, and thank the boys for understanding when I couldn't be with them.

My coaches molded me as a player, and I learned so much from them. My high school coaches Janis Tupesis and Kurt Schneider did a great job of instilling a love of the game in me. Niels Pedersen, my Junior Olympic coach in Madison, gave me my first opportunity to coach volleyball full-time, with the 2nd City Volleyball Club in Chicago. Don Shondell, Jerry McManama, Scott Nelson, Russ Carney, and Denise Van De Walle all had a part in shaping who I was as a college player. I thank all of these coaches for sharing with me their time, effort, and passion for the game of volleyball. In addition, after coaching a wide variety of players over the course of 28 years, I apologize to my coaches if I was ever a pain in the butt. Of course, my memory is fading as I get older, so I don't remember anything I might've done wrong. That's the nice thing about aging—you mostly remember the good things.

This list of thank-yous suggests the process by which I became the coach and person I am today. There are so many other people I'd like to mention as well, but to do so would be impossible. My bosses and administrators over the years have given me the opportunity to hone my craft and learn as I go. Trainers, academic advisors, and facility managers have all had a hand in keeping our teams rolling. They've also been there as I've found that there is much more to coaching than just what you do in the gym. If you can handle the paperwork, parents, recruiting, and budget while remaining successful, *that's* impressive. Coaching is a tough job, and just when you think you've got the hang of it, some player issue comes along that you've never experienced before. Coaching also seems to be a job that everyone has an opinion about, even if they don't have the knowledge or experience to be an expert. I have a great deal of respect for anyone who has ever been a coach, especially when he or she is a good person who stays within the rules.

I want to thank my players, current and former, and colleagues for their help in creating this book. I am especially grateful to the models and players who helped to demonstrate the skills that you'll see pictured in this book. Taylor Braun, Erin Byrd, Brittney Dolgner, Jenelle Gabrielsen, Jill Odenthal, and Eli Sharping all did a great job.

I've also benefited from the people I've coached with and the players I've come up against. I've had many great assistants who have shared their knowledge and viewpoints and made me a better person and coach. They have all helped me strive for success while trying to balance professional and personal life. Players on opposing teams have always made me work to find ways for our team to slow them down, and the best ones set the bar ever higher. Russ Rose of Penn State once told me something about the greatest players in the Big Ten Conference: "They can only ruin my day eight times!" Now it's my turn to give back to the sport and give you some of my thoughts about the game. Whether you are a player or a coach, I hope you'll take some of these ideas and make them part of who you are—and who you will become.

# Key to Diagrams

| | |
|---|---|
| B | Blocker |
| C | Covering player |
| CO | Coach |
| D | Defender |
| H | Hitter |
| HA | Hander |
| L | Libero |
| LB | Left back |
| LF | Left front |
| MB | Middle back |
| MF | Middle front |
| P | Passer |
| RB | Right back |
| RF | Right front |
| S | Setter |
| SH | Shagger |
| SV | Server |
| T | Target |
| X | Player |
| _____ | Player movement |
| --------- | Ball movement |

Numbers indicate order of movement

# Understanding Aggressive Volleyball

*Aggressive play*. Taken separately, these two words can mean very different things, but put them together and you have an attitude and game style to strive for. Many people *play* volleyball, and they do so for a variety of reasons. They play for the exercise, the socializing, and the fun of a team-oriented game in which both young and old folks can participate. Then there are those who truly want to compete at the highest level possible. They are the ones who thrive on the competition and intensity that can be enjoyed when two aggressive teams collide. These coaches and players want to win—they want to be champions—but playing aggressive volleyball is an art in itself. It is a balance of skill and will that everyone strives for yet only a few truly understand. To develop and consistently execute this type of play, one must first understand the specific objectives and structure of aggressive volleyball. Doing so will guide you toward promoting the mentality and preparing the game plans that foster the aggressive style of play. This chapter defines aggressive play and explains how you and your team can benefit from using this style. I discuss how to get players to buy into this mind-set and how being *overly* aggressive can hurt your team more than help it. Whether you are a coach or a player, this chapter can help you understand the structure of—and the need for playing—aggressive volleyball.

## Characteristics of Aggressive Play

Certain characteristics are inherent to aggressive play, and these traits of players and coaches are practiced like any other skill in the sport. In order to determine whether your team is playing aggressive volleyball, you can make two lists for comparison. First, look at your team both as a member would and as an outsider would, and make a list of descriptive words that characterize the team. Think both about individual players and about the team as a whole. If the list includes words like *cautious, passive, error-prone, timid, quiet, nervous, hesitant, mindless,* and *disorganized*, then you will know that your team is not playing aggressive volleyball. Next, make a similar list that describes your favorite championship team in any sport. This list will most likely include words such as *intense, competitive, active, purposeful, thinking, assertive, confident,* and *organized*. These words suggest the goals of aggressive volleyball, and coaches and players alike must move intentionally toward the aggressive style if they want to be champions.

Playing aggressive volleyball requires mastery of certain skills—some physical, others mental or emotional. Physically, playing aggressive volleyball can mean jump-setting to speed up the offense rather than setting from the ground, or attacking a jump topspin or floater to put opponents on their heels rather than staying with a standing serve. Mentally, it means employing a serving strategy to disrupt the opponent's offense rather than just serving the ball into the court; it means playing volleyball like you would play a game of chess and knowing how to think two plays ahead. Emotionally, playing aggressive volleyball means knowing how to avoid the highs and lows that allow your opponent to score points in streaks; it means knowing how to deal confidently with the stress that the opponent or the crowd is putting on you and still play your best. Learning all of these skills of aggressive volleyball—physical, mental, and emotional—allows you and your team to come out winners in the big matches. When the game is tied 14-14 in the fifth set, you will come out on top more often than not. When you are down by 6, you will know how to come back, and when you're up by 5 near the end of the game, you will have the confidence to close the deal.

Here are 10 keys to playing aggressive volleyball:

1. Aggressive attitude
2. Correct techniques
3. Identical repetitions
4. Good offensive and defensive systems
5. Experience
6. Physical conditioning
7. Strong mental abilities
8. Emotional stability
9. Cohesiveness
10. Trust

These are the keys to earning success at the highest levels of any sport. The first and last items on the list—aggressive attitude and trust—were placed in their respective positions intentionally, because they are two of the most important and they allow the rest to happen. Without these two keys, you might field a good team, but not a great one. Anyone can coach these keys, and anyone can learn them, but it is important to understand that the process of change takes time. Both coaches and players need to be patient with themselves and with others as each week goes by. If steps along the way are skipped or patience is lost, the team may implode and experience a major setback. Patience, persistence, enthusiasm, and energy: Anyone can do it with the right tools.

Certain tendencies characterize any team that plays aggressively. These are the coaches and players who are always looking for the edge over their opponent. They intentionally take themselves out of their comfort zone in order to continually raise the bar and reach new heights. In training, they simulate situations that are carbon

Courtesy of University of Wisconsin Athletic Communications

The battle at the net is won by those not afraid to take risks and those unwilling to back down.

copies of the most difficult scenarios they may face in the course of the season. These teams are not afraid of trying new things to push the envelope and work their way through the learning curve.

Here is a common slogan used in advertising and motivational situations: "Attitude is everything." These words encapsulate the philosophy of aggressive volleyball. It's a mentality that focuses on being the best in every part of the sport, in everything that affects training and competition. Coaches and players work to absorb as much information as possible, then use that information to gain an advantage. When your team is serving, are players chatting with each other, waving to their friends, or not talking at all? Before they serve, they should be aggressively pursuing the edge that can win the next point. They should call out the hitters, know if the setter is front-row, and decide how they will pick up the next off-speed shot. They can look at the setter or coach to pick up the next play, or they can tell their own hitters what areas are open. These are just a few examples of what can and should be done in that short period of time. If your players are not doing this sort of thing, then they are falling behind teams who are. With every point gained by outsmarting an opponent, you will see your team's attitude strengthen and passion grow.

The only downside of this attitude is the possibility that players will make more errors because of their aggressive play. If coaches and players are willing to accept the fact that errors are part of the game and part of the process, they will gradually work toward their ultimate goal. The old theory of "two steps forward and one step back" definitely applies to aggressive volleyball. As long as everyone learns from mistakes, they can continue to climb the ladder step by step, and adopting a more aggressive style of play will be well worth it.

Just as aggressive play brings eventual rewards, it also involves some definite risks, and they are related to the specific skills needed to play aggressively. Physically, players risk injury on defense when they swarm the court to pursue a ball. Some people consider "contact sports" to be those in which you collide with your opponent, but aggressive play in volleyball can involve contact with teammates, the chairs on the bench, and the floor itself. Mentally, players must risk being tested and challenged to use their brain as much as their body in order to win. If you are outmatched physically, can you still outwit the opponent? You might even risk making the wrong decision about who to set or what set to make because you think the more aggressive set would be best. Emotionally, the risk comes from teammates, coaches, and opponents. Aggressive players and coaches can be more vocal, which often means they will be more demanding of team members. To yell at players or push them too far out of their comfort zone risks prompting them to check out emotionally and curl up within themselves. When opponents raise their emotional level in a match, you want your team to rise to the occasion and thrive in an intense environment, yet both in practices and in matches there is a fine line between pushing players to be better and having them take offense to a comment and give up the fight.

One way to see examples of aggressive volleyball in action is to watch high-level college or professional teams. This is, in fact, a great way for younger players to learn the style. After watching a match, players can make a list of key observations, then use the list to set their goals for future practices and matches. The aggressive play of great teams can be seen in many forms. In most people's minds, it's the obvious—the players who get the loudest, hit the hardest, fly after balls defensively, and bring the most intensity. But aggressive volleyball can also be seen in other manifestations. It might be the soft, short serve intentionally placed to clog up the offense of the opposition's top hitter. Maybe it's a blocking system that risks leaving a weaker hitter alone in order to double up on the top threat. Or perhaps the block will involve intentionally taking the line in order to channel the hitter to the phenomenal defenders waiting crosscourt. One of the most common examples is the hitter who is given a bad set. The cautious option is to tip or roll the ball over the net in order to avoid making an error. The aggressive option, however, is to do everything possible to get to the ball while it's above the net and take an aggressive swing. Is it a risk? Yes, but teams and players who consistently make aggressive plays learn that good things happen when they play with an aggressive mind-set and intent.

The rewards are why we take the risks, since taking risks is the only way to get to the top. The rewards are, in fact, unlimited, and they are both personal and team oriented: the ace, the critical dig, the monster block, the perfect pass, the backbreaking kill, the quiet player who finally talks, the new skill finally learned, the confused sub who blossoms into a confident player, and the team chemistry that emerges from a group of individuals. The rewards continue to build on themselves as each team member grows to understand the philosophy and the intent of playing aggressive volleyball. The ultimate rewards are the wins and the championships, but along the way the small rewards can be among the most satisfying.

## A Tip From the Top

We were playing Colorado State for the Mountain West Conference Championship on our home court. It was senior night, the arena was full, and everything was in place for us to win that day. Nonetheless, we started out horribly and lost the first set, and we were down 21-19 in the second set when my starting right side went down with a bad ankle sprain. I knew that if we went down two sets to none we would be in trouble against a very good CSU team. I walked down my bench to put in a sub and stopped at my back-up right side, a 6-foot-6-inch (2 meter) redshirt freshman who had played in only three matches all season. I looked at her and said, "Jen, are you ready?" She said yes, but she knew, as did the rest of the team and everyone else in the gym, that this was going to be a tough situation. I called a time-out and told the team, "We can do this." The players looked at each other, and someone said, "Let's everyone step up and get this done." I told my setter to get Jen some sets in good situations and she would get it done for us. We won the second set 29-27 after being down 22-24, then went on to win the match in four sets. Jen had three kills and two blocks. She did her job, and the team rallied around her and responded to the challenge. I believe that performance in adversity shows the true character of an individual and a team. We had an amazing season because of the strong character the players showed on that night and at many other times throughout the year.

—Beth Launiere, Head Women's Coach, University of Utah

# Promoting the Aggressive Style With Players

Coaches can introduce the concept of aggressive volleyball to players by placing it front and center in team meetings, practices, and games. Every program should have a handbook that spells out the philosophy and mentality that will be used to pursue the team's goals. If the program is to succeed, coaches must instill a degree of discipline in every aspect of the athletes' lives. The team must buy into an aggressive style similar to that used by people in successful businesses. The following sections discuss the cycle of aggressive play, as well as how and when to cultivate an aggressive mind-set in your team.

## Cycle of Aggressive Play

A team that plays aggressively and plays with desire will win many matches. Even better, they'll have fun in the process and become hungry to do it all the time. Thus, it's a positive cycle that feeds off itself once you get it started.

It all starts with the vision. Once everyone understands the vision for the team and for individual roles, there is a path to follow. The aggressive mind-set can then be nurtured in team meetings, practices, and games. For the mind-set to really take hold, you need to find ways to make practices exciting, challenging, and fun. (Yes, even college teams need to enjoy what they're doing, or it becomes a burden.) This excitement and love of the game creates an eagerness to meet every challenge. Once players are hungry to play, the team experiences more success and wins more games, which in turn increases the desire to compete and play with a passion. And when players play with passion and emotion, they have more invested in what they are doing. In short, with passion and emotion comes ownership, and ownership brings more effort. The positive and aggressive play grows, creating an upward spiral that continues to take your team to higher levels. The cycle goes full circle. Players naturally play with an aggressive mind-set because it brings so many positive feelings and results. They win more games, enjoy it more, and realize that their aggressive play is making good things happen. They continue to fight to get that great feeling again and again. As soon as the team can complete the cycle a few times, an aggressive attitude and playing style will be the norm. Players will continue to develop naturally with the hunger and desire that promotes better play and positive results.

Now that I've described the cycle in full, let's break it down into individual stages. If you follow each step of the process to begin raising the bar, you will begin to improve the mind-set of your team.

**Understand and develop a vision of playing aggressively.**    The first stage of the cycle involves introducing the vision. Everyone needs to be on the same page in terms of understanding the aggressive playing style. From the first team meeting, you should help your players develop an understanding of how aggressive play works (the characteristics and tendencies) and why it is the preferred style of play (the benefits). As the season progresses, player and team assessment will determine how aggressive play can best be used within the team's capabilities. The vision then gets redefined as players cycle through the aggressive play process. The vision should become sharper or more specific in terms of team goals, individual roles, and the plan for achieving the vision. See chapter 2 for guidance on how to adapt the aggressive style based on player and team assessment.

**Define and develop a focused and aggressive mind-set.**   The desired mind-set is first defined in terms of the thought processes communicated to staff and players. The mind-set may even take written form as a statement of program philosophy or governing values. In any case, it will dictate how coaches plan to progress through each week of the season. These thought processes are then further solidified through drills that prompt the players to respond as desired. Thus, players who were once considered mindless or spacey will have the tools to begin improving their mind-set. When these thought processes become part of the game plan, the cycle is almost complete. With all players on the team connected mentally, they will be able to move together in the desired direction.

**Create and practice aggressive play tactics.**   Both players and coaches can bring forward ideas for simulating match conditions and allowing the team to practice aggressive skills and techniques. Asking players to be creative fosters new ideas and gives them ownership in the overall plan. One or two creative wrinkles can be the key to winning a match.

**Set challenging and fun goals for executing aggressive plays.**   Use drills that spark players to dig deeper than they could imagine, and give them challenging goals that they will enjoy achieving. Players who can figure out how to beat a drill tend to jell into a team that loves finding ways to beat an opponent. Ask them to reach higher numbers or complete tasks in less time. Create an urgency to win within your players so they'll defeat the opponent as efficiently and convincingly as possible.

**Play with an aggressive attitude and game plan during matches.**   Match time is go time. Every part of the match needs to be approached with an aggressive attitude and played with a strategic game plan. Matches are the time for players to use what they have learned in practice—to play hard, play with a purpose, and play with a passion. This is not a time to be cautious. It's a time to test the limits of aggressive play within each individual and the team as a whole. It's a time to play hard and have fun for love of the sport. Even players on the bench are critical to the team's success. It's important for them to stay tuned in and support the players on the court. Helping call balls in or out, staying positive, and paying attention can all help the team win. Coaches also need players who can come off the bench and raise the level of play or get the team out of a jam. Coaches love players who are ready at a moment's notice to go in and prove themselves.

**Evaluate and recognize improvement and success within the team.**   Players and coaches should evaluate the results of their aggressive play after each match. Effective evaluation involves both statistical data and subjective opinion. *The most important part is to recognize improvement and success within the team.* Even if the match was lost, you can recognize the small victories that showed progress in the effort to develop more aggressive play. To dwell on the loss takes the focus off the long-term goal, which is to be more aggressive as a team. Improving personal numbers can explain a lot. A good passer will have numbers in the 2.2 to 2.4 range on a 3-point scale. Strong middles will hit percentages in the .300s, and outsides will be in the .220 to .240 hitting range; right sides may even be a little higher than that. Defenders should aim for two to four digs per game, and aces should prevail two to one over errors. As long as a player individually improves his or her statistics (no matter how low he or she starts), the team will become stronger. Progress must be acknowledged by coaches and players alike so that everyone knows their efforts have been worthwhile. When everyone sees that progress is being made, they will buy into the plan and be more eager to get back in the gym for practice. As soon as the athletes realize that more aggressive talking, thinking, and playing pays off, they will bring a new passion to everything they do.

**Go back to the vision and set your sights on the next level.**    Recognize the positives and build on them. Look at the negatives as areas of weakness where the team needs to grow stronger. Maintain the vision of aggressive play from day to day and week to week as the season continues. Sometimes improvement will seem slow; at other times, it will be dramatic. Eventually, the cycle will feed off itself, and the team's energy will become more positive and aggressive.

## Maximize Coaching Opportunities

Several specific situations provide key opportunities to define and develop the appropriate mind-set for playing aggressive volleyball. These opportunities are often overlooked by teams as they rank priorities and how they affect the outcome of a match. The best coaches, however, do a great job of utilizing every team contact they have in order to help athletes achieve the right frame of mind for the match.

**Team Meetings**    Certain characteristics define a team meeting that cultivates focus and the aggressive mind-set. The tone you set in your first meeting will carry over to all future meetings. When athletes walk into the room, they should show proper respect for the situation. As the meeting begins, they need to stop talking, focus on the speaker, and give him or her their full attention. (It's good to have a no-cell-phone policy during all team functions.) The players should always look the speaker in the eye and indicate that they understand the information being shared. The atmosphere in team meetings is a good indicator of what your team will be like in a time-out during a game. If players pay attention and are engaged during team meetings, they will likely listen to the game plan during a time-out. If, on the other hand, meetings are disorganized and chaotic, then you can expect time-outs to be the same way.

Playing aggressive volleyball isn't just about what you do on the court; it's a mentality that can also eliminate distractions off the court. It's important for your players to be active listeners at all times—to be people who listen and ask questions if they don't understand. Coaches are always talking about how critical it is for everyone to be of one mind. This is where it starts—in every team meeting. Players should know how listening in meetings is related to listening during a time-out. When the game is tied at 23, they will want to come right out of the time-out and score, but that can happen only if they respect what the coaches are doing for them and take ownership in the process. You can ask players questions during meetings to help them understand the major points they'll need to remember when they leave the room. Many coaches talk so much that players lose their concentration and disengage from the group. Players must stay focused during meetings so that everyone will be on the same page.

**Time-Outs**   Each time-out offers the team an opportunity for players to rest, gather their thoughts, and prepare a plan. You can take specific steps to conduct constructive time-outs that cultivate focus and encourage the aggressive mind-set. The top teams usually conduct their time-outs in a calm, assertive, organized fashion. Their players have been taught to look the coaches in the eye and refuse to be distracted. It's also helpful if players give the coach a nod to acknowledge they have heard and understood what was said. In the best atmosphere, players feel comfortable enough to contribute through information, motivation, or inspiration; these are players who have become strong personalities and can help lead the team in the toughest of times. Even so, the teams who really struggle are those with no leadership coming from their coach. During time-outs, players are looking for guidance and confidence, and coaches must convince them that playing aggressive volleyball gives them a shot at beating anyone. If they take aggressive swings, chances are that good things will happen. The time-out is a critical part of every game, and the best coaches know how to maximize that time together. They know when to calm their players and when to crank up the intensity. The team has to come out of the time-out with great focus so that the players can continue their momentum—or grab it away from the other team.

**Off the Court**   In order for your team to use an aggressive mind-set on the court, it is important that the players also take an aggressive attitude toward everything they do off the court. In some areas of life, aggressiveness may be viewed more as assertiveness. If players are forward-thinking in their lives outside the gym, it will carry over to what they do in the gym. Pursuing a championship takes total focus on one's opponents, and your team's off-court distractions can ruin your season.

An athlete who pays attention in class will know how to employ that same mind-set during team activities. Players should learn how to attack an assignment in class like they attack a drill in practice—view it, analyze it, and then put the necessary effort into solving it. If they lack attention skills in class, they may also fail to pay attention to the coach at critical times. Players should attack their homework and get the most out of their abilities. Taking mental or written notes in class is similar to making notes on an opponent's tendencies. In the classroom, there is always something going on that students should be paying attention to, and it's exactly the same on the court. There is always something going on that players can absorb and use to help them win. Set academic goals and expect each player to improve his or her grades; poor grades cause stress for the player, the team, and the staff.

It's the same with players' social lives. Some kids are inclined or brought up to avoid problems that can derail them. Others seem drawn to trouble. Being socially forward-thinking and assertive means the player should steer clear of social circles that can be detrimental to his or her role on the team and life overall. Players must aggressively and intentionally avoid situations that can take them down. If the staff and team constantly have to deal with distractions within the program, it is hard to focus on moving forward as a team. The vision you have for your team to play aggressive volleyball and win championships cannot be realized if players are lost to academic probation or if their friends or family distract them severely. Take an aggressive attitude and aim to take care of responsibilities. This approach makes playing on the court much easier.

## Managing Aggressive Play

This discussion has been concerned largely with how to take a team to a higher level by creating a certain atmosphere, focusing more effectively, and developing an environment that promotes aggressive play. As a coach guides a team toward that championship level, however, it is important not to rush it or take shortcuts. If players are asked to be ultra aggressive at the wrong times, the rhythm of the game will be lost. In the era of rally scoring, you have to have a good understanding of how much to risk in light of what you could lose in the process.

Every skill in the sport can be analyzed and broken down to see where your team is gaining or losing points. Rally scoring makes it clearer because every one of your errors results in a point for the opposition. The best coaches not only find ways for their team to score points, but also work hard to minimize instances when their team gives points away to the opponent. Here are a few skill areas in which overaggressive play can lose matches for you:

• Serving errors exceed aces. Some players really get back and crank on the ball regardless of whether they are jump-serving or staying on the ground. While their aces are exciting, you can't tolerate too many errors. It's simple math. If the bad outweighs the good, the player should dial it down a notch to get the ball in more often. The other option is to use a more reliable type of serve.

• Passing errors can result if one player is too aggressive in going for serves out of his or her assigned zone. Each passer should be given a specific zone or area of responsibility. Unfortunately, some players don't trust their teammates and thus move well out of their zone to play a ball. This type of overly aggressive play can result in a passing error or in other passing problems in the future. The player whose zone was encroached upon will likely become more passive about taking the ball. He or she will flinch a bit upon sensing that a teammate is coming over to take the ball. Each time this happens, the team is burdened with a higher risk that on an upcoming point the ball will just drop, as the person who usually takes everyone else's balls suddenly decides to let them have one when they are no longer ready. If a three-person passing formation is used, the court doesn't have to be split into equal thirds. The best passer can take up to half of the court while the other two share the remaining half. As long as boundaries are established, you can make good use of the skills of the overly aggressive passer.

• Setters can be overly aggressive and lose points when they force things. The problem can be as simple as forcing the back set when the setter is really out of position on the left side of the court; players have to use great footwork and technique to execute that play without a mishandle being called. Trouble can also arise when players try to force the quick attack in the wrong situation or when they really don't have the skills to accomplish it. Opposing teams and coaches like nothing more than getting a free point from a mishandle or a miscue.

• Overaggressive blocking is a common mistake. Blockers big and small often try too hard to block every ball. Blocking is one of the most difficult skills because of the proximity to the net. The blocker has

Attacking aggressively makes good things happen. Passive play leads to errors.

to be very disciplined in order to resist the temptation to swat at the ball. This is a skill that many coaches overlook, yet their teams give up a lot of points because they get called for being in the net.

What coach hasn't said to his or her team, "Come on! We need to pick it up and be more aggressive!" Yet coaches need to be careful in choosing when to say it. There is an optimal level of aggressive play, and it is the coach's challenge to teach the team how to maximize it and how to sustain it. Along the way, coaches must keep a keen eye on every aspect of the program—on the athletes' individual skills and on their team play. Coaches are always testing athletes to get them ready for competition, and they are continually trying to raise their level of play. It's very common for coaches and players to make mistakes during the course of a season, so it is essential to develop an equal amount of trust, understanding, patience, and commitment on both sides. Whatever tactics, techniques, or methods are used, it's important that they are producing good *results*. That is the key word to use when evaluating a coach, a staff, or a team. Is what we are doing getting the *results* we want? If not, it's time to be creative and find a new way to get there. Be flexible, be patient, and be creative. That's a good motto for player and coach alike.

# 2

# Player and Team Assessment

From the first day of practice, players want to know how they compare with their teammates. In individual sports (e.g., swimming or track), athletes who are not in the top spot still get to participate. In volleyball, however, a team may include 12 to 15 players, but only 8 or 9 get to play in matches. Volleyball coaches need to determine which players will form the best lineup every time they get ready for a match. They also have to evaluate how their team compares with the competition from the first match of the season through the last. Thus, talent assessment is one of the many jobs a coach must do on a daily basis throughout the season in order to implement an aggressive volleyball program.

Coaches can gather information through various forms of assessment to develop practices and create lineups. Each practice provides an opportunity to strengthen the weaknesses of each player and mold the team into a unit that works as one. If your goal is to get your team to play aggressive volleyball, then it is imperative to use all available means to gather information about your team. In this chapter, you'll learn ways to assess both individual players and your team as a whole. You'll also read about assessing by position and by roles played on the team. Your team must understand your expectations and the standards they need to reach in order to raise their game to the next level. In this way, players and coaches can take hold of the process and share in the vision of playing volleyball aggressively.

## Player Assessment

Every time the players are on the court, coaches have the opportunity to assess their skills and progress. Coaches should make mental notes during practices and matches to compare players and their contributions to the team. It is often an easy call to select the best and most valuable player to the team, but deciding who is the last player in the lineup or the first off the bench can be the toughest—and may be even more critical to the outcome of the match. Who is the best player? Who is the best athlete? Are these the same questions? No. The best player is the one who plays the best volleyball. This person may not be a great athlete, but he or she is well trained, has a good court IQ, and consistently brings the skills needed to win. The best athlete, on the other hand, is usually the quickest, the most agile, and probably the highest jumping. He or she can take over a match physically and literally rise above the rest. You need both the great players and the great athletes to win at the highest levels.

In order to separate one player from another and select effective lineups, a coach must of course assess the abilities of individual players. Of the various tools available for this purpose, the most commonly used is simply the watchful eye of the coaching staff. Most of the best coaches have experienced so many different situations during their careers that they know how to make the right adjustments to help individual players and the whole team improve. Beyond their subjective opinions, coaches also use other tools to test, confirm, and clarify their thoughts. As with players, some coaches learn better through visual means, whereas others are excellent with numbers. Here are some of the categories that should be addressed in assessing individual players.

## *Physical*

Individual players should be assessed in the areas of vertical jump, strength, speed, and fitness and body composition. Each of these components plays a part in a player's success on the court. Vertical jump is a good indicator of a player's explosive potential, which can be seen in how far he or she gets off the ground at the net, as well as how well he or she covers the backcourt. Strength is also important. Without it, players fade as long matches intensify, and their skills disintegrate. Speed pays off in transition footwork, defensive moves, and arm swings that generate more power. Finally, players must be fit in order to sustain long rallies and be free of the mental distractions caused by a body that cannot keep up. With these components in place, your team has a much better shot at competing with anyone in the conference.

**Vertical Jump**    One of the most telling tests related to excellence in volleyball is the approach vertical jump. It's important to know if a player can transfer forward speed into upward momentum, and the criterion that college coaches use most for front-row players is the top reach from a spike approach, which indicates how far above the net a player can play. If a player can hit over people or put up a huge block, then he or she has the ability to wreak havoc on opponents. Conversely, if a player can get only the wrists above the net when blocking, that player could represent a weak spot on the court.

Some players have extremely long arms, which can be a real bonus in net play. For those who must rely on a very good vertical jump, good flexibility is known to be a factor. Some players are born with this capability, and others can improve their vertical jump by working to become more flexible. Very few players, however, make huge improvements in their vertical jump even after extensive training. The average improvement that I've encountered is 2 to 3 inches (about 5 to 7.5 centimeters), even with the benefit of college strength programs. Some of the biggest improvements in jumps have been made after correcting approach speed and coordinating the timing of arm swing and foot plant. It is still very important, whether the athlete is in high school or college, to do plyometrics and work on jumping and landing techniques.

Playing high above the net puts stress on the opposing players and forces them to change their tactics. Coaches always notice the great vertical jumps.

The vertical jump may improve a bit, but the most noticeable benefit is that the player will be able to jump to his or her maximum height many more times before tiring.

When testing vertical jumps, the Vertec tool can give precise measurements. The Vertec is freestanding, which allows athletes to take a full approach (devices attached to a wall tend to be more limiting). To conduct testing, allow each athlete to continue jumping as long as he or she keeps improving the score. Once a player misses three attempts in a row, he or she is usually done, and the jump starts fading. To figure vertical jump from the ground up, subtract the player's standing reach from the best approach jump during the test. The measurement from the ground up is not as valuable to volleyball coaches, but strength coaches sometimes prefer to chart progress in those terms. In making lineup decisions, however, it is very helpful to know how high a player can play *above the net*. For example, if a player can't get his or her hands over the net, then he or she may prove most valuable in the backcourt positions. A player who can jump-touch higher than anyone on the team is worth investing in even if he or she is raw and can't yet play at a high skill level. Such a player will usually be the kind who comes on late but eventually dominates the competition.

**Strength**    Very few volleyball players work on improving body strength during high school, but those who do gain a definite advantage. Once a player begins regular strength training (a minimum of 3 days per week throughout the year), it takes 8 to 12 months to see considerable change in his or her body and on the court. Players who lift for a month or two and stop will lose anything they gained within 2 weeks of stopping. Players should not focus on lifting to get big—volleyball players need to stay quick and agile—but improving core body strength helps prevent chronic injuries and allows them to move more easily on the court. Defensive players will more easily make low moves, blockers will be stronger against powerful hitters, and attackers will bring more dynamic hits. Areas to pinpoint include the abdominals, the back and shoulders, and the hamstrings and quadriceps.

Strength assessment can be done with very little equipment, so every program has the ability to do this. Leg strength can be tested with the vertical jump, as explained previously. The explosiveness that is measured in inches correlates to attacking, blocking, setting, and defensive moves. Lower-body strength is needed for hitters to get to balls, blockers to explode off the ground, setters to use their legs to jump-set, and passers and defenders to surround the ball. Core body strength can be tested using sit-ups, push-ups, and the medicine ball throw. Testing maximum sit-ups in 1 minute will gauge abdominal strength, while testing maximum push-ups in 1 minute will gauge chest strength. Abdominal strength is needed for every attack and block during play. Abdominal injuries are some of the slowest to heal, so improving abdominal strength is vital. Push-ups demonstrate a combination of abdominal strength, back and shoulder strength, and chest strength. Chest strength is needed for blocking, setting, and getting up from the floor after a defensive move. The medicine ball toss is done from the knees with a two-handed overhead throw for distance. It gauges the upper-body strength of the core muscles along with the speed as they work in combination. More complicated tests can be done to gauge a player's strength, but these will usually tell a coach who the strongest members of the team are as it relates to volleyball.

**Speed**    Some players are naturally fast and quick, and others can make improvements with speed training. Because the volleyball court is relatively small, quickness is an important part of the game. Quick players can move aggressively to a bad set on offense or an off-speed shot on defense. A middle blocker with quick feet can move laterally to block in either direction, and a fast setter can run down bad passes. Slower players, in contrast, may fail to get to the ball soon enough or may be generally unable to keep up with the opposition or the pace of a high-level match.

The two most important types of speed for volleyball are foot speed and arm speed. Foot speed can be assessed in any type of shuttle drill on the volleyball court. Keep the duration of the test the same as or shorter than the length of a normal rally; if you make the test too long, it will be an endurance drill rather than a speed test. To conduct the test, position cones at four or five spots on the court and tell players what pattern to follow. A star pattern with the cones located about 3.3 yards (3 meters) apart allows players to demonstrate speed and quickness.

Foot speed is important in volleyball because there are so many times players must change direction. If their feet are slow, they will have trouble every time they stop and must get going again. A player with good foot speed is considered quick and able to play the game at a fast pace. Quickness can be improved through ladder drills or movement training on the court. One way to perform movement training is to do high repetitions of blocking footwork or passing shuffle patterns. The keys to becoming quicker are moving efficiently and being light off the ground. You can learn some great training exercises for foot speed by asking your top local soccer coach. Soccer players live and breathe foot speed, and their drills can be adapted to help volleyball players. Having said all this, I will offer the following caveat: Some of my best defenders have not been blessed with quickness. Some players are able to compensate with a great work ethic and an ability to read and anticipate situations. Don't abruptly cut or give up on a player who doesn't win the speed and agility drills. Make sure you give them a chance to show their volleyball skills in game situations before making a decision. Speed and agility drills are simply a tool to help assess players' physical traits. They don't tell you everything about mental and emotional gifts.

Arm speed is more difficult to test, and much of its evaluation will be subjective. One simple way to determine arm speed is to have players partner up and stand about 10 yards (9 meters) apart. Initially, have them throw the ball back and forth while you observe their body movement, which should look just like that of a baseball outfielder. Here are some keys to watch for:

- Stepping with the opposite foot. For example, a player who steps with the right foot while throwing with the right arm will have trouble generating arm speed.
- Hips and shoulders opening up. If the hips and shoulders stay square to the partner, the player will generate no power.
- Opposite arm up. As a player draws the throwing arm back, the opposite arm should be up high in front of the body.
- Finish. As a player throws, the sequence (once the arm has been drawn back) should be as follows: Step with the opposite foot, close the hips, close and rotate the shoulders, draw the opposite arm back toward the body, and follow through to the target.

You can progress to having players self-toss and hit to their partner; again, the sequence should look very similar to that of a baseball player. If hitters are missing a part of this sequence, they won't generate the speed and power they are capable of. This problem is not as uncommon as you might think. Since so many athletes these days play only one sport, some have never learned the right throwing motion. I've had high school All-Americans enter my program without the knowledge or skills to functionally throw a ball correctly. With practice, however, all players can learn to use their entire body better, and the results will show up in their serving and attacking power.

Arm speed can also be seen in hitting drills. Some players have trouble bringing their arm through; others have a natural whip. Arm speed can be improved by throwing tennis balls and loosening up the arm. Each hitter should hold a tennis ball in his or her throwing hand and go through a normal approach at the net. After jumping, the player should reach above the net and snap his or her wrist down toward the opposing court, releasing the ball at the highest point he or she can reach. High repetitions of this drill will help speed up the arm since the player is dealing with a much smaller ball than a volleyball. Making the drawback motion more compact allows the arm to move faster and become more of a whip. To do this, a player should have his or her elbow bent as he or she draws it back and then lead with the elbow as he or she throws. A straight arm moves slower than a bent arm, so more bend means more speed. Another approach is to have players stand at the end of the gym and throw volleyballs as fast and far as they can. Some players with slow arms try to compensate by using their shoulders to initiate the arm swing. This puts a great deal of stress on the shoulder, and over time they will develop shoulder problems. A fast arm brings more speed to the ball on contact, and that becomes a harder hit. Improving arm speed will increase the velocity of attacks and take pressure off the shoulder joint. Some players are born with great natural arm speed, and coaches should be careful not to change a motion just to make it look a certain way. But if the arms are slow, you can help them become more functional, and the results can be dramatic and exciting.

**Fitness and Body Composition**   If your players are not fit, they will fade at the end of long or intense matches. They will not have the lung capacity to sustain long rallies, and their performance of skills will decline dramatically. Playing volleyball will not, in and of itself, keep your players in proper shape. Because of the constant rest time between plays, volleyball is not an aerobic activity, and, if a player takes in more calories than he or she burns, it is even possible to gain weight over the course of the season.

The smartest way to maintain good body composition is to eat well—that is, to avoid overeating or eating late at night and to begin eating healthy foods. Limiting sugary foods and drinks (e.g., soda, candy, dessert, and white bread) can help considerably. An occasional treat is not bad if the athlete regularly does a good job of eating the right foods. Society moves at such a fast pace these days that people rarely take time to eat well, but athletes should not skip meals because they feel too busy to eat; they need nutrients before they practice and play. Breakfast is extremely important and should be the start of every athlete's day. Eating correctly gives players the brain and body energy they need in the late stages of a long match. There is no room in sport for disordered eating, but discipline and good decision making about food can make a huge difference in a player's game. Poor nutrition and fitness can lead to illness and injury. Your body is like a car: If you put sludge in the tank, the car won't perform well. Prioritize fitness and good body composition so you can play at the highest level.

**Technical Skill**   Assessing a team's technical skill level requires a knowledgeable coach. The benefits of doing so are clear. If you identify which skills are subpar in individual players, you can design practice plans to help them improve in those areas. It's important that either the head coach or an assistant coach knows how to teach each skill; otherwise, a skill area can become a weakness for the team. Each skill should be evaluated separately because individual skills form the basis for team success. The following list identifies the technical areas in which your team must be strong; many of them involve good footwork, which is one of the core concepts of aggressive volleyball.

- Approach footwork: Begin slow, finish fast and dynamic.
- Arm swings: Make them fast, strong, and intentional.
- Efficient shuffle (passing): Use a wide base and forward posture.
- Passing technique and location: Make compact movements to achieve good results.
- Floor moves (e.g., single- and double-knee drops, rolls, pancakes): Be comfortable with making good plays while going to the floor.
- Setting footwork patterns: Be quick and efficient.
- Setting technique and location: Achieve good, consistent results.
- Blocking footwork: Use quick feet and good balance.
- Blocking hand positioning: Use high, strong hands with fingers spread.
- Blocking setup positioning: Use proper eye sequencing from setter to hitter.
- Service arm swing and hand contact: Use an open chest and a strong hand.
- Defensive control: Maintain good posture and patience.
- Coverage posture and positioning: Pause before the hit and balance the court.

### Statistical

If you have enough personnel (coaches, managers, players), it's good to keep statistics during practices as well as matches. Assessing individual players during practice gives coaches much of the information they need for making lineup decisions. Even basic information such as positive or negative points that each player contributes can be helpful. One good way to use statistics to motivate players is to post the top three players' names in each category after every scrimmage in practice. Players whose names do not appear will know that they are at risk of not playing in matches, and this realization will motivate them to improve and get their names on the board. Categories that can be posted include digs, aces, stuff blocks, assists, kills, hitting percentage, and passing numbers. Statistics from matches can also be used, but this approach leaves team members who don't play without a way to set goals for themselves.

Many teams keep statistics by hand, and the information they gain is valuable. If you have the financial means, however, you can choose from a variety of statistical software designed to help players and coaches understand their strengths and weaknesses. These options range from US$100 for software for a handheld device to US$10,000 or more for software for a laptop; thus, a volleyball program's budget generally dictates which software to choose. The more expensive options can handle a combination of statistics and video. For example, some software allows you to see all the attacks by hitter number 23 in rotation 5. It can pull together all of the clips featuring a specific server or attacker for the entire match. It can make shot charts that show exactly where the attack came from and where the ball landed. Such programs require that someone on staff learn how to input the information either during the match or later, and they tend to be very complicated and finicky since they have so many processes going on at once. The trend seems to be the same in football and basketball programs that use digital video statistical software: It's great when it works, but at times you may need a computer technician to help after it crashes. You can find a variety of sample statistical charts and explanations in chapter 8. In the end, you must decide which statistics can help your team the most—and which options make a good fit with your staff and budget.

## Emotional

It's important to continually assess the emotional status of each player. Some are steady, and others experience extreme highs and lows. Those who are steady can be enjoyable to coach, but they may not know how to bring the extreme intensity needed for play at the highest levels. On the other hand, those who have big emotional swings may bring that burning fire you want but then hit rock bottom if things don't go well. Since volleyball is a game of errors, players need to learn how to let mistakes go and move on to the next play. Thus, the goal for each player is to be as emotionally consistent as possible yet raise his or her emotional level when the situation requires it. Players can also become emotionally drained from the general daily grind of school, life, and volleyball. If a player seems too emotionally flat to contribute to the team, then it's time to give him or her a break from practice. Some players put so much emotion into their play that they need time to reenergize, and they will rarely know that they need it. In extreme cases, it's possible to enlist the aid of companies that perform personality inventories for each player. Such services use a battery of questions to predict how a person will react emotionally to various situations, and this kind of insight could help coaches and teammates understand how to get along better as a group and how to recognize red flags when they pop up. Prices for these services can range from a couple of hundred to a couple of thousand dollars, so again, your budget may limit you. If this is the case, some great books and Web sites, specifically business and self-help related, can help you accomplish the same goals.

## Mental

Assessment of an individual's mental abilities can be divided into three categories: volleyball IQ, ability to learn, and mental toughness. These areas are important because they serve as building blocks of a complete player. A player who is smart on the court but slow to learn will have trouble taking his or her game to the next level. If a player learns easily but cracks under pressure, it won't matter what he or she has learned. To play aggressive volleyball, individuals and teams need to be good in all three areas, and assessing them gives a coach knowledge that is crucial to gearing practices and meetings to improve all three.

Like street smarts, volleyball IQ involves the ability to use available information to anticipate what will happen next. A player's volleyball IQ tends to increase with every year of participation, yet some young players have a great volleyball IQ while some older players do not. Examples of good knowledge of the game include knowing when and where to tip, where the defense will be in various situations, and why (or why not) to set players at various points in a match. Defensively, volleyball IQ means understanding, for example, when a setter or hitter is likely to tip and being able to make the play. Players with a poor volleyball IQ make the same mistakes over and over, no matter how experienced they are. Coaches would like to think that players become smarter on the court as they get older, but there are a few who just don't seem to catch on. Conversely, some first-year students come in with great common sense, which may have a lot to do with their previous sports experiences and the household they were brought up in.

The second category—ability to learn—relates to how quickly a player can understand concepts and use them in gamelike conditions. Examples include learning a new physical skill or new offensive and defensive strategies. Some players grasp concepts very quickly; others do not. If a player needs to be reminded over and over about the same thing, this stumbling block hinders his or her progress and becomes a weakness on the court. Ability to learn can be assessed during every contact a coach has with a player. Coaches are teachers, and they are trying to pass their knowledge of the game on to the players. Realizing that a player is a slow learner gives the coach a chance to try various methods and be persistent. Players may also hinder their own progress by being resistant to learning. These players either make excuses for why they don't want to change or they are offended by the coach's attempt to help them. Both types of players put up a wall between themselves and the very people who can teach them. Players need to be open-minded and willing to try new things without taking critique personally.

The third category to assess is mental toughness—the ability to stay focused during even the most chaotic and difficult times on the court. It's important to know which players will step up and play well when the opponent or the coach puts them in a stressful situation. Some players thrive in challenging and stressful conditions; others become quiet, passive, and error prone. Mental and physical toughness often go hand in hand. Why are coaches always trying to toughen players up? Why do they think the athletes are softer and less hungry than even 5 years ago? From the Great Depression in the 1930s, many people in America were brought up to be tough and strong, and for decades that mentality filtered down through families. People understood that sacrifices needed to be made in order to have a chance at surviving. They knew that if they could be strong mentally and emotionally, they were likely to succeed. Since then, we have softened up to the point that some athletes feel they are entitled to enjoy great things before they have earned them.

Much of society today does not teach young people to be aggressive. They are taught from kindergarten on to be polite and nice, yet coaches want them to be tough and aggressive. Take a look at the parents of the players on your team and the households they grew up in. From a young age, more and more kids have their parents do almost everything for them, and as a result they don't learn how to be independent. Yet when they get to high school and college, coaches need those passive, nice players to be strong and mentally tough. Many athletes are drawn to this sport because it is not as rough as, say, basketball, where elbows fly and bodies get knocked around. Indeed, some players like volleyball in part because the teams are separated by a net. They like the separation, because no one can hit them or hurt them. Thus, coaches may face the challenging task of helping players who don't like being physical develop into a tough, aggressive team.

The best way to improve mental toughness in individuals is to put them in stressful drills during practice that force them to fight their way out. Most of the drills included in this book challenge the athletes physically and mentally so they will become tougher and more independent. Many of the drills also require players to complete a skill multiple times in a row in order to become consistent. As players become physically taxed during a difficult drill, they reach a point where they fight harder to complete the drill. That's when you see the aggressive attitude become a more regular feature of the team.

### Applying Individual Assessment Results

Coaches use information gained from individual assessments in various ways, depending on their level and situation. At the high school and club levels, they will likely use the results to make cuts during tryouts or to form teams. It is very difficult to decide who will make the team when it has to be done in a short period of time, though most coaches would agree that the toughest part is telling the players who did not make the squad. Once the team is selected, the process becomes more similar to that of the college game, as coaches turn their attention to picking starters and deciding what roles each player will have.

Good coaches should be analyzing and testing players all the time. They should be watching everything players do, from ball-handling drills in warm-ups to their interactions with each other on and off the court. In some individual sports, coaches can use times, distances, or scores to select players, but in volleyball they must often make subjective decisions based on all of the assessment areas already listed, along with players' volleyball skills in the team setting. Some players may look good in controlled drills but fall apart when a game is played. Coaches should be sure to give players ample opportunity to play variations of the game; doubles, triples, quads, and sixes will expose some players' weaknesses, and others may surprise you with how they excel. Synthesizing all of the assessment information gives a coach the basis for choosing a starting lineup and points out the weaknesses that individual players need to improve. It also helps the coach gear practice drills to strengthen each player. I strongly believe that a team is only as good as its weakest link and that a good coach finds ways to improve every player. A team's lineup will likely change from week to week, depending on the consistency shown by team members, and one of the goals for any coach should be to find a role for each player and help him or her be great in that role.

## Team Assessment

As individual players improve, the team will naturally become stronger as a group, and it becomes more difficult for opponents to break any given player down. The coach must also consider how the individuals perform as a group. Here are some categories that should be used in assessing the team as a whole.

## Communication

Volleyball is a team sport that requires good communication (covered in depth in chapter 7), and there are two basic types: informational and inspirational. Players need to be taught that there is a place for both. Informational communication involves, for example, calling out that the setter is in the front row or back row, or telling a hitter if one or two blockers are up and where a good place to tip would be. It might also mean calling for the ball in serve receive, telling a teammate if the ball is headed in or out, or calling to set the ball (in case a nonsetter is stepping in to set). Inspirational communication involves exactly what it sounds like—words and actions that inspire others to be great—and might range from cheering a teammate on to looking a fellow defender in the eye and saying, *"Nothing hits the floor!"* It might also include using body language—such as fist pumps, high fives, or a huge jump in the air after a great block—that motivates or excites teammates to rise to a higher level. Both words and actions can be inspiring to teammates, but this type of communication doesn't always come naturally. In fact, coaches have to be very aware of the opposite: negative communicators. They can tear a team apart and ruin a season. It is useful to keep in mind a great question I've seen on motivational posters: "ATTITUDE. Is yours worth catching?"

At the lower levels of the sport, a lot less is happening during games, but in order to play aggressive volleyball at the elite levels, teammates must share constructive information. Watch your team during drills, scrimmages, matches, and time-outs. Some players rarely speak, some talk too much, and others talk a lot but don't say much. Quiet players need to practice their gym voice, and all players should know what information is important enough pass on. Look for communication that is short and concise to avoid confusion about what is said. Teammates with poor communication skills will play balls that are headed out, run into each other, and give away easy points.

## Positioning

Coaches must conduct visual assessments to determine whether players know where they should be at the start of each play and where they should go as each situation develops. Base positions on defense, blocking, and free-ball situations have to be covered repeatedly in practice so that everyone knows their responsibilities. Players should memorize primary passing formations, as well as a secondary formation in case the passers are struggling. Coverage positioning involves a different formation for each possible attacker, and it's important to position players in key spots to cover both the short and deep areas of the court. It's common for players to cover the hitter too tightly, leaving no one in the deep court, whereas balancing the court will enable the team to play all blocked balls. It is also important to assess the timing of the hitter coverage. Players moving to coverage position should get as close as possible to their base, then stop their feet before the hitter contacts the ball. This technique helps them make an immediate move to the ball once it comes off the blocker's hands.

One of the best ways to assess and teach positioning, as well as individual techniques, is to use video. Coaches should first draw the positions for each team formation (on a whiteboard or on paper) to give players a visual picture in their minds of where they should go when they step onto the court. Once the team has practiced positioning, coaches can take video footage during practices and matches in order to show players where they are actually going, so that they can make corrections and improve their positioning as a unit. As much as players think they know where they are and what their technique looks like, the pictures never lie.

For recording the performance of an individual's skills, the camera can be set at whatever angle is needed to get the view you want. Filming practice repetitions for any skill allows the coach and player to review them either right on the court or in a separate meeting. Setting up a monitor at courtside allows the player to be filmed, get immediate feedback, and return to the court to work on improving the skill. When filming team play, it is best to put the camera on a tripod behind the service line so that the camera is at least as high as the net—the higher the camera, the better your view of your players' movement and spacing. Zoom in close enough that the lens frames the two corners of the end line and the antennae. Any of various video formats (from VHS to digital) will serve the purpose; I recommend using a playback device with good still-frame and frame-by-frame capability. When players and coaches review individual techniques and team play, it's important to watch not only for the good plays but also for what caused the errors.

## Flow

Being in base position is one thing, but moving to play the ball after it is contacted is another. Inexperienced or low-level teams often stand still, and they rarely move more than a step or two. To play aggressive volleyball, however, players must be confident enough in themselves to run across the court to make a play if needed. Assess your players' movement patterns out of each of their bases and make sure they understand their assignments. If a team is to remain organized during chaotic rallies, teammates must engage in an intentional and orchestrated flow with each other. Indeed, when two great teams are in the middle of a long rally, there seems to be a fluid dance among teammates; when a team is clicking or flowing together, it's one of the most entertaining parts of the sport of volleyball. A team that is inclined to stand still and stagnate must practice the flow patterns out of every base position in the game. Chapter 4 describes a great drill called Speed Ball that helps all teams with their flow. You will soon find out who knows how to balance the court with a teammate during play, and it's an easy drill to learn, so you'll see rapid progress in the flow between your players.

## Chemistry

This is one of the most mysterious and elusive ingredients of a team. Everyone wants to know how to develop good team chemistry. To assess chemistry, watch how players on a team interact with each other, both on and off the court. If they turn away from each other on the court or argue with each other off the court, the odds are good that they will separate from each other when games become stressful. Some players will always sit apart from the team and never make a connection. This is a big red flag, and it needs to be addressed. Coaches must also prevent cliques from forming within the team; over time, such separations divide a team. Every player brings a different background, attitude, personality, and perception to the team. To blend all of them together, bonds have to be created and trust has to be earned. Coaches should provide opportunities for players to share experiences together off the court so that they have something to draw on when times get tough on the court. Examples include pregame team meals, planned team-building activities, or even roommate rotations on road trips. In the gym, you can rotate ball-handling partners or groups who train together, and team chemistry will begin to improve. Some teams can succeed without great chemistry if they have great skills, physical gifts, or phenomenal determination. But teams who have genuine chemistry bring an X factor that is hard to explain and truly difficult to beat. Every tournament has a team whose players seem to "play above their heads," and it is usually the team with the best chemistry.

## Sideout Percentages

This area of team assessment needs to be done statistically in order to eliminate the human element of subjective decision making. Use the following formula to determine what percentage of the time your team scores out of serve receive: number of sideout scores divided by total number of serves received (e.g., 12 ÷ 36 = .333 whereas 22 ÷ 36 = .611). Compare all six rotations to determine which are your strongest and which need work. You can improve sideout percentages by altering passing formations or attack patterns.

## Transition and Free-Ball Scoring

You can use the same type of formula for transition and free-ball scoring: number of transition scores divided by the total number of transitions attempted. A separate percentage can be determined for attempts to score off a free-ball play also. Calculating these percentages will help to determine how successful your team is in defending and transitioning to the offensive set. Comparing percentages between rotations allows you to identify the weaker ones and change defensive looks or personnel as needed. Free-ball percentages tell you how well your team is scoring with easy balls and whether the offensive patterns you have chosen are providing the best opportunity to score. Low percentages in transition and free-ball plays can also be connected to poor ball handling that prevents the setter from using all the options available and splitting the block.

## Out-of-System Scoring

This may be the most important category in determining success at the highest levels. The most aggressive opponents consistently bring strong attacks that are hard to dig into the target area. Any dig that prevents the setter from running a quick offense results in a higher likelihood of an out-of-system set to the outsides. Lower-level teams tend to make errors on these plays or give an easier ball to the opponent, whereas the best teams are able to terminate out-of-system balls on a regular basis.

Hitters must be trained to alter their approach angles, their timing, and the shots they are attempting in order to improve their percentages.

## Applying Team Assessment

Assessing the team is a continuous process. It begins the day you meet the team and ends just after your last competition. Coaches who select one lineup and never change it are probably not getting everything out of their team. By making slight changes in personnel, coaches can create a more competitive environment on the team as players work hard to earn a spot. Players can become complacent if they know they will never come out, but they may raise their level if they know someone else could take their position. Inevitably, the coach will face matches where the players are struggling and he or she needs to ignite them; at these times, information gained during individual and team assessment pays off. Matches themselves provide an opportunity to assess performance under stressful conditions where expectations are much higher and some players tend to falter. If a coach selects a player to sub

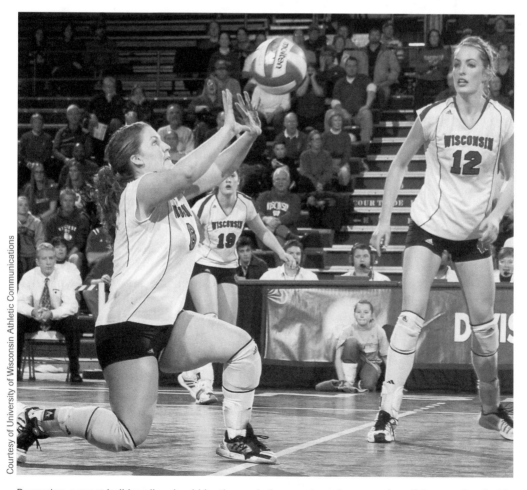

Becoming a great ball handler should be the goal of every player because she will become invaluable to her team.

Courtesy of University of Wisconsin Athletic Communications

in and serve in a critical situation, the player has to prove that he or she can do it; if not, the coach won't likely make that move again. If the goal is to progress as a team throughout the season, assessment must be constant. As the saying goes, if you're not moving forward, someone is passing you.

# Player Roles

Each position player on the court has a different role in playing aggressive volleyball, but one thread ties them together—the aggressive mentality required to play at the highest level. Here are some examples of player roles by position. You might also call them job descriptions for success.

**Setter**   Needs to have consistent overhand skills and a desire to be involved in every play and be relied upon. Should have the ability to analyze situations quickly and make instant decisions. Must be able to communicate and connect with teammates on a regular basis while bringing a strong leadership mentality.

**Middle Hitter**   Needs to have good movement skills and a never-say-quit mentality. Must know that he or she will not get all the sets yet must always approach aggressively to draw attention from the block. Should bring a great work ethic and have the ability to quickly analyze situations in order to cover the most territory of any attacker or blocker.

**Left-Side Hitters**   Must be able to carry a large offensive load because the setter will go to them a majority of the time when the team is out of system. Should be able to stay aggressive in difficult situations, knowing that they will often have to deal with a double block. Must be mentally sharp as blockers to deal with front-row setters and slide hitters during the same play. Great back-row skills are a bonus so they can stay in the game for six rotations.

**Right-Side Hitters**   Should have strong blocking skills to deal with what is usually the opponent's strongest attacker. Being opposite the setter, they should also be well rounded in case the setter digs the first contact and they are required to set. In the past, this has been called "the technique position" because the player often plays multiple roles and needs to be good at a variety of techniques. Again, solid back-row skills are preferred.

**Libero**   Must have strong serve-receive and defensive skills because his or her main responsibility is to start the offense. Should be aggressive in controlling and patrolling the backcourt. Will often be in charge of the passing formations and must be able to communicate that information to teammates. Must have a passion for stopping the opponent's best attack and thrive on starting the offense for the setter and hitters.

To be truly great at any of these positions, athletes must play with an aggressive attitude. Look at any all-conference, all-region, all-state, or All-American team and you'll see one similar trait: Each athlete had to play aggressive volleyball to excel in his or her position.

## A Tip From the Top

At the USA Junior Olympic Championships back in the mid-90s, my 18s team was playing in the second round of pool play. To advance to the quarterfinals, we had to win our pool, which came down to a match against the defending national champions, Team Mizuno of the Bay Area. We lost the first set and were down a couple of points (using sideout scoring) near the end of a very close second set, and we were running out of subs. We decided to use our final sub for our back-row player, meaning that she might have to play in the front row, but we felt that without making the sub we would have a very tough time winning the set and match. Therefore, we took a chance that we could come back *and* win the set before the specialist made it to the front row. We were partly correct. We made up the deficit, but we couldn't close the set before the specialist rotated to the front row and was matched up against Kerri Walsh! We were able to move the specialist around to disguise her position in the front row, and for whatever reason our opponent chose not to set Walsh. We rotated the specialist through the front row and ended up winning the set. Though some luck was probably involved, this gutsy effort by the back-row specialist and by our entire team enabled us to win that match and the following quarterfinal match before bowing out of the tournament in the semis.

—Tom Pingel, Managing Director,
High Performance Indoor National Programs, USA Volleyball

Having great role players can help a team win against an opponent that looks much stronger on paper. Some hitters put up huge numbers on a regular basis, and their teams rely on them. Other hitters put up small kill totals but are great at serving and passing. Their role is to get points with their serve, keep the opponent out of its preferred offense, and make precise passes in order to limit points lost to aces and begin a great offense. In fact, the big hitter would probably not get huge kill numbers if his or her teammates didn't pass so well. Even players on the bench can play critical roles. They can inspire others with their attitude, calm teammates during stressful times, and keep players focused when they tend to drift. They also have to be ready in an instant if a player on the court gets injured or if the coach makes a last-minute decision. In addition, they may be asked to do statistics that help with strategy during the game or to actively learn from more experienced players so they are ready when called upon. Great role players understand that even though their name may not appear in the newspaper after every match, they are vital to the success of the team. Most players have weaknesses in their game, but teams with great role players blend together in phenomenal ways that make them extremely difficult to beat.

## Ingredients of Winning Teams

Call it a recipe for success, or compare it to fitting together the pieces of a puzzle. By any description, coaches are searching for the right group of individuals to form the best team. To do so, they must analyze players' skills, personalities, emotions, and learning abilities (and disabilities) while trying to defeat an opponent who's also trying to win. Even the best coaches make mistakes in judging which players will get the job done. In some years, it seems like the stars align and everything falls into place; in others, it seems like a couple of important puzzle pieces have fallen under the table. All great coaches have vision, but they also admit that their vision is best when they look back at their team after the season. Hindsight is indeed 20/20.

In all my years as a coach, I've seen definite similarities between my championship teams. They have just the right mix of skills, athleticism, attitude, and personalities. Once the initial assessments are done and the season is underway, teams with the potential to be great have players who can generally be placed into one of six common categories. Each of these player types needs to be coached in a slightly different way in order to reach full potential, but they are all critical to the success of the group. Players' individual makeups dictate how they interact as a team both socially and athletically. The best teams have a good combination of these traits, whereas average teams are lacking in one or more of these areas.

**Stud Athletes**   Every winning team needs to have one or more stud athletes—and the more you have, the higher you'll probably finish in the final standings. These are the players who jump higher, move quicker, and hit harder than most anyone else. The strange thing is that they may not be your hardest workers or deepest thinkers, but they can simply beat people with their physical gifts. There will be many times when these players put the team on their shoulders and carry it to victory. After working with athletes of this type, you might compare them to a car such as a Maserati. They can be temperamental at times, but if you take care of them they can really get up and go. Many elite athletes seem to have quirks that set them apart from other players. If coaches can deal with their high-maintenance behavior, they'll find that the rewards are worth the effort.

**Hard-Shells**   These players resist change, may seem to question authority, and possess a rebellious side. They offer something valuable to the team, but it's not easy to get to it. They may be compared to a stallion and what it can bring to the herd. Too much discipline can break their spirit, but with just enough they can do some amazing things if you nurture their competitive nature and take advantage of their toughness. The key is to come to an understanding with them. They have to be willing to try new things so they can improve their game. Call them stubborn or call them competitive—either way, patience is needed, because they may be frustrating to coach. One phrase that comes to mind is "tough nut to crack." These players may have a hard shell on the outside, and you have to find a way to reach them and connect with them. Like any shell, it won't open up until it is ripe, but when it's ready you'll find something great inside.

**Perfectionists**   There are two kinds. One group has a healthy level of perfectionism and gets the most out of their bodies. They work harder than the rest to be technically perfect, and they make corrections quickly after an error. These kids may not be great athletes, but they can compete with the best because of an unbelievable work ethic. The second group goes overboard in their pursuit of perfection. If they don't get it right every time, they become so negative that they distract the team or themselves from making the next play. This problem may take the form of yelling, pouting, or even crying; regardless, it is a habit that you have to try to change because it takes too much energy away from the pursuit of team goals. Volleyball is a game of errors, and players need to understand that they can't be perfect all the time. Perfectionists can be difficult to coach, because they may react negatively to any coaching. They are so hard on themselves that any comment from the coach can put them over the edge. Yet perfectionists can be very good if they are able to be reasonable and find a workable balance.

**Relievers**    These players are perfectly suited to come off the bench and give the team a lift. They may not be able to maintain their play at a high level for an extended period of time, but in short bursts they're invaluable. You can compare this role to that of a short-relief pitcher in baseball; they come in and help close out the game. In volleyball, relievers might offer a different tempo of attack or a new variety in your serves. These are the players who really understand the question, "Which is it better to be—a starter or a finisher?" Even as seniors, some players are better off the bench than as starters. Coaches need to find out what each player does best and use each in the appropriate role. Relievers can be the hero who comes in and saves the day. Convince them of that, and they will relish the role.

**Clowns**    These players bring comic relief to the team and staff. In competitive sport, considerable tension can build up over the course of a season, and you need these players to lighten the mood. They often have a hearty laugh and can tell a good joke or story. You may see them at the center of attention on the bus or on the plane. The most valuable ones also know when to get serious on the court. If you have nothing but serious players, they will probably be at each other's throats at the time you need it least. Loose teams are the ones who will be calm when you're in the thick of the battle. Some kids are born this way, and others emerge as they get comfortable with their surroundings. Either way, you'll all be better off if you have a couple of players who give you what might be called "high entertainment value."

**Leaders**    These players aren't always the most physically gifted, but they are the glue that holds the team together. They have a good sense of the team's mental and emotional status. They can cool tempers or motivate teammates depending on what is needed. They may also be your best ball control players—steady with low error rates. You absolutely need one or two of these players if you want to make a run at a championship. You could have six studs, but they might not be able to play together and stay organized. Leaders have the ability to drag the others to a win even when things aren't going well. They use their brain to find ways to beat drills and opponents. They give their teammates confidence and at times think for them. They are willing to speak up even if they risk offending someone, and they play with an urgency to win. These players are often the unsung heroes because there isn't a statistic for their contribution in the box score. Without them, you just have six people on the court. With them, you have a team that can win championships.

# Assessment Drills

## FREE-BALL MAX

**Purpose**   To assess a player's ability to pass consecutive free balls on target.

**Goal**   To consecutively pass as many balls as possible on target and to improve on personal bests.

**Equipment Needed**   Balls; targets.

**Explanation**

- One player is on the court at a time. The coach punches or throws the ball over. The player must put the first ball in the target to get another; play continues until the player misses.

- The coach starts by hitting right to the player in early rounds, then moves the player around some as he or she improves.

- Players rotate out as soon as they miss; they should keep track of their highest total. After 20 minutes, write everyone's totals on a whiteboard so they can aim to beat those totals the next time they try the drill.

- More than one court can be used, and players can serve as tossers. Players who excel in this drill can be relied on in games.

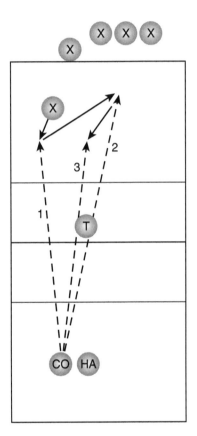

## HAWAII DEFEND-AND-SET

**Purpose**   To assess ball handling and improve defensive and setting consistency. This is a great drill because players need back-to-back digs and sets. Nonsetters are put in the setter role to improve their skills.

**Goal**   To score 5 big points by earning consecutive points with high-quality plays.

**Equipment Needed**   Balls; coaching boxes.

## Explanation

- Two coaches on boxes at the right and left front positions alternate hits to three defenders, who dig to one setter. Coaches hit both balls to the same player. The setter sets each ball to one of the two targets located at the right and left front attacking positions. A small point is scored by making a dig and set to either of the targets. Players need 2 small points in a row to score a big point. After 5 big points, new players rotate in, using three defenders and a middle blocker to set.

- Use nonsetters in the role of the setter to improve their setting skills.

- Challenge the players with off-speed shots that make them run down balls with control. Halfway through, remove the setter and have one of the defenders bump-set the ball to the outside.

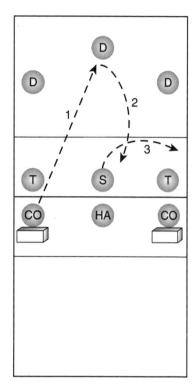

# MIDDLE BLOCKER MOVES

**Purpose**   To mimic the moves that a middle blocker would make during a match.

**Goal**   To have one hitter score on three attacks and block two balls.

**Equipment Needed**   Balls; coaching boxes.

## Explanation

- Start with the coach's toss to the hitter. The hitter uses his or her hands to pass to the setter.

- The hitter follows this sequence:
  1. Hit a 1 ball.
  2. Move left and block.
  3. Transition to the middle 3-meter (10 foot) line, approach, and hit a 1 ball.
  4. Move right and block.
  5. Sprint to the middle 3-meter line and hit a 1 ball.

- This drill can be adjusted by having a player pass a ball to the setter. The attacks can also include a 31 and a tight slide.

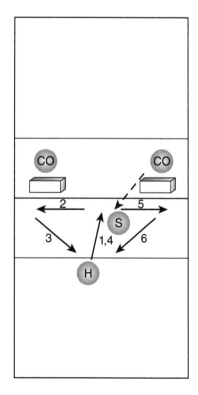

## OFF-SPEED TEST

**Purpose**   To assess a player's ability to make off-speed plays and hit off-speed shots.

**Goal**   To defend off-speed shots and get 10 on target; to hit off-speed shots as a defense plays those shots and transitions to offense.

**Equipment Needed**   Balls.

**Explanation**

- From across the net, the coach tosses off-speed balls to players by position (figure *a*): first right backs, then middles, then lefts. Each group needs 10 on target to get out. (Do right and left front blockers coming across the court as well.) Do two rounds for each position.

- Put one player in each defensive position, including three blockers. Have a player self-toss and hit, tip, roll, or throw the ball anywhere (figure *b*). The defense needs 10 good points (i.e., kills) to get out. Self-tossing hitters start at the 3-meter (10 foot) line.

- For more advanced teams, each ball that they do not get up *subtracts* 1 point from the total. If they play it up and don't attack it but do get it across the net, it is a wash (i.e., no point is scored or lost). You can also have advanced teams work into strong transitions to earn each point.

- One benefit of doing this drill is that players learn how to self-toss and comfortably hit or tip the ball anywhere. This gives them ownership in the drill and lets them make decisions on shots.

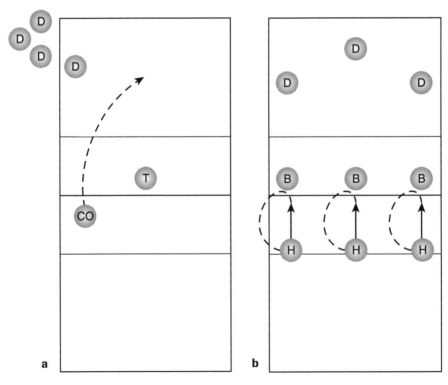

## OLYMPIC FEST HITTER TEST

**Purpose**   To rate a hitter's ability to score against a full defense.

**Goal**   To compete against a teammate to see who can score more consistently against a full defense.

**Equipment Needed**   Balls.

**Explanation**

- Two hitters go up against a full defense. Each hitter receives four balls. Hitter 1 and hitter 2 alternate attempts to score. The coach tosses or punches a free ball to the hitter, who passes to the setter. The hitter then calls the set that he or she wants and approaches to attack. Scoring is kept head-to-head between the hitters.

- If both players get a kill (or get dug, or make an error), the round is a wash. If one player gets a kill and the other is dug, the first player gets 1 point. If one player gets a kill and the other makes an error, the first player gets 2 points. If one player is dug and the other makes an error, it is also a wash. Points are only given if one player scores.

- Middle blocker goes against middle blocker, outside hitter goes against outside hitter, and right-side hitter goes against right-side hitter. Alternate setters with different groups and post the results as each group completes its round.

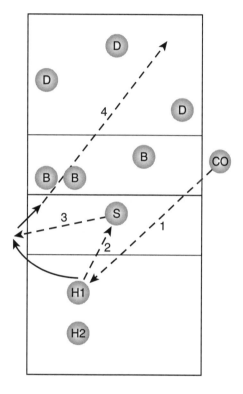

## PASSER'S TOUCH

**Purpose**    To teach passers to cushion the ball and help them develop a feel for slowing it down for the setter.

**Goal**    To pass two balls into a ball basket before rotating.

**Equipment Needed**    Balls; ball basket(s) for each set of passers.

### Explanation

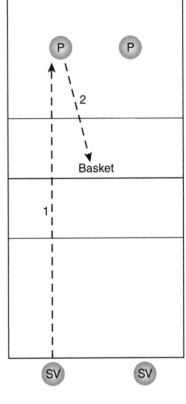

- Groups of three to six players (depending on the number of courts available) try to pass the ball into ball baskets (or buckets) so that the ball stays inside. Doing so requires an accurate pass and a soft touch. Groups of three are best, since they reflect gamelike conditions in a three-passer system.

- Each group of passers takes turns passing until one of them gets two balls to stay in the basket.

- The server throws to the passers in round 1, throws deep to the end line in round 2, and throws to the area inside the 3-meter (10 foot) line in round 3. The server *serves* to the end line in round 4, serves to the area inside the 3-meter line in round 5, and serves topspin to the end line in round 6.

- One variation is the 10 before 4 game. The server needs 10 aces before the passers hit the basket four times (passers work together to win).

- On the second day of trying this drill, do only one round of throwing before moving on to the serve. You can then advance to pass-set-hit triangles, with each hitter needing three kills to rotate. Subtract 1 point for each error. Starting with the basket should reinforce the soft touch, which should be maintained as players begin passing to a setter before hitting.

# SINGLES ON TWO COURTS

**Purpose**    To assess ability to control the ball and plan ahead.

**Goal**    To win a one-on-one game to 3 points and get to the winner's court.

**Equipment Needed**    Balls; two extra antennae for each court used; floor tape or discs to designate sidelines.

## Explanation

- Players play one-on-one, starting with a serve. They pass to themselves, set to themselves, and hit the ball back over the net. Attacks must be made from behind the 3-meter (10 foot) line, and no tipping is allowed into the area in front of the opponent's 3-meter line.

- Each game goes to 3 points (win by 1); as players improve, games can go to 5 or 7 points. After each round, winners move one court toward the top court, whereas losing players move one court away.

- This is a great drill for ball control and strategy. Players can send the ball across the net on the first, second, or third contact.

- Use extra antennae to separate the courts; if you have room, space the courts apart from each other.

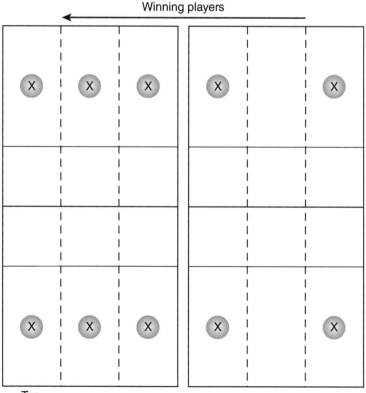

# 3

# Offensive Techniques and Strategies

The increased athleticism of volleyball players in recent years has given teams the chance to try new offensive skills and schemes. Both the men's and women's games have become acrobatic and exciting as the players have grown taller and improved their vertical jumps. In the early 1980s, front-row players stood an average of 6 feet 4 inches (about 1.9 meters) for men and 5 feet 11 inches (about 1.8 meters) for women. The top men could jump-touch just over 11 feet (3.4 meters) and the top women 10 feet 4 inches (3.1 meters). Now, the men are averaging 6 feet 7 inches in height and jumping closer to 12 feet (3.7 meters), and the top women's teams feature front-row players who stand between 6 feet and 6 feet 6 inches (1.8 and 2 meters) with top vertical jumps of 10 feet 9 inches or even higher. With their increased height and athleticism, the men are playing almost 4 feet (1.2 meters) above the net and the top women 3 feet (0.9 meter) above. As the players have evolved, so have their abilities on offense. Coaches and players are always trying new and exciting offensive plays, and the higher angle of attack can wreak havoc on opposing defenses.

The beauty of volleyball, however, is that the biggest team doesn't always win. Championship teams can still involve a variety of sizes and styles, as long as they master the offensive techniques and strategies of aggressive play. This chapter covers everything that is part of an offensive attack. If you were watching a match, you would easily pick these areas out, since they follow each other in sequence. Each play begins with the serve, which, if done aggressively, is meant to disrupt the opponent's offense or score an immediate point. Next come passing and setting, along with strategies needed in order to prepare for the attack. The last part of the chapter discusses hitter coverage, which is often overlooked as part of the offense. When an opponent blocks your best shot, coverage set up with an aggressive mind-set is the only thing that can keep your offense alive.

# Serving

Almost every coach at any level is asked the same question prior to a big match: "What do you need to do to win today, Coach?" The answer is usually something like this: "We need to serve tough." The theory is that a tough serve keeps the opponent out of its quick offense and gives the serving team an easy ball to defend.

The following sections outline serving techniques and strategies that players need to learn in order to wield a better, more aggressive serve.

## Serving Techniques

Several factors characterize a great serving team, and the first is finding the correct serve for each player. The main serves now being used are the floater, the standing topspin, the jump floater, the jump topspin, and the hybrid (a combination of the jump floater and the topspin). To be effective, they all need to be done with an aggressive mentality and strong hand contact. The hand contact for any floater serve is meant to make the ball travel without spin, since a ball without spin tends to float and shift like a knuckleball in baseball and thus is very hard to pass. The hand contact for any topspin serve must include a strong wrist snap from the top to the front side of the ball. The resultant fast spin creates air currents that pull the ball down to the ground faster. Any strong wrist snap with follow-through to the left or right creates real problems, since it causes the serve to break sideways in front of the passers. Here are some keys to aggressively executing each of the main serving techniques.

The serve is an offensive weapon meant to put opponents on their heels and slow down their offense.

### Standing Floater Serve

- Hold the ball in the nonhitting hand with the arm fully extended directly in front of the hitting shoulder.
- Position the foot opposite the hitting arm so that it is forward and pointing toward the target.
- Draw the hitting arm back fully so that the chest is wide open (figure 3.1*a*).
- Position the hitting hand above the head with the elbow pulled back fully (figure 3.1*b*).
- The toss should be 1 to 2 feet (0.3 to 0.6 meter) high and should land right back in the tossing hand if not contacted.
- The hitting hand should be fully open and rigid on contact; it should be perpendicular to the ground (figure 3.1*c*).
- Follow-through should be made with a straight arm pointing directly to the target.
- Power should be generated first through hip rotation, then through shoulder rotation, and finally by bringing the arm and hand through.
- To aim deeper into the court, hold the follow-through higher.
- The full sequence should be as follows: Toss, step, swing, follow through, and hold on target.

**FIGURE 3.1**   Standing floater serve.

*Jump Floater Serve*

- Toss the ball with two hands so that it is 1 to 2 feet (0.3 to 0.6 meter) high and out in front of the hitting shoulder (figure 3.2, *a-b*).
- After the toss, the step sequence for right-handers is left, right, left, and the jump takes place after the right-left, two-foot plant.
- Draw the hitting arm back fully so that the chest is wide open.
- Position the hitting hand above the head with the elbow pulled back fully.
- The hitting hand should be fully open and rigid on contact; it should be perpendicular to the ground (figure 3.2*c*).
- Follow-through should be made with a straight arm pointing directly to the target.
- What makes this serve more difficult to pass is the height at which the ball is contacted. The ball should go straighter over the net on the jump floater rather than arcing like a standing serve, which must go up and then over the net.
- The jump floater can also be done with a one-handed toss and the hitting arm pulled back.

**FIGURE 3.2**  Jump floater serve.

### Jump Topspin Serve

- Toss the ball with topspin out in front of the hitting hand (some people use the opposite hand).
- Toss it high and far enough in front to have time and distance to do an approach jump (figure 3.3, *a-b*).
- Once the ball is released on the toss, begin a normal three-step attack approach (figure 3.3*c*).
- Contact the ball at the peak of the jump and snap the wrist forward.
- Be sure to take off behind the end line and to land balanced on two feet.
- Aim for the opposing team's end line so that the topspin will not pull the ball down into the net.

**FIGURE 3.3**    Jump topspin serve.

*Hybrid Jump Serve*

As its name suggests, this serve is a combination of the topspin and floater jump serves. The difference resides in the hand contact on the ball. Instead of fully snapping the wrist, snap it partway and swing through the ball. The goal is to hit the ball so that it spins, floats, or does both. Not knowing what the ball will do or where it will go makes it very difficult to pass. Right now, this serve is seen mostly in the men's game.

# Serving Strategies

Some float servers can serve short to the opponent's 3-meter (10 foot) line; others can go back 30 feet (about 9 meters) from the end line and hit the long serve. If the gym space allows it, the serve from deep can be extremely effective. It can also be a great serve for the player who doesn't excel at other serves, because all that is required is

## A Tip From the Top

Prior to the 2008 season, we had not won the really big conference match in my three seasons as coach at UK. In contrast, Florida had won the SEC conference for 17 straight years. This year, however, we thought that we had a chance to win it. We knew it would be a tough challenge; in fact, Kentucky hadn't beaten Florida since 1990. We played them twice during the season. The first match was down in Gainesville during October. Both teams came into the match unblemished during the conference season, but we started out poorly and went down two sets to none. One of the biggest problems was our lack of aggression in serving the ball. In order to beat a powerhouse team, you must serve tough to get them out of rhythm and slow down their attackers with terminal velocity, but during the first two sets we had made 5 serving errors and produced only 1 ace. Obviously, we had put insufficient stress on Florida to give ourselves a chance to win the match, and we had to make an adjustment during the intermission in order to have a chance. During the next three sets, we produced 9 aces and only 5 serving errors, and we put ourselves in a position to win the match. Though we ended up losing the fifth set, our team gained an understanding of the need for aggressive serving that would help us next time around.

When we played Florida in Lexington, we won the first set with an intense, aggressive serving plan. We lost the second set convincingly, and though we made the third set more competitive, we still lost. Our fourth- and fifth-set wins were set up by attacking with our serve. Of our 7 aces in the match, 4 came in those last two sets, including the first 2 points of the fourth set to set the tone. Our team got back to being aggressive with the serve, which allowed our block and defense to score points for us. Our identity as a team rested on our block and defense—all started by aggressive serving to get opposing teams out of system. After the first two sets of the first match, our aggressiveness allowed us to take advantage of our strength as a team. From that point on, we had 16 aces and 10 errors from the service line in the next eight sets of those two matches.

—Craig Skinner, Head Women's Coach, University of Kentucky

to go back and hit it hard; this serve requires less accuracy, and the power generated to get the serve all the way to the far end line makes for a heavy ball that is hard to pass. In college, I was one of those players, and we worked out a pretty good system. I told the coaches that since I couldn't be very accurate from that far back, they should give me just one half of the court or the other to hit into. They agreed and would use three fingers to signal either west (three fingers up) or east (three fingers sideways). It seemed like a funny way to do it, but it was a simple and effective system. Another good serve is the high archer to the opponent's end line. If the server can place it on the last 2 feet of the court, it forces the passers to back up and wait for the ball to drop. A good, high serve to the end line often makes the passer alter the height of the pass to the setter, and it causes problems for the hitters waiting to attack.

The best teams vary their serves so that the opponent's passers cannot hone in on a specific style. Realistically, however, not all players are capable of mastering all serves, and players' limitations may dictate the coach's decision about who uses which types of serves. It will take some experimenting during practice to determine a serve type or two for each player. Even with players who are good at jump serving, it's important to have them practice a serve from the ground as well, because sometimes their jump serve will be off (e.g., a shoulder or knee starts hurting and reduces their consistency) and they'll make too many mistakes that lead to points for the opponent. Surprisingly, some players who have a good jump serve don't have a strong standing serve, but it's still vital to have a second serve to fall back on when necessary or to use when the opponent is passing the first serve too well.

Simply serving the ball in across the net isn't good enough for teams who want to win championships. The serve is your first opportunity to break down your opponent and take the opposing players out of their rhythm. Both players and coaches can look for weak spots evident in opponents' statistics, warm-ups, or performance in the early part of a match. A weakness might involve a specific player or a certain alignment. If it involves a specific player, serve to him or her until the coach puts in a sub or you win the game. It's also important to designate the opponent's top passer; sometimes, if you don't serve to him or her for a good part of the match, the player loses concentration and passing touch. Then, if suddenly served to after a long drought, he or she may be caught by surprise and fail to pass a good ball. Another point to remember is that some teams and some players just don't handle the jump serve very well; they'll end up overpassing the ball or shanking it to the side.

Target serving, whether designated by a coach's signal or by a player determining the spot, can work well with any type of serve. A coach giving target zones to the server can disrupt an opponent enough to gain a couple of points in a row at the service line. Good areas to serve to include the deep end line, the sidelines, the seams between passers, and the area inside the 3-meter (10 foot) line. Serving to deep zones can make it hard for passers who are also front-row hitters; they have to move backward before beginning their approach. Short serves, on the other hand, can cause the same sort of trouble for hitters; one who starts back deep to pass will have to come up short to play the ball and thus won't be able to get a full approach. Serving short to the front-row players can keep them from running their patterns efficiently. Some middle blockers aren't good passers at all, and serving to them can cause their entire play to fall apart. Serving to zone 2 (right front) can create real difficulties for the setter. Since the setter is often farther along the net in front of that zone, it makes him or her turn to the left in order to see the pass coming. When that happens, it's hard for the setter to see the middle hitter coming in for the quick set in front, and he or she may be forced to set the ball to the outside.

### Serving Strategy Keys

- Find the right serve(s) for each player.
- Determine your opponent's passing weaknesses.
- Attack weak players or zones to disrupt the opponent's offense.

# Passing

Although some people might place passing in the category of defense, it must be understood as offensive by an aggressive player. Consistently accurate passing in serve receive is critical for teams who wish to run an efficient offense, and it is especially important for smaller players facing bigger teams. If they can pass the ball to the center-court target area, then their setter has the opportunity to hold the middle blockers and split the block on the outside. The following sections discuss both individual passing techniques and team passing formations. If you want to build a high-level team, you first have to build a strong foundation of individual skills. Once each individual on the team can execute the needed skills, you'll be able to establish good team passing formations in an effective system. Aggressive passing techniques and strategies are crucial to becoming a great team. Who would want passive passers?

## Passing Techniques

If you want a team that can compete with anyone, you need consistent passers. They must bring confidence and use aggressive technique to hold up to the rigors of serve receive. Passing is one of the most vital skills in the sport of volleyball; without it, you will have no offense. Passers who are slow, soft, and weak will get torn apart by the opponent's serves. Passers who are quick, solid, and strong have the best chance at success. In fact, these three words—*quick, solid, strong*—should form the vision that guides coaches and players to develop aggressive passing. Fulfill this vision and you have a chance to beat anyone. The following explanation of passing techniques includes information about the skill as it has evolved in response to rule changes.

There are two common passing techniques: overhead and forearm. In 1998, the National Collegiate Athletic Association (NCAA) followed the Federation of International Volleyball (FIVB) and inserted a rule to allow double contacts on the first ball coming across the net. Now, every top player trains to receive serves in the overhead position, which allows players to start closer to the net in serve receive and take any balls coming above their shoulders with their hands. The pre-serve posture of the player is identical to the ready position for the overhead pass. Feet should be shoulder-width apart, and knees should be flexed in an athletic stance. The key is

**FIGURE 3.4**   Overhead pass.

to contact the ball above the head and in front of the body (figure 3.4, *a-b*). Any ball contacted directly above or to the side of the shoulders will likely be called a lift by the official. The fingers must be strong or the ball will continue through the hands and on past the passer. This skill is especially efficient when playing the floater serve, which can rise or move from side to side at any moment. If the ball suddenly moves lower than expected, the player should lower his or her hips and get directly behind the ball. The beauty of this rule change is that a play which used to be considered ugly and illegal now constitutes an exciting form of defense.

As with the overhead pass, a successful forearm pass requires players to use the ready stance and posture (figure 3.5*a*). The passer should have his or her platform fully extended and locked out by the time the served ball is crossing the net (figure 3.5*b*). The platform should look like what its name indicates—a platform or board. With arms fully extended in front of the body, the passer should connect his or her hands from the tips of the thumbs to the bottoms of the wrists. From there, the arms should form a perfect triangle, in which the area from 2 inches (5 centimeters) above the wrists to 2 inches below the elbows serves as the contact zone for the ball. Common errors include putting the arms together too late and dropping the platform to a horizontal position. One way to correct these problems is for the player to hold the arms stretched out in a forward but separated position before the serve. As the ball crosses the net, the player should already have formed the platform by extending the arms and bringing them together in a position that allows the player to *see the ball and his or her arms at the*

**FIGURE 3.5** Forearm pass.

*same time.* The player may drop the arms slightly as the ball arrives to achieve the correct angle for hitting to target, but this technique should help them connect the ball and their platform on a more regular basis.

This approach slightly exaggerates the technique, but it's very similar to the way in which baseball coaches teach outfielders to catch the ball. For a ball hit higher than their head, outfielders are taught to get their glove above and in front of their face so that they can watch the ball all the way into their glove. In volleyball, passers should position their platform away from their body so that they can put their arms in the path of the ball. Watching or filming a passer from the side will show you if he or she drops the platform. A good starting position for a platform is a 45-degree angle to the floor with the elbows fully locked out early. In the ideal starting and finishing posture for the forearm pass, the player stands with hips back and shoulders forward (over or in front of the toes). The passer should also round his or her shoulders to establish a strong frame around the ball. Maintaining this posture helps the passer keep the arms in front of the body rather than reaching to the sides, standing up, or letting the arms get too close to the body.

Whether using the overhead or the forearm technique, the next part of the process involves attitude. All passers, especially liberos and defensive specialists, must take great pride in starting the offense. The passer's first goal should be to give the setter a pass in the target area so that he or she then has the option to jump-set to the quick attacker or dump the ball. The target area is a rectangle along the net which starts 10 feet (3 meters) from the right sideline. The area starts 1 foot (0.3 meter) off the net, so the overpass isn't a concern, and is 8 to 10 feet (2.4 to about 3 meters) long by 3 to 4 feet (0.9 to 1.2 meters) wide. These dimensions allow the setter to make the blocker follow him or her and spread out the offense by setting either forward or backward with the same ease. If the pass is pushed too far to the left, the opposing middle blocker can make an easy move to the outside in order to block. If it's pushed too far to the right and set to the right, it is again very easy for the middle blocker to get there. Passing to the center third of the court allows the setter easier options for setting in front or behind.

Without aggressive passers who get good results, setters lose their options and the sets become predictable to the outside hitters. Passers should shuffle or sprint to the spot to which they anticipate the serve is heading and set their feet when the ball is still 10 feet (3 meters) away. In short, beat the ball to the spot. If the ball floats, they can move or shift again to get their platform in the right spot. Once they feel that the ball is in a good spot in relation to their body, they should attack the ball with their platform or hands. They should shove the ball aggressively toward the target and hold their platform or arms strong and still after the ball is gone. Lower-level teams should have a target goal that is twice as big and a little off the net in order to avoid overpasses. When using the overhead pass, holding the follow-through allows players to see exactly where their arms were facing at the finish. The same concept works when holding the platform and freezing after the pass. Thus, players can analyze their own technique and make adjustments to their passing angles.

The final adjustment to make is the tempo of the pass. To create a faster and more aggressive offense, the pass should head to the setter with a lower trajectory. Balls should arc no higher than the antennae, so that blockers and defenders have less time to react to the movement of the setter and the hitters. In addition, if pass tempo is consistent, hitters will be better able to time their approaches correctly. With all passes, players should remember to stay on task, and the task at hand is to make a good pass for the setter. Because a ball that is served or attacked often floats and moves around, it is not always possible to use picture-perfect technique. The bottom line, for both players and coaches, is good results, and top passers find a way to make the right adjustments to consistently get good results.

### Passing Technique Keys

- Use ready or athletic stance and posture.
- Beat the ball to the spot.
- Attack the ball.
- Shove to the target.
- Lower the trajectory.
- Stay on task.
- Make adjustments to obtain good results.

## Passing Formations

Teams choose passing formations based on their offensive systems and the skills of their passers. Over the years, different trends make their way through the volleyball world, and coaches experiment to find the best formation for their team. Each formation has benefits and drawbacks, and the best teams are willing to experiment aggressively to find the best fit.

**Two Back**    This style was made famous in the early 1980s by the U.S. Men's National Team. Karch Kiraly and Aldis Berzins were the two best passers in the world, and they could cover the entire court by themselves. In winning the Olympic gold medal in 1984, they inspired coaches and players across the United States to pass with two back (figure 3.6). The benefit of this formation is that there are fewer seams between passers to worry about. With three passers there are two seams, and with two passers there is only one seam. By using two-back passing, the two players involved know that they have to cover the entire court, so they'll move more aggressively and confidently to balls. It also allows the hitters to begin their approaches without slowing down to pass the ball. The drawback is that there are huge open areas for the opponent to serve into. As a result, you must have two amazing ball handlers in order to use this formation, and most teams have found it to be too difficult. Kiraly and Berzins were great players, and very few men or women have been able to match their talents since.

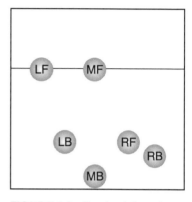

**FIGURE 3.6**    Two-back formation.

**Three Back**    In the 1990s, three back became the most popular formation—and it may still be. It offers the advantage that three players can each take a third of the court (figure 3.7); or, if the team features one passer who really excels, he or she can take half the court while the other two share the remaining half. The drawbacks are that your team will have to protect more passing seams and that one of your passers could be a front-row hitter. When a hitter is passing, you always risk having the opposition serve to that player in order to take him or her out of the offense. However, you need three good passers in order to use this formation, and usually one of them must be a front-row player.

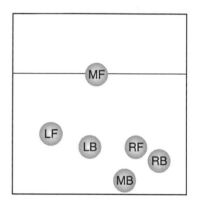

**FIGURE 3.7**    Three-back formation.

**Four Back**    This formation was also popular in the 1990s, and it is still used by many teams. It is a good formation to use if you have four players who can pass the ball comfortably, and it can be done in a cup shape (figure 3.8) or with three back and

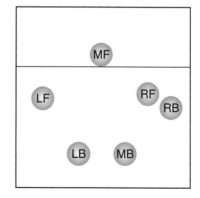

**FIGURE 3.8**    Four-back formation.

one at the 3-meter (10 foot) line. Although this formation involves more seams to protect, it makes it tougher for servers to find open spaces to serve into. It also helps teams play short serves, because they are able to assign specific players to handle them. With the advent of the jump topspin serve, this formation has allowed teams to have passers cover more of the floor without moving a great distance.

**Five Back**    This formation was very common in the 1980s and is starting to make a comeback. Originally called the "W formation," it was set up between the 3-meter (10 foot) line and the end line. Players were positioned as if they were the points of an imaginary W, with the players at the top three points standing near the 3-meter line (figure 3.9). Lower-level teams whose players didn't move much liked it because it put more bodies on the court. Now, however, teams are using it in reaction to the fairly recent let-serve rule change. Since a let serve can now stay in play, players must be alert to the ball that hits the net and dribbles over inside the 3-meter line. I'm not a fan

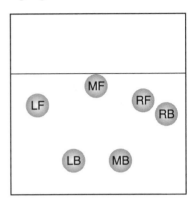

**FIGURE 3.9**    Five-back formation.

of the rule change for the women's game because I believe it was meant more for the men. Men used more hard topspin serves and made so many errors that play kept stopping. By allowing a serve that hits the net to stay in play, the game can keep going. Hard topspin serves usually continue on to the middle of the backcourt after hitting the net, so they are still easy to play. In the women's game, more floater serves are used. When a floater serve hits the net, it is with less velocity, so it just dribbles over the net. While the current five back is not the true W formation of old, it can be a great way to both limit the open areas and play the let serve. It can also be a useful formation for teams who feature no great passers, since each player is responsible for a smaller area.

Once a team has selected a formation (which could vary between rotations), it must form an aggressive plan of action. Each individual within the system has to know his or her role, and the players as a group must flow together. First, they have to identify the type of serve that is coming. If it is a jump topspin serve, they should add an extra player in the formation since the ball is arriving faster. Once the ball is served, the passers must move into position to claim and pass the ball. Claiming the ball means calling it with attitude. It also means arriving there first and claiming the area with one's body. You can compare claiming the ball to boxing out for a rebound in basketball. Passers should claim the ball and the area with body and voice. When the serve goes between players and into a seam, the person claiming the ball should increase the volume of his or her call to avoid collisions with teammates. As one passer claims the ball, the others should open up to that player and make helpful calls. Being positioned to the side of the serve, they have a better angle from which to view short serves and end lines. Opening up to the passer also helps him or her start running off the court if the ball is shanked. The passers' final role is to cover their hitters. If they stay focused throughout, they can alter the game by keeping the ball in play.

### Passing Formation Keys

- Identify the type of serve.
- Claim the ball with body and voice.
- Teammates should open to the passer and make calls.

## Passing Strategies

For every pass attempted, there is one single-minded goal: Put the very first ball in the target area so the setter can easily make decisions and set the attackers. If passers accomplish this goal, they have fulfilled their role. Realistically, though, some great serves will cause even the best passers to struggle, and when that happens, the passers can make adjustments to improve their odds of success.

No matter what passing formation is used, the most basic strategy is to hide your weaker passers and allow your better passers to take more territory. For example, short serves are intended to disrupt the offense and clog up hitters' approach lines, and coaches must decide who they want passing the short serve—the front-row hitters or the back-row players. If your hitters are good ball handlers, then it's not bad if they play the ball. The only drawback is that they must make an accurate pass and therefore delay their approach. If you want to avoid that situation, or if your hitters are poor ball handlers, put the back-row players in charge of all short serves. They will learn to be more aggressive in moving to the short serve, and the hitters will know that they can begin their transition to hitting.

Another passing strategy involves shifting the backcourt passers according to their talents. If you are using a three-passer formation and you have one outstanding passer, allow him or her to pass half the court while the other two share passing responsibility in the remaining half. Since this approach gives the weaker passers less court to cover, they will probably be more successful. The same holds true if one of your passers is a front-row hitter. Many opposing coaches will attack such a player with the serve to distract him or her from starting the approach, but you can have your passers shift to give the hitter less area to cover and, if possible, use the sideline to protect him or her. The same holds true for the weakest passer in the group. Give this player just a sliver of court to cover near the sideline, and if the opposing servers still go after him or her, there is a chance that they will serve it out of bounds. The only time the three passers should divide the court equally is if they are of equal talent. In all other cases, shift to protect and let your top passer have more freedom.

Yet another passing strategy can be used after one of your passers has been aced. I believe that you should shift the formation immediately to protect that passer and give the server something else to think about. You don't want the server to get comfortable and get in a good rhythm that results in a string of points. The main goal is to get the next sideout and prevent more points from being scored. There is no real reason to wait to see if the player who was aced can work his or her way out of a bad situation. Help that player now, and later he or she can be more relaxed and get back into the usual passing formation.

### Passing Strategy Keys

- Hide your weaker passers.
- Allow your better passers to take more territory.
- Have your best back-row passers take the short serves for the hitters.
- Shift the formation after an ace.

# Setting

The setter is the most critical position on the court. A good pass to an average setter will likely result in an average set, and a good hitter is nothing without a good setter because it's impossible to get into a consistent rhythm. A *good* setter, however, can take an *average* pass and deliver a good set to the hitters, and a *great* setter can take a *bad* pass, make a great set on location and in perfect tempo, and get the hitter a split block by making the blocker flinch or travel a long distance. Every team would love to have a great setter, whether recruited or found through tryouts, but the hard fact is that most great setters aren't born that way—they are trained through hundreds and thousands of repetitions. The best setters are not the passive, cautious ones. They are the ones who work tirelessly and think and play aggressively.

## Setting Techniques

The first key to creating a great setter is to train him or her to always be ready in an athletic stance. Whether releasing from the back row on a serve or waiting at the net during a hitting drill, a great setter should always be ready to sprint 30 feet (about 9 meters) to set the next ball. When you look at a setter at the net, you should see an athletic stance similar to what you would look for in a variety of sports: knees flexed, feet slightly staggered (with right foot forward), body leaning slightly forward, and hands at chest height (figure 3.10*a*). Picture a distance runner at the starting line or a football wide receiver at the line of scrimmage. Setters should give the image of an athlete ready to move quickly and efficiently. They know that they'll likely have to sprint from 10 to 20 feet (3 to 6 meters) on every single play, so they have to be alert. Average setters get lazy and stand more upright as the game or drill goes on. They have trouble getting to any ball that is passed off the net because their first move is not toward the ball; rather, their first movement is to flex their legs to get ready to run, and their *second* move is toward the ball. Setters can improve their quickness simply by slightly flexing their legs and being ready to go.

Passers and defenders will do their best to deliver a settable ball to the target area, but the setter has to be prepared for the worst. The first thing every setter should do is defend, whether blocking at the net or protecting an area of the backcourt. If a setter doesn't stuff-block the ball or play the first ball as a digger, then he or she

**FIGURE 3.10**  Setting technique.

must immediately react in the direction in which the ball was hit. Setters must have great vision to read where the ball has gone after the opponent's attack and then pick up where their own team digs or passes the ball. The setter's attitude must be that he or she takes *every* second ball. The setter must sprint to the spot toward which the ball is dropping and clear the path along the way. If teammates are in the way, the setter should assert him- or herself and call for the ball loudly while running— and, if necessary, push teammates aside along the way. Of course, no setter wants to hurt a teammate, but setters must claim the spot under the ball and establish an attitude on the court. Nonsetters should take the ball only if the setter dug the ball or is unable to get to the ball in time to set it.

As with passing, the most important body part is the setter's feet. Ideally, setters should get their feet directly under the ball no matter where it goes, whether on or off the court. As they arrive, they should center themselves under the ball so they can more easily set forward or backward. If the setter's hands are in front of his or her face, it's very hard to set backward; it's also easier for blockers to read where he or she is setting. If hands or feet are off to the side of the ball before contact, the result will likely be a mishandle. Ideally, the setter's hands should be waiting directly above the head so that he or she can easily set forward or backward (figure 3.10*b*). One of the best ways for a setter to learn to get centered on the ball is to jump-set as much as possible and alternate setting in both directions. Another good way to practice centering the ball is to have setters set to themselves, then set to target.

Whether they are setting forward or backward, this drill forces them to be directly under the ball with hands centered above the head. When jump-setting in either direction, an athlete will find a way to get directly under the ball with his or her feet. Once off the ground, the setter will have a still core and a balanced upper body.

When watching a setter, most people notice the hands as they contact the ball and follow through to target. It is more important, however, to watch the preparation of the hands and arms. As setters move around the court, their hands should never go below waist level. In fact, the hands should be at chest height and then be brought above the setter's head just as the ball passes its peak. Setters can achieve consistent tempo and accuracy by employing an aggressive follow-through to target with the elbows fully locked out (figure 3.10c, page 51); they can dictate the tempo and distance of the set by controlling arm speed. Late hands, separated hands, and undisciplined hands result in poor location and ball-handling errors, whereas a strong finish to target with the hands and arms allows the setter to deliver consistent tempo and location.

One of the more advanced sets is the one-handed set (figure 3.11). It is normally used when the ball is passed tight to the top of the net and the setter can't get two hands on the ball. It can be very effective because at least one blocker will stay on the setter in an attempt to get the overpass or block the setter dump. If the setter can save the pass, he or she can give the hitter a one-on-one hitting opportunity and a great chance to score.

Many players and coaches focus so much on the set and the attack that they forget how often hitters get blocked. With this in mind, after setting the hitter, the setter's next assignment is hitter coverage. Location of the coverage spot depends on where the setter releases the ball. One common mistake for setters is to watch their set (analyze it, admire it) and fail to get low and close for coverage. Well-rounded setters will be down and ready as the hitter contacts the ball so they can pop the blocked ball up and continue the play. If the hitter does get the ball by the block, the setter then needs to sprint to base defensive position. Setters are often criticized for not playing good defense because they're thinking about setting the next ball, but good setters cover *and* play great defense by anticipating what the opposing setter might do next. They should know specific situations when the other setter might want to dump, and they should rarely be caught off guard. If setters think only about offense, they hurt their team, whereas thinking about defense as well gives the whole team a boost and creates an aggressive attitude instead of a defensive void. In fact, setters who play great defense are often recognized with MVP honors.

**FIGURE 3.11**   One-handed set.

Setters must be fearless in play and consistent in delivery.

Courtesy of University of Wisconsin Athletic Communications

## Setting Technique Keys

- Use a ready or athletic stance.
- Sprint to the spot.
- Get feet and body under the ball.
- Hold hands at chest height.
- Move hands up quickly and early.
- Finish to target.
- Cover your hitter.
- Sprint to base.
- Play defense.

# Setting Strategies

Setting consistency and technique must be handled before strategies can be considered. Once a setter can deliver a good, hittable ball, then you can establish an aggressive mind-set and game plan. The goal of every setter should be to give his or her hitters the easiest opportunity to score. To do so, a setter must make it hard for the opposing blockers to set up a double block. One simple approach to use is setting the ball from pin to pin, or antenna to antenna. By setting the ball the full width of the court in both directions, the setter forces the middle blocker to travel farther to close the block with the outside blocker. In contrast, setting the ball in just one direction a majority of the time or letting the ball drop inside allows the opposition more frequent chances to set up a double block.

The second level of setting from pin to pin involves setting opposite of the flow. Setting with the flow means that the pass takes the setter to the left half of the court and the setter then sets to the hitter on the left side. Generally, the opposition's middle blocker will follow the setter in order to reduce the distance that he or she must travel to close the block. Thus, a setter who aggressively sets opposite of the flow gives the opposing middle fits by making him or her run long distances. If the pass is to the right half of the court, the setter will set to the outside hitter. If the pass takes the setter to the left half of the court, he or she will set the ball to a hitter in the right half of the court. This strategy usually results in a single or split blocker that the hitter can take advantage of. Setters usually use their hands to set these distances. If they are precise enough with their back bump set, then they will be even more effective. Only a few elite setters use this strategy, and it is very deceptive.

To speed up the game and make the offense even harder to defend, the setter should jump-set at every possible opportunity. When the setter contacts the ball at a higher point, the set takes less time to get to target, which means the opposition has less time to decide which way to move to close the block. If the setter jump-sets when he or she is in the front row and back row, the block will flinch and not always know whether the setter is available to attack. All setters should learn to act as an offensive weapon by attacking on the second contact when they are in the front row. If they never dump, the block doesn't have to honor them and can instead double up on the other attackers. The best time for setters to attack is when they are in motion along the net. Some setters dump or tip when the pass is going perfectly to target; unfortunately, when the pass is right on target, the opposing middle blocker doesn't have to move. One way to get this point across is to designate the "perfect" pass area as the "No Dumping Zone." Setters should learn to attack as they move forward and back through the setting zone in order to make the opposition chase them. They'll enjoy much more success and put blockers off balance.

As setters advance their skills, they should use a variety of tempos and locations. First-tempo sets stay low to the net, such as 31s, front 1s, and back 1s. Every team uses its own terminology, but first-tempo sets are attacked very quickly out of the setter's hands. Second-tempo sets range between 3 and 6 feet (0.9 and 1.8 meters) above the net and resemble more of a loop set. Third- and fourth-tempo sets tend to be outside sets to the pin. Again, a faster-tempo set system going from pin to pin is very hard for opposing blockers to keep up with. With sets of different tempos available, setters should know what blocking scheme the opposition is using so they can set in the gaps. If the blockers are pinched into the middle, the sets should move them to the sidelines. If the blockers start by an antenna, some sets can be placed in the gaps between blockers to take advantage of the seams; they can be first- or second-tempo sets to give the hitters the advantage over the blockers. The hitters will be off the ground sooner, and the blockers will have to move from their base and jump earlier.

Another advanced strategy is to overload the blocking zones. By bringing two attackers into one zone, you force the blocker to choose one attacker to key on. This is when the setter will bring in one hitter using a first-tempo set and the other hitter using a second-tempo set. Using crossing patterns makes this strategy even more difficult to defend against; thus, it usually gives offensive players an advantage. Examples of overloading patterns include the X (front or back 1 and a front 2), a double slide (back 1 off one foot and a slide to the antenna), and a 31 with a go (outside set) overloading the right-side blocker. All of these advanced techniques and strategies can be used individually or in combination to keep the opposition off balance and make it easier to score on the attack.

### Setting Strategy Keys

- Set from pin to pin.
- Set opposite of the flow.
- Jump-set.
- Be an offensive weapon.
- Vary tempo.
- Set in the gaps.
- Overload the blocking zones.

# Attacking

Most spectators and players say that the attack is the most exciting play in volleyball. From the initial pass or dig on target to the attacking patterns and the setter's decisions, the main goal is to keep the defense off balance. If your team always runs the same patterns in the same zones at the same tempo, they become easy for blockers to read and defend. The following sections cover attacking techniques and strategies.

## Attacking Techniques

In order to succeed, any hitter must be dynamic and explosive. The two basic types of attack approach being used today are the running slide attack off one foot and the three- or four-step approach with a two-foot takeoff. The slide attack has become much lower and faster over the last 10 years, and it is much more prominent in the women's game. The combination of the lower, faster set to the slide hitter and bigger, more athletic players has created the need to move the standards (poles) farther from the sideline. Previously, the poles were placed only 18 inches (just under half a meter) from the sideline, and players would sometimes land on them and suffer a turned ankle or broken bone. In 2007, the NCAA rules committee recommended that the poles be moved to a minimum of 1 meter (3 feet 3 inches) from the court, and all newly constructed NCAA courts are now required to have the poles at that distance (1 meter) from the sideline. Seeing that players were hitting the pole on a regular basis, however, we moved ours out even farther, to about 4 feet (1.2 meters) in 2006. It works great, and our players don't have to be concerned with where they land. When we go to schools who haven't changed to the wider distance, we definitely see how cramped it is. In fact, while playing at Ohio State, we had a run-in with a pole when our middle hitter came down after a slide with her toes up on the pole pad and her heel on the ground. She suffered a heel bruise that kept her out of the lineup for two matches and hindered her play for the final month of the season. It was a real reminder of what great athletes the sport is developing, along with the importance of providing them with safe environments.

The single-leg takeoff, or slide attack, can be performed in front of the setter (from the sideline to midcourt) or behind the setter. Both approaches allow hitters to rise to their vertical max while flying along the net horizontally, and this horizontal movement makes it hard for blockers to position themselves. Most hitters who use this technique are right-handers, but it can be executed just as well by a left-hander moving from right to left along the net. The slide attack simply begins with a running motion to where the ball will be set. The tempo of the approach should build from slow to fast. The takeoff leg will be the one opposite the hitting arm (figure 3.12a, page 56). As this leg is planted, both forearms should be lifted above the hitter's shoulders. From there, the hitter will draw the hitting arm behind his or her head, lifting the elbow high (figure 3.12b). As the set arrives to the correct location in front of the attacker, the hitting arm will come through to contact the ball.

**FIGURE 3.12**    Single-leg takeoff.

The two-foot takeoff is the most common plant for an attack because the slide attack requires more precise timing. For right-handers, the four-step approach begins with a simple right-left-right-left stepping sequence. The first two are smaller adjustment steps that allow the hitter to head toward the spot where he or she will intercept the set. The third step is more elongated in order to convert the forward momentum into vertical height. The fourth step finishes simultaneously with the third, thus creating the two-foot takeoff. The tempo of the approach should build from slow to fast. It is important to properly coordinate the motion of drawing back the arms with that of the final two-foot plant. As the hitter's feet hit the ground, he or she should have his or her arms pulled back fully behind his or her body in order to begin the forward and upward motion. Novice players often confuse this timing by leaving their arms forward as they plant their feet to jump, thus completely stopping the flow of the jump and decreasing their vertical potential. After the plant, the attacker drives the arms forward and then up above the head to begin the attack arm swing.

With both the single- and double-leg takeoffs, it is important to the hitter's safety that he or she land on both feet. On double-leg takeoffs, a hitter often leans over his or her nonhitting shoulder while reaching for a ball, ends up tilted in the air, and thus lands on one leg. Such plays can lead to ankle and knee injuries because the body cannot support all of that force upon landing. Hitters should practice the correct two-foot landing in training sessions so that it will be ingrained as a habit come game time.

### Attacking Technique Keys

- Build speed during the approach.
- Be dynamic and aggressive.
- Land well balanced on two feet.

## Attacking Strategies

It should be every hitter's goal to master shots to all areas of the court and know how to hit the perimeters. Hitting to the perimeters (sidelines and end lines) creates real problems for defenders, who often come off the sidelines and into the court to play balls. Attackers who hit down into the court risk being blocked (even by small blockers) or hitting the top of the net. All players want to score on the initial swing, but a good attack also means keeping the opposition from running its quick offense. One mistake that hitters often make is thinking that they can always score without having the ball touched by the block; as a result, either they put the ball to the ground and score or they avoid the block but hit the ball out of bounds. I would call such an attacker a terminator because the play will end after he or she hits the ball. Being this kind of terminator is not usually a good thing. In actuality, one of the best strategies for a hitter is to attack the block. At almost all levels, a majority of the blocks put up are bad blocks—late and split, soft, or failing to penetrate the plane of the net. Thus, an aggressive attacker has a great opportunity to score off the edges, at the top, or in the seam of the block. Well-rounded players will use off-speed shots as part of their arsenal in order to keep defenses from setting up only in the perimeter digging bases. Every player should be able to tip or hit roll shots with intention, every attack and arm swing should look similar, and the decision to tip or roll should be made just as the arm comes forward so as not to show the shot too early.

The hitter should still have the advantage even when receiving a trap set—that is, a ball set so close to the net that the block is practically touching the ball before the hitter is. As soon as the hitter recognizes that the set is tight, he or she should take a

Great arm speed and wrist snap give hitters the power to avoid the block.

huge first step toward the net; this move ensures that the hitter can plant and take off straight up, next to the net, and therefore avoid drifting into or under the net. Once in the air, the hitter should press the ball against the blocker and, in a separate move, shove it off the block and out of bounds. Some hitters make the mistake of shoving the ball toward the center of the court or of losing contact with the ball before it touches the block. In order to seize control of the play, it's important that the hitter maintain contact with the ball until he or she feels the ball against the block. This technique can also be used by the setter anytime he or she is handling a tight pass within 3 to 4 feet (0.9 to 1.2 meters) of either sideline. Both hitters and setters should practice the wipe-off technique often in order to be comfortable using it during a game. It's a skill that might be used only once or twice during a match, but this is the kind of point that every team needs in order to win.

## Attacking Strategy Keys

- Attack to get the opponent out of system.
- Hit both at and off the block—don't always avoid it.
- Swing to the sidelines and end lines (the perimeter).
- Use off-speed shots to open areas.
- Wipe off the block on trap sets.

# Hitter Coverage

Many players and teams need to improve their efforts at hitter coverage. If they approach hitter coverage with an aggressive attitude, they'll create opportunities to keep a majority of blocked shots in play. Unfortunately, many players don't give coverage the attention it deserves, and as a result the team misses a chance to keep the play alive. It can be a great inspiration to a team to pick up a ball on a coverage play and transition to win the point.

As the hitter jumps to attack the ball, all five teammates should fight to be in position. Most teams use a similar formation, putting three players in close to the hitter and having two players share the deep court. The position of the setter varies according to where he or she ends up after setting the ball. It's important for the setter to cover immediately after the ball is set. The three players who are closest to the hitter should assume a very low position, with their hands up and in front of their body. They must be ready for a ball that deflects quickly toward them, in which case they may have to use their hands or forearms to make the play. The players sharing the deep court should be in a medium position, with their knees slightly flexed so they can turn and run to cover longer distances. If a hitter attacks from the back row, the team should position a couple of players very close to the net. Since back-row attacks that are blocked often head straight down, near the net, getting a couple of players in tight improves your odds of making a play.

Once the players have hustled to their positions, it's vital that they stop before the hitter contacts the ball. Making a true effort to pause before the ball is contacted gives coverage players a chance to react quickly in any direction to make the play. In contrast, if they are still running to their coverage spots when the attacker hits the ball, they won't be able to make the play on a ball that deflects in the opposite direction. You can record video footage of your team during a match or scrimmage to show them whether they are stopped before the hit. Position the camera at an end line, then show the footage in slow motion. If you can pause the playback right before the hitter contacts the ball, it will be easy to see whether the court is balanced and whether the whole team has paused before the hitter attacks.

After the players are in position and stopped, they should all focus their eyes on the block to enable a quicker reaction to the ball. If, instead, they watch the hitter, they will have to turn their head from the hitter to the block, which can cost them important reaction time and result in a missed play.

The final part of hitter coverage is to make a controlled play to center court so that the offense can start to attack again. The ability to control the ball is determined by how hard the ball comes off the block. A good hitter takes some tight sets and intentionally taps the ball into the block in order to provide an easy coverage play. While a teammate plays the ball to target, the hitter should sprint off the net to prepare for another approach. Teams who work hard on their coverage skills can provide themselves with multiple opportunities to score, whereas teams who lack an aggressive attitude about hitter coverage will be caught off guard and off balance.

### Hitter Coverage Keys

- Fight to be in position.
- Stop before the hitter contacts the ball.
- Focus on the block, not on the hitter.
- Make a controlled play to center court.

# Offensive Drills

## ATTACK TO SCORE

**Purpose**    To improve attackers' ability to score on back-to-back plays and teach setters and passers to cover their hitters.

**Goal**    Attackers compete against each other to earn 3 big points first (2 scores in a row constitute 1 big point).

**Equipment Needed**    Balls.

**Explanation**

- The coach initiates play with a down ball from the sideline to the opposing backcourt. Attackers start at the net and transition to hit as the coach's ball crosses the net. Two passers work together to pass the ball on target. If the pass is not on target, that player rotates out. Two setters come from the right back and rotate for each attacker.

- Hitter 1 attacks first. If hitter 1 scores, the coach hits in another ball and hitter 1 gets a second set. If hitter 1's attack is blocked, the setter and both passers can cover and set the hitter again. If hitter 1's attack is dug, the defense sends the ball over to the offense on the second contact and hitter 2 attacks next. Use the same sequence from hitter 2 to hitter 3 to hitter 1.

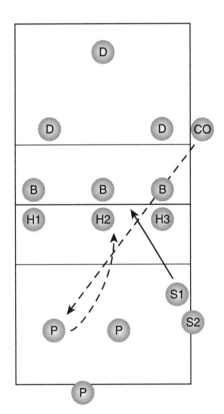

## HITTER SELF-TOSS TO ATTACK

**Purpose**   To learn body control and scoring around a single block and improve arm swing, court vision, and shot selection.

**Goal**   For each hitter to score five times against a single block and three defenders.

**Equipment Needed**   Balls; floor tape or discs to designate target areas.

**Explanation**

- Begin by teaching the hitters to toss to themselves and attack on the net. For some players, it takes time to learn how to toss well and not go into the net. Use the self-toss-and-hit as a warm-up for a couple of practices or until your players can do it with some degree of control.

- In the first round, there is no block, and a group of three hitters needs 10 kills to the corners in order to get out (figure *a*). Subtract for errors; a ball that hits the tape is a wash.

- In the second round, put up a single block and three defenders (figure *b*). Each hitter must score five times to complete the round and rotate a new hitter in. Each hitter does two rounds. Defenders stay in if they dig the ball to the setting target; if they miss the target, a new defender steps in. Hitters take turns so that the defense can attempt to play all the attacks.

- Allow time to clear one ball out before hitting the next.

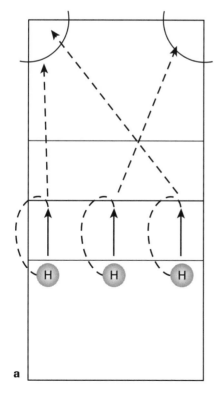

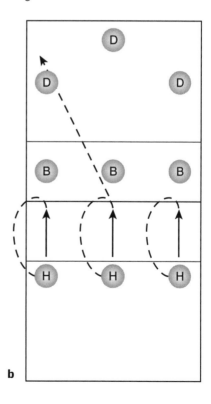

a                                    b

## PASS-AND-HIT CONTROL

**Purpose**   To teach players to pass with control, move to an attack spot, and score with a deep shot.

**Goal**   Each group needs three kills per player to the designated area in order to rotate out. The designated area is the right back corner in round 1 and the left back corner in round 2. In round 3, players need five kills to each corner as a team. For overpasses, subtract 1 point from the group's total.

**Equipment Needed**   Balls; cones or dots to designate kill zones.

**Explanation**

*   The coach initiates to the passer; he or she passes to the target area and sprints to the approach spots. Two (or three) setters run from a base spot to take turns making sets.

*   Figure *a* shows attacking from the left side, figure *b* shows attacking from the right side, and figure *c* shows middle blockers hitting from in front of or behind the setter.

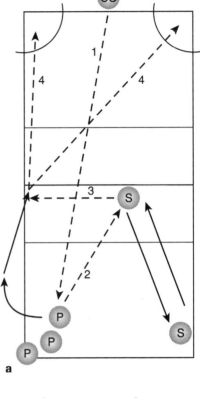

a

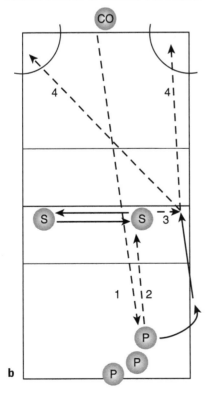

b

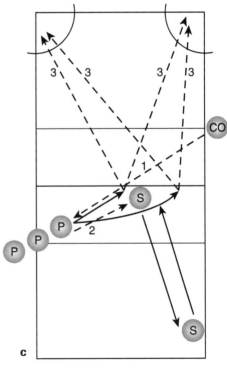

c

- In order to make this a challenging drill for the setters as well, they have to sprint back to the base area each time. Thus, the setters and the hitters must maintain their poise and control even as they tire. Each passer's success is based on his or her own ball control and then on the setter's accuracy.

## SERVE TO DEFEND

**Purpose**   To teach players how to serve tough *and* contribute by making a defensive play.

**Goal**   To score 3 big points. Either a tough serve or a dig to target earns 0.5 point. Subtract a big point for a service error or overpass.

**Equipment Needed**   Balls; one coaching box for each set of three players going on a court.

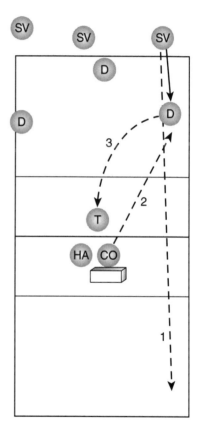

### Explanation

- Three players are stationed on the end line, and each first serves a ball, then sprints into his or her defensive base. The serve must be gamelike and tough in order to earn the half point.

- After the serve is contacted, the server turns into a defender and heads off to his or her defensive base as the coach tosses the ball. As the player nears the defensive base, the coach hits the ball in that area for the player to dig; meanwhile, the next player hits his or her serve and runs into the court. The dig must be controlled to the setting target in order to earn the other half point, and the serve and dig must be made in succession to count as 1 big point.

- When a player earns 3 big points, he or she rotates out and a new player rotates in. Each player does three rounds to complete the drill.

## SET THE STANDARD

**Purpose**    To teach players to score in sideout situations and to defend.

**Goal**    To win more rallies than your opponent in each rotation and to complete six rotations.

**Equipment Needed**    Balls.

### Explanation

- This drill is done in 6v6 form, and each team serves seven balls in each rotation. Team A serves seven times and tries to set the standard as high as possible. If team A wins all 7 points, then team B must also win all 7 in order to avoid losing the rotation. If team A scores, say, 5 points, then team B needs 6 to win the rotation.

- Each time a team wins a rotation by setting the highest standard, it earns 1 big point. Play all six rotations to determine the winner. If the game is tied after six rotations, play one rally-scoring game to 5 points to determine the champion.

## SETTER DIG

**Purpose**    To teach players how to react if the setter digs the first ball across the net. One drill is intended for teams who want the right front setting the next ball; the other is for teams who prefer to have the middle front set the ball.

**Goal**    To execute 10 sets to target (the coach) and then switch positions. Novice: 10 sets. Advanced: 10 sets in a row.

**Equipment Needed**    Balls.

### Explanation

- For the right-side drill, the coach stands at the left front and hits balls at either the right front or the right back. The two defenders work as a team by having one player dig and the other set the ball back to the coach, who then hits the set ball back to them so that they have to get back to base (figure *a*). The keys to this drill are communication, controlled digging, and accurate setting.

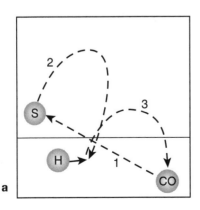

a

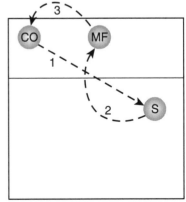

b

- The other option is to always have the middle blocker set when the setter digs (figure *b*). This strategy allows a good right-side hitter and outside hitter to score more. The middle blocker should start facing the net and turn to the digger as the ball is hit by the coach. Once the ball is dug, the middle blocker sets every ball to target. This drill can be done with targets or hitters at the right-side and left-side spots. If both sides of the court are available, the coach can be positioned on a box at the middle back spot on the other side.

## TIP CONTROL

**Purpose**    To teach players to be comfortable and accurate in using the open-hand tip.

**Goal**    To score two times in the bucket. (Vary the types of approach and the bucket locations.)

**Equipment Needed**    Balls; 55-gallon (about 208-liter) trash cans.

### Explanation

- Players must first learn how to soft-tip. Have them toss to themselves and work on tipping into buckets placed in a variety of locations inside the 3-meter (10 foot) line. Once they have a feel for it, they can move on to the drill.

- In the drill, the coach tosses balls to two players, who compete to see who can tip two balls into the bucket first. To ensure a soft touch, the ball must stay in the bucket to count.

- After each round, switch hitters and move the buckets to different spots. You can use a blocker or have someone hold up a Blockette—a padded board measuring at least 2 by 4 feet (0.6 by 1.2 meters)—over which the hitters can tip.

- It's important to have setters take balls tossed from outside the 3-meter line and tip as well. This drill helps all players greatly improve their touch on the soft tip.

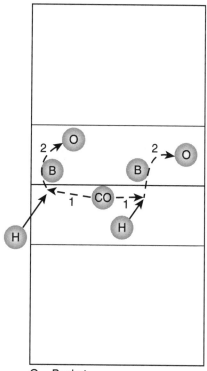

O = Bucket

## TRANSITION COMPETITION

**Purpose**    To teach players how to aggressively attack the block and to transition and score multiple times.

**Goal**    For a hitter to score three consecutive times for 1 big point and earn 3 big points in order to win.

**Equipment Needed**    Balls; Blockette.

### Explanation

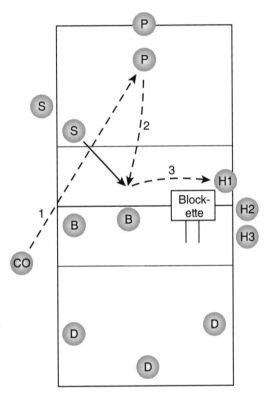

- Challenge the outside hitters by putting a full defense around the Blockette. The coach hits a down ball to two passers. If it's a 3-point pass, they stay; if not, the passer who received the ball rotates out. Setters rotate through after each hitter.

- Three outside hitters compete against each other to be the first to score 3 big points against the defense. As long as the hitter scores (or teammates cover the hitter and keep the blocked ball in play), the hitter stays in the drill. A hitter who errs or is dug must rotate out and run to the bleachers and then back to the end of the line. When his or her next turn comes around, the hitter tries to build on any points earned previously. The first player to win 3 big points wins and goes out, at which point you bring in a new hitter. The other two hitters remain in the drill to try again, and all three players start over with 0 points. If a player does not win after three rounds, he or she is automatically out. This drill can begin anywhere on the court; if performed on the left side first, do the same drill in the middle and on the right side.

# 4

# Defensive Techniques and Strategies

It's one of the most common statements in all of sport: "Defense wins championships." For years, coaches and players have realized that it's not enough to have a good offense if you want to win. You also have to be able to stop, or at least slow down, your opponent's offense. Volleyball generally involves two areas of defense: blocking in the front row and floor defense in the back. Teams often focus on what their physical attributes give them. A bigger team wants to stop the ball at the net with the block, whereas a medium or smaller team focuses its energies on the back row. If a team is well balanced, featuring both height and good ball handlers, it will be able to mount a well-rounded defense that is hard to score on. Whatever your team's makeup, you can play an aggressive style and stress your opponent enough to alter the course of the game. This chapter covers blocking, anticipation, and defensive systems and tactics, as well as the process of selecting a defense. Addressing all of these areas will help you solidify your defense so that you can put forth a well-balanced team capable of playing with anyone.

## Defending the Net

Blocking has changed dramatically over the years, and many younger coaches and players probably don't even know the original strategies. My only knowledge of traditional blocking has evolved from old photos I've seen or from stories I've heard from older players (much older—this was well before my time!). At one point, teams were allowed to have more than three people blocking, and I've seen photos of a four-person block that put up a pretty good wall. In the early days, blockers weren't allowed to penetrate the plane of the net with their hands, so they had to reach straight up. In addition, players weren't as tall, which meant that blockers weren't quite as menacing as they are today.

The main focuses of modern-day blocking at the highest level are to create stress for the opposition's attackers and to play in a defensive system that blends net play with backcourt play. The first line of defense is blocking in the front row. If you can stop your opponent at the net, you won't have to be as concerned about your transition offense. Since offenses have become faster and more complex, great blockers are at a premium, and they can change the outcome of a match.

## Blocking Techniques

Some players are naturally good blockers—they seem to have a knack for putting their hands on more attacks than anyone else. Other blockers have to work very hard at being technically correct in order to improve their odds at the net. Here are some keys to making a good block.

First, each blocker should stand at a forearm's distance from the net with the feet slightly more than shoulder-width apart. The knees should be flexed so that the blocker can instantly jump up rather than having to lower and gather first. The hands should be held at shoulder width, slightly higher than the blocker's head, and should be open with the fingers fanned apart; the hands should also be rounded, as if each is separately holding a bowl (figure 4.1, a-b). Once the hitter has committed to a spot at which to contact the ball, the blocker should explode upward and press his or her hands across the net (figure 4.2). The hands should stay in front of the blocker's body; in fact, the blocker should be able to see the back of the hands as he or she jumps. As soon as the blocker is high enough, he or she should press the palms of the hands across the net. It is helpful to press the heels of the hands over the net first, rather than the fingertips, to prevent the fingers from being injured. This technique should also help prevent balls from being hit between the blocker and the net (i.e., down the blocker's front). As the blocker peaks—and just before the hitter contacts the ball—the blocker should shrug his or her shoulders forward and fully lock out the elbows.

**FIGURE 4.1**  Blocking ready stance: *(a)* front view; *(b)* side view.

At hitter contact, the blocker should flex from the fingertips down to the abdominals in order to match the impact of the strong attack. On the way down from the block, the blocker should keep the elbows locked out until he or she is back on the ground. This technique improves blockers' chances of blocking balls even when they mistime their jump, since it may help them deflect the ball on the way up if they jumped late or on the way down if they jumped early. During the jump, the blocker's eyes should be fixed on the hitter in order to determine when to jump and where the attacker might be hitting the ball. Blockers should land balanced on two feet and be ready to transition to attack if the ball is still in play.

When done correctly, blocking is a very aggressive technique. First, the blocker has to work hard with his or her feet in order to put him- or herself in the best position to jump. Then, at the peak of the jump, the blocker has to aggressively push the hands across the plane of the net and prepare for the impact of the attacker's strongest hit. All of this requires great discipline because the technique is performed at full speed just inches from the net. If done aggressively, the block can be intimidating and psychologically traumatizing to attackers. If done passively,

**FIGURE 4.2** The blocker explodes upward and presses the hands across the net.

it can energize opposing players and allow them to swing with great confidence.

One way to train the upper body in the correct blocking technique is to put the blocker on a box and position a mirror opposite the blocker. This way, the blocker can see his or her own movement and hand positioning without having to do all the jumping. We improvised with this technique by stacking our coaching boxes and using a mirror from the crew team. Each player spent time alone on a box putting his or her hands in the correct position, locking out the elbows, and fanning out the fingers. After practicing a good locked-out upper body from a standing position on the box, players can start from a flexed-knee position to mimic the jumping motion. Eventually, you can remove the box and have players jump and go to a full block while continuing to watch their hands and arms. If you can't get a mirror system at the net, any full-length mirror will work; you can also use mirrors in the rest room or locker room. Players should perform the motion slowly and really watch themselves as they go through the entire sequence. Doing repetitions in front of a mirror helps blockers develop good muscle memory.

The most important aspect of successful blocking is timing. There is no guarantee that tall players and those with good jumps will be great blockers; often, the best blockers are the ones who know how to time their jump. Against quick hitters, some teams use the commit block, wherein the coach asks the blocker to totally commit and jump at the same time the hitter does. If the quick attacker is truly taking off when the ball is in the setter's hands, then the commit block may be the only way to stop or alter the hit. This strategy carries a big risk because the blocker is dedicating all of his or her efforts to one hitter, and if the setter sets the ball to a different attacker, it's nearly impossible for the commit blocker to help out anywhere else.

On higher sets, the blocker can wait longer to set up the block and jump. The blocker usually wants to set up on the angle of attack, but the decision could change depending on scouting reports. Once the blocker decides where to set the block along the net, his or her focus should go to the hitter.

On slower sets, every hitter has to go through the same sequence. It is important for blockers to know hitters' tendencies so they can improve their block setup location and block timing. First, the attackers move toward the anticipated end location of the set, meanwhile looking to see where the block is being set up. Then their focus must go to the ball, and their eyes will therefore come off the blocker. An eye

## A Tip From the Top

In 2001, my first year as head coach, we had a team of hard-nosed Iowa kids who were hardworking, competitive, and looking to prove to the world that they were a great volleyball team. We had an amazing season, upsetting several teams and winning the conference, and we were hosting the first and second rounds of the NCAA tourney. We had beaten Northern Illinois in the first round and were matched up against a tough Minnesota team in the second. We had dropped the first two games, 26-30 and 21-30. Going into the locker room between games two and three, I felt completely overwhelmed by the look in the players' eyes and the words they were saying. I did not know if we were going to win the match, but I did know that it was going to be a battle. In game three, every part of our play was taken up several notches—especially our defense, both at the net and in the backcourt. We fought our way back and won the next two games, 30-21 and 30-19. The ensuing fifth game was everything a deciding game should be and more! We found ourselves down 14-15 with our team serving. Even though we had picked up every part of our game, we had remained unable to handle the slide of All-American Stephanie Hagen. With the match on the line and Minnesota receiving with their best front-row combo up, I saw one of the most aggressive blocks of the night when our left side went one-on-one with the slide, dove in, and blocked for a point to tie it up. She did a "hot lap" around the court in pure excitement from making an aggressive move that finally paid off! We went on to win the match 17-15 to head to the Sweet 16. This team was made up of an amazing, special group of student-athletes who were competitive and aggressive every time they stepped on the court.

—Bobbi Petersen, Head Women's Coach, University of Northern Iowa sequence that will help the blocker is "ball, ball, hitter": Watch the ball from the passer; watch the ball as the setter releases it to see if it is set inside or out and if it is on the net or off; and then look at the hitter to see the angle of attack and pick up hints about where the hitter is going. It is at this point that the blocker chooses the final blocking spot and where to penetrate the net with his or her hands and arms. The blocker should wait until the hitter has left the ground and committed to the attack itself.

Once the blocker jumps, he or she should press the hands across the net as fast and as far as possible (figure 4.3). Coaches often use the word *penetrate* to get blockers to push to the opponent's side of the net. Whether it's small blockers getting 2 inches (5 centimeters) across or big players with big jumps getting 2 feet (0.6 meter) across, they can block much better if they penetrate. The blocker's hands and arms should be across the net and locked out just before the hitter swings at the ball. After the attack is made, the blocker should leave the arms in a locked-out position until he or she lands on the ground. This technique was taught by Toshi Yoshida, the U.S. Women's National Team coach from 2001 to 2004. It's based on the theory that if you leave your arms locked out above your head as you

**FIGURE 4.3** The blocker presses the hands across the net.

land, you have a better chance to deflect the ball even if you jumped too early. Our blockers have enjoyed good success with this technique.

## Blocking Technique Keys

- Stand a forearm's distance from the net.
- Position the feet shoulder-width apart.
- Flex the knees.
- Hold the hands head-high and shoulder-width apart; fan the fingers.
- Flex the legs in order to jump (flex less on quick sets, more on high sets).
- Press the heels of the hands to the tape (top of the net) as soon as possible.
- Push across the plane of the net as far as possible.
- Lock out the elbows, shrug the shoulders forward, and lock the abs before the ball is hit.
- Continue to press across—long and strong.

- Keep the head tilted forward and chin down, and look up at the hitter.
- Keep the elbows locked and the hands strong through the landing.

## Blocking Strategies

Once players have developed good basic blocking technique, teams can use certain blocking strategies to improve their odds of succeeding. Poor blocking teams use little or no strategy; it may seem that they are always late to the outside block or that they don't set up the block in the right place. Blocking strategies contribute to the aggressive style of play because they put players in a mind-set of staying one step ahead of the opponent, and nothing frustrates hitters more than having a block already waiting for them when they arrive to attack.

Tactically, what constitutes a good block? It does one or more of the following:

1. Alters the hitter's intentions. Most hitters have their favorite shots, and a block set up in the right spot can push them away from what they prefer to do. A hitter who is forced to swing or tip to areas with which he or she is not comfortable often makes errors and begins to lose confidence.

2. Channels the ball to the defense. Blockers need to understand that while a stuff block is the most exciting form of block, many matches are won by simply channeling the hitter toward the defensive scheme. Many blockers, especially shorter ones, become frustrated when they aren't stuffing the balls. If they work hard to use the right technique and perform a good double block with their teammate, they can get the better of most hitters.

3. Directs the ball back into the opponent's court (ideally resulting in a stuff block for a point). Shorter blockers' main goal should be to steer the hitter toward the defense or deflect the ball so that their team can make an easy transition play. Most teams and hitters try to score by attacking smaller blockers, but this strategy can play right into the hands of a good small blocker who knows how to slow the ball down with a good deflection (soft) block.

4. Does not give a point to the opposition. A good block must be disciplined enough not to touch the net and cause a violation that gives the other team an easy point.

These basic tactics should form your blockers' mind-set. If blockers think their entire goal is to block balls, they may become overzealous in their desire to terminate the ball. This attitude often leads blockers to play out of control and leave separations in the block or commit net violations. Blockers need to know that they can be good even if they don't stuff the ball on a regular basis. They should feel that they are helping their team if they deflect the ball so it can be played by a teammate or if they channel it in the direction of the defense.

It's important for blockers to prepare at the beginning of a play. As you serve or attack the ball to your opponent, there will always be a specific sequence for which blockers should be prepared. If they anticipate situations addressed in the next three sections, they will be ready to react in time to make a high-quality play.

**The Overpass**   The block is responsible for controlling the top of the net. If the ball comes immediately within range of the blockers from an opponent's pass or a dig, they should do one of three things (discussed here in order of potential success). The first option, if possible, is to sweep the ball along the net to an unoccupied area on the side (figure 4.4). Many hitters who try to attack an overpass make hitting errors into the net or out of bounds; they also risk being blocked by a front-row player, especially the setter. If a blocker attacks the ball and sends it back into the defense, there is a chance that it will be dug. In contrast, being prepared to sweep the ball allows the player to be ready to joust with the opposing blocker if he or she is right on the ball. Sweeping the ball along the net also makes it hard for the defense to begin its transition offense. Occasionally, a blocker will bounce an overpass to the ground and give a huge emotional lift to the team, but more often than not the blocker will make a mistake, thus wasting an opportunity for an easy score. In my early years as a coach, I

**FIGURE 4.4**   The blocker sweeps the ball along the net.

had my teams attack the overpass, but beginning in 2006 I emphasized sweeping the ball. I think this is the most effective and highest-percentage play that can be made. It reduces errors, and our blockers are very efficient with the sweep.

The second option is to attack the ball, and this can be one of the most exciting plays in the sport; indeed, it can change momentum and energize a team. It is also, however, more risky, especially for smaller or lower-level teams, and coaches must evaluate their players' abilities and determine whether the benefits outweigh the risks. When attacking, players should try to change the direction of the ball and hit to the open court. If there is no block up, they can take a strong swing and put the ball down as quickly as possible. When using this technique, players should be careful not to follow through into the net—a good wrist snap is more effective.

The last technique is the most basic, but it is often very effective. If the overpass is arcing higher toward the top of the net and no defending blocker is nearby, they can simply put their hands at the plane of the net and let the ball hit their hands and fall straight down. Defenders will be on their heels expecting an attack or a sweep, and they'll struggle to pick up the ball that goes straight down in front of the blocker. To make sure blockers aren't called for reaching over the net before the opponent can play the ball, they should keep their hands above the plane of the net. If the ball doesn't get to the plane of the net, the blocker should still go up, since showing that he or she might hit or sweep the ball will keep defenders away from the area. The defense will freeze for a split second, and the ball will fall straight to the ground next to the net.

**The Setter Dump**   Responsibility for stopping the setter from dumping usually falls to the middle or left-side blocker. It helps to have a scouting report on the opposing setter so that you know if he or she is very active or tends to dump only in certain situations. It is also important to know where the setter likes to dump, as well as the usual tempo of his or her attack. As the pass or dig nears the setting zone, blockers should keep their hands high and their legs slightly flexed. If a blocker believes that the setter will dump, he or she should quickly press the hands into the expected path of the ball. If the setter is good, he or she may fake the dump and set the ball to a hitter. In that case, the blocker should just do an ankle jump and be prepared to quickly move to the next spot to jump a second time.

**Attack by a Hitter**   On very rare occasions, the dig or pass will go directly to one of the hitters, and they will hit it over on second contact. This may be done intentionally or accidentally. In either case, the block should be alert and react as they usually would; this type of play might happen only once or twice in a season. Otherwise, defenders go back to being ready for the normal sequence of pass or dig, followed by set and attack. Once the overpass and dumping options are gone, blockers can focus on stopping the attackers. Every team's goal should be to have at least two blockers ready to defend every ball as it is being attacked. The middle blocking position is the most rigorous, and excelling at it requires great focus, determination, and athletic ability. Blockers have to deal with varying tempos, hitting styles, and locations of sets. If the opponent is good at using the back-row attack, their job gets even tougher.

Advanced blockers are more mobile and can use certain special moves. One strategy is to show the hitter what he or she wants, then take it away. For example, the blocker could set up in such a way as to show the hitter that the crosscourt or seam shot is open, then at the last second reach outside his or her body line and jump into the hole for the block (figure 4.5). Some coaches teach their blockers to drop their hands into the seam or hole. I prefer to tell them to shove their hands into the seam at a 45-degree angle outside their body line. This technique can work well and makes sense when you look at the play from a hitter's perspective: Once the ball is set to the hitter, he or she finalizes the approach and plants the feet for takeoff near the ball. Just as the hitter takes off, he or she sees the general area of the blocker's body and decides where to hit the ball. The hitter must then raise his or her head and look above the blocker to find the ball, and it is at this moment that the blocker can make one more shuffle move or reach into the expected path of the ball. It's a bit of a risky move for the blocker, but it is one that elite players use on a regular basis. A really good hitter may anticipate the blocker jumping into the path of the ball and quickly change his or her shot. Generally, though, the blocker is making a very aggressive move, and it will often pay off.

**FIGURE 4.5**  The blocker reaches outside the body line and jumps into the hole for the block.

Right- and left-side blockers must be alert for sets that drop in from the sideline. If the set is coming down a couple of feet (less than a meter) inside of where the outside blocker initially set up, he or she should first yell, "In, In, In!" to alert the middle blocker. Then the outside blocker should stick his or her inside arm out horizontally, toward the middle blocker, to stop him or her from traveling too far. The outside blocker is trying to put the middle blocker in the right position to block the sharp crosscourt attack. This technique also prevents the middle blocker from crashing into the outside blocker, who is shuffling inside. Once the middle blocker makes contact with the outside blocker's hand, it is the outside blocker's responsibility to fill that space in the seam.

Let's now consider two special blocking situations that arise only a few times per match. Both must be addressed aggressively. The first is the joust—the ball that comes down toward the plane of the net, where both players can reach it at practically the same time. In my years of coaching, it seems that most jousts have been won by setters, due perhaps in part to the strength in their hands and forearms but mostly to the way they time their jump and press. It is often the player who contacts the ball *second* who wins. The player who contacts it first presses across the net but at a certain point loses his or her initial strength, and at that moment the second player can begin his or her initial press and overtake the first. This move requires good upper-body strength and good hand speed. If one player is too tight to the net, his or her arms will be straighter up and therefore easier to push back. In contrast, keeping the arms out in front of the body provides the best leverage and allows a player to lock the shoulders in a strong position.

The other special blocking situation involves an overpass that the opponent wants to attack. One of volleyball's most exciting plays occurs when the blocker can attack an overpass, and it can change the momentum of a game. It is also a play that can often be shut down by an alert front-row player on the team that sent the ball over. As the ball heads toward the net, the blocker should track the ball and move to where he or she feels it will cross the net. As the ball heads over, the blocker should look at the opposing hitter to see where his or her shoulders are facing. Then, as the opponent draws back the arm to swing, the blocker must get his or her hands across the net and into the path of the ball. The formation of the block should be completed just before the hitter swings so that the ball can be directed right back at the hitter. Thus, what was about to be a momentum-swinging play for the opponent can be turned into a great save for the offense. Both the joust and the block of the overpass can be accomplished only by alert, aggressive players.

© AP Photo/Koji Sasahara

A great team block will put stress on the attacker and force her to make an error.

### Blocking Strategy Keys

- Alter the hitter's intentions.
- Channel the ball to the defense.
- Deflect or stuff the ball.
- Be disciplined; don't overblock and get into the net.
- Anticipate the overpass.
- Be ready on the setter's contact.
- Shift focus to the hitter and move to block.

# Backcourt Defense

The second part of the defense is the floor or backcourt defense. Once the ball gets by the block, it is the rest of the team's responsibility to keep it in play and try to start the offense. Since there are generally four players behind the block available to defend the court, they must be aggressive and cover a lot of area. Attacks come in all speeds and to all spots on the floor, and players must be willing to swarm the court to make the right defensive play in each situation. In order to do that, they need instruction in basic defensive techniques that may be needed on any given play.

The coach's first job is to make sure that every player is comfortable with using a variety of defensive techniques. Every position player on the court should be taught to make defensive moves—even the big middle blocker who only serves and runs in to make one play. Once all the players are competent at using defensive techniques, coaches can teach strategies that help the defense work better together. When the techniques and strategies are combined, players can play with confidence and be more aggressive in defending every attack.

## Backcourt Defensive Techniques

Correct defensive posture (figure 4.6, *a-b*, page 78) gives players the best opportunity to make a variety of plays. Each player's feet should be a little more than shoulder-width apart. The right foot should be slightly forward of the left; this position can be established by putting the toe of the left foot in line with the arch of the right foot. The knees should be flexed, and the head and shoulders should be just in front of the toes so that the heels come slightly off the ground. With the entire body thus balanced, the player can move to the left or the right or forward without taking a false step (i.e., a step that has to be made in one direction before the body can move in another). A false step makes a player slow, and when this problem is corrected, the player can make a faster first step in order to make the play. The arms should be held out in front of the body so that the player is ready to make a play with the hands (above the head) or the platform (to the side and lower areas).

When teaching defensive posture, the keys are balance and the ability to move from base if needed. If the feet are even, then the player can't make an immediate move to the ball. Try it. It's a faster move if the feet are staggered. Think of sprinters

**FIGURE 4.6**    Defensive posture: *(a)* front view; *(b)* side view.

on the track. They don't start with their feet even; they want a foot to push off of. Even a slight stagger helps volleyball players move better on defense, and it keeps them from being back on their heels. Players also need a false step in order to get going if their feet are too close together. Again, when playing aggressive, high-level volleyball, the attacks come fast, and saving a split second can be vital in making the play.

Some defenders are too often in motion; they aren't stopped when the hitter contacts the ball. If they are still moving when the ball is hit, they can dig the ball only if it is hit right at them or in the direction they happen to be going. To improve their odds, defenders should pause before contact is made with the ball. Doing so allows them to step immediately to where the ball is headed. Do not teach a prehop unless the player can be done with it and have both feet on the ground before the hit. If you take video footage of your defenders, you will see that players who prehop often land only after the ball is halfway to them; in addition, as they land, their muscles still have to flex to absorb the move, so it will take another fraction of a second for them to make a move in any other direction. Many players feel like they're slow and have insufficient time to react, but the real problem is that the prehop uses valuable time, and therefore the ball is only 10 feet (3 meters) away by the time they are ready. It can be helpful to watch older players on defense. Some people think they are just old and slow and therefore don't move much. That may be true in some cases, but these players make plays because they move with the contact of the hit; they don't waste any motion.

The best players need to be comfortable with various defensive moves: the upright dig, the step-and-surround, the single-knee drop, the double-knee drop, the collapse, the chase-and-pop, and the pancake in a prone position. Here are some simple hints:

*Upright dig* (figure 4.7, *a-b*). Beat the ball to the spot and form a strong leg base and platform.

**FIGURE 4.7**    Upright dig: *(a)* front view; *(b)* side view.

*Step-and-surround* (figure 4.8). Make a jab step forward (45 degrees) and surround the ball with the outside foot.

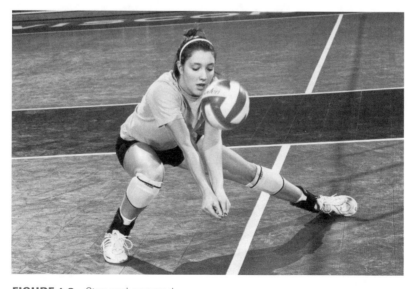

**FIGURE 4.8**    Step-and-surround.

*Single-knee drop* (figure 4.9). Go to one knee in order to keep the hips below the ball and the platform in a good position.

**FIGURE 4.9**　Single-knee drop.

*Collapse* (figure 4.10). To get fully under a ball hit hard at the defender, collapse to the floor while keeping the platform intact.

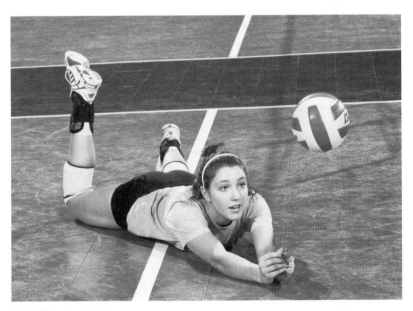

**FIGURE 4.10**　Collapse.

*Chase-and-pop* (figure 4.11). An off-speed ball away from the body must be pursued and played high enough for a setter to come from the back row to play it. Reach under and past the ball, then use a J stroke (bend at the wrists and elbows) to pop the ball up.

**FIGURE 4.11**   Chase-and-pop.

*Pancake* (figure 4.12). Use only for off-speed balls that are away from the defender and coming down more vertically. Balls coming to the defender at an angle (horizontally) are more difficult to pancake. Shove off the back leg, slide to the stomach and chest, and fully extend the arm and hand with the palm down under the ball. Fingers should be fanned out and the hand should be held flat and strong against the floor as the ball arrives. The hand is like a spatula, and if it is flat on the floor, the ball should bounce up high enough for a teammate to make the next play.

**FIGURE 4.12**   Pancake.

It's important to teach players to be comfortable with defending aggressively. Individually, they must each go all out for a ball and hit the floor at full speed if needed. What used to be viewed as an emergency technique (e.g., sprawl, dive, pancake, or dig and roll) is now simply a necessary skill for all backcourt players to learn. Taller players often have a harder time with such skills because of their distance from the ground and the length of their limbs. Teach them how to gradually get lower as they step toward the ball so they can make a smooth move like a plane coming in for a landing, finishing with a light touchdown. The opposite is the plane, or player, who heads straight down to the ground from a high position and crashes and burns on impact. Some people wouldn't call volleyball an impact sport, but it is. The impact comes on a regular basis—with the floor and with teammates.

To help players get comfortable going to the floor, try using soft (cotton) gardening or work gloves. They are fairly inexpensive, and you can find them at most lumberyards in a wide variety of sizes. Have players put on the gloves, start on one knee, and see how far they can shove off with their legs and slide forward on the floor (figure 4.13). They should make contact with the ground with their lead hand and that same side of their body. Don't have them run and slide yet—you'll get some injured players if you try that right away. Once they try a few slides, mark the farthest spot their hand reached. Then ask them to be sure to shove off their back leg just before their body hits the ground in order to get better distance and a smoother landing. Start slowly with this technique and practice some reps every other day (if

**FIGURE 4.13**    Glove slide exercise.

you do it every day, players' hips and sides will be so bruised that they won't be able to walk). You may want to have the players use hip pads if they are doing dozens of reps; even cut-up carpet padding will give you an inexpensive way to avoid injury and keep players on the court.

Once your players are comfortable sliding to the front and sides, have them use the gloves in a defensive drill. You'll find that they are less inhibited and more aggressive in going for the ball. As they grow more confident with their move to the ground, they can start doing the same drills without the gloves. After a few weeks without the gloves, bring them back for drills to remind them how much more court they can cover with the shove-and-slide move. Your defenders will play with more explosive moves to the ball and will cover more of the court. Many players who were all-state or All-American in high school get to college without good floor-defense skills, and using the gloves is a great way to get all of them playing the aggressive style of defense that every coach wants to see.

Defense is a vital part of the game that every team must master in order to win on a regular basis. Like anything else, however, it doesn't just happen by itself. Teams must work on basic movement patterns and techniques before progressing to team defenses. Sometimes, repetitive digging drills are needed so that players can develop muscle memory for a variety of moves. Team practices should also involve pairs digging side by side, blockers working together, and front- and backcourts playing as a unit. All the while, the attitude must be aggressive or the team will not reach its maximum potential.

### Defensive Technique Keys

- Maintain a wide base with the feet slightly greater than shoulder-width apart.
- Stagger the feet slightly (position the left toe at the instep of the right foot); heels should be slightly off the ground.
- Flex the knees and keep the body in balance.
- Shoulders should be forward, slightly in front of the lead toe.
- Hold the arms out in front and be ready to use the platform or the hands to defend.

## Backcourt Defensive Strategies

Within the defensive scheme being used, each player has to anticipate what might be done by the opposition. The first part of the sequence is the same as for the blockers. Defenders have to be ready for the overpass, the dump, and the attack. They can improve their odds by anticipating what kind of shot the hitter or attacker might make. Scouting reports can help, but experience also counts. Here are a few basic examples:

1. If the setter on one side tries to dump but does not score, it is possible that the opposition's setter will dump on the next play within the rally.

2. If a hitter has been blocked two or three consecutive times in previous rallies, he or she is likely to bring an off-speed shot on the next set.

3. A hitter who knows he or she is facing a triple block may back off and tip.

4. A right-side hitter who runs an X (a 2 in front) may tip to the zone 4 sideline if the left-side blocker follows him or her in.

5. If a left-side hitter runs a 32 (gap) and the right-side blocker follows him or her in, the hitter may tip to the zone 2 sideline.

6. A hitter who is showing tip from the left side will usually go short behind the block or assume that the right back is coming up the line to play the tip and then throw it to the deep zone 1 corner.

7. When a hitter gets a bad set or is off balance, he or she will often make an off-speed play.

Knowing that they will see these ploys on a regular basis, defenders can be alert and ready when the opponent tries the shot. On the other hand, the best hitters know that bad sets trigger certain responses from defenders who can make easy plays once they know an attacker's tendencies. As a result, top hitters have learned to be aggressive with every swing and to hit off-speed shots only when they are approaching a good set.

The coach should assign a specific territory to every defender. The size of the area depends on the defender's speed and skill, and it will overlap the territory of other defenders. Each individual must know that he or she is in charge of a circle 5 feet (1.5 meters) in diameter around his or her body for hard-hit balls, as well as a circle 15 feet (4.6 meters) in diameter for off-speed hits. Each player must want and expect each attack to come into his or her territory. Players should play defense in the same way they play pepper with a partner to warm up. In pepper, they know that every ball is coming their way, so they're able to anticipate the speed and direction of the attack. Defenders will make many more plays if they pretend the attacker is a pepper partner and thus expect every ball to come in their direction. The defender can then just dig the ball to target rather than back to the hitter. Defenders should also understand that a majority of the balls will be off-speed shots (tips, dumps, deflections) that require them to move their feet two or three steps. Too many defenders get dug in with their weight on their heels and can't move anywhere to pursue a ball.

In volleyball, we always know that when we walk into a gym the dimensions on our side of the court will be identical (29 feet 6 inches by 29 feet 6 inches, or 9 meters by 9 meters). Since volleyball courts are always the same size, we know just how much court a team must defend. In the younger age groups, it seems like a lot, but as the block gets bigger there is less area to cover. This fact was demonstrated to me by Niels Pedersen, my Junior Olympic coach in high school and later a partner at the 2nd City Volleyball Club of Chicago. Pedersen taught me this drill, and I think it makes a good impression on the players as defenders. To show players just how much court they can cover on defense, have them line up across the end line. Next, have them sprint into the court toward the 3-meter (10 foot) line while you count out loud: "one one thousand, two one thousand." Then mark their progress to make clear to them just how far they can run in 2 seconds. Now, stand on the other side of the net in one of the hitting positions. You can also stand on a chair or coaching box. Toss the ball to yourself and execute a tip, arcing it over an imaginary block to the 3-meter line in the middle of the court. As you do this, have the team count out loud, beginning at the moment you touch the ball to tip it; they should be able to count to 2 by the time the ball drops. This exercise should help players understand that if they are alert and ready to be mobile on defense, they can run from the end line and pick up a ball tipped to center court. With at least four defenders available during every game, they should now feel like they can easily cover the entire court.

One of the best drills you can do to help a team learn to cover the court better is called Speed Ball. Players from seventh grade through college can benefit from this drill, and they enjoy it at all levels. It can be used as a warm-up game, and it will improve movement, anticipation, and the use of strategy. Have the players form doubles teams and start each game by having the players on the incoming challenger's team serve. Play 1-point rally-scoring games and have the winning teams rotate to the far side of the net. The near side of the net will be the challenger's court. Start with throwing and catching, then work up to making one, two, and finally three contacts. With the throw-and-catch game, the player catching the ball can take only two steps before having to throw it back across the net. The most important concept the players initially learn is moving to get a ball. After that, they learn to throw to the open spots. It sounds basic, but some players will throw right back to the areas already occupied by the opposing players. Very quickly, however, you'll begin to see them throwing short, deep, and into the seam between players. You'll see the two players on defense start communicating and balancing the court to cover the open spaces.

After a few minutes, change the rules so that catching the ball is not allowed. Players must now hit the ball back over the net with only one contact. You'll see the pace of the game increase. After a few more minutes, move on to two contacts and then to three. Once at three contacts, you can either *require* three contacts or allow players to send it across on the first, second, or third contact. You will have a great game of doubles going, and the players will immensely improve their coverage of the court.

Another variation of the game is to have doubles teams lined up on both end lines. This time, immediately after playing the ball over the net, each team sprints around the poles to the far end line and gets ready to enter the court again. Teams rapidly rotate through and are eliminated if their team makes an error while on the court. As teams get eliminated it gets tougher, because as soon as a team sprints to the opposite court, the players have to jump right in and play. If they don't get there in time to make a play, they will lose that point and be out of the game. Eventually, two teams will remain to play for the final point, during which they stay on their court. Both variations of Speed Ball are great for enhancing competitiveness, movement, and problem solving.

## The Badger Defensive Pledge

Desire is a key to being a great defender. Defensive players must truly want the ball to come their way, and they have to want to make a good play to start the offense. In defense, however, as in every part of playing aggressive volleyball, desire is nothing without effort. Several years ago, in an attempt to improve our defensive effort, I asked assistant Christy Johnson to put together a defensive pledge. We printed it up and handed it out to the team. Before every practice, the players would stand together and recite the pledge. It was our intent to have the words of the pledge create a great defensive attitude in their hearts and minds.

### The Badger Defensive Pledge

1. I will make every effort to play great defense. It doesn't matter that the ball looks undiggable or unretrievable—I will do everything possible to bring the ball up.
2. I will not let a tip, roll, or deflection drop in my defensive zone.
3. I will try my best to dig a hard-hit ball, but I will NEVER get beat by a tip or roll.

Our team defense improved dramatically over the course of the season, and the team's mind-set became much more aggressive and confident. In fact, after a few days of reciting the pledge, the whole team had it memorized and said it in unison without the handout. They probably thought we were a little crazy, but you have to be creative when you're trying to solve problems.

# Team Defense

Learning the individual skills and techniques involved in defense is vital if your team wants any kind of shot at playing good team defense. Once the individual skills become habit, the improved ball control can be used to play defense as a team. The players will now be challenged with learning their responsibilities in a variety of situations so they can react instinctively during a match. When players combine individual techniques with team defense, their confidence and aggressive mentality catch fire. The following sections explain how to work as a unit, how to read specific situations, and how to select the right defense for your team.

## Working as a Defensive Unit

The best defensive teams not only play good individual defense but also flow together as a unit. Every player knows where he or she should be in every situation, and players react well to every different type of shot that crosses the net. While players begin with individual assignments in specific zones, they must be alert to balls heading to the outskirts of their areas of responsibility. A team that has practiced every possible scenario won't miss a beat, and the shifting of roles will be seamless. How do you know when it's time to make an adjustment? Basically, it's time when an opponent beats you with the same play again and again. If you don't adjust, the opponent will continue to score points until the match is won. There are hundreds of situations that arise regularly, and savvy coaches pick up on the trend and know it's time to make a correction. Here are some examples of the adjustments that players have to make as a team.

• Some left-side hitters tip every time they get a bad set, and others show early signs of a tip by extending the arm to tip instead of drawing it back to hit. In both cases, the two most common spots to tip to are right over the block and straight down the line. As the left-side hitter shows tip, the right back defender should run in for the short tip. The middle back is ready to move to the right corner to cover the deep line, and the left back covers center-court tips. The left front comes across for the tip or roll just inside the block (figure 4.14).

• The same scenario can be involved in defending the right-side hitter (figure 4.15).

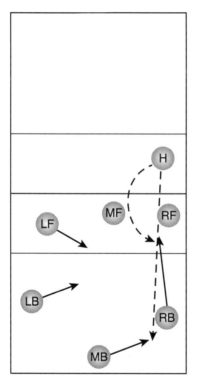

**FIGURE 4.14**  Adjusting the defense against a left-side attacker.

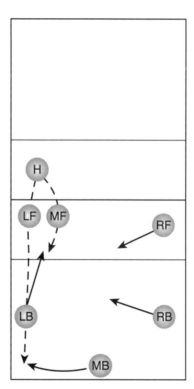

**FIGURE 4.15**  Adjusting the defense against a right-side attacker.

• The coach should designate who will set if the setter digs the ball. Some teams have the right front set (figure 4.16a, page 88), some use the middle blocker (figure 4.16b), and some bring in the libero from the back row (figure 4.16c). Using the

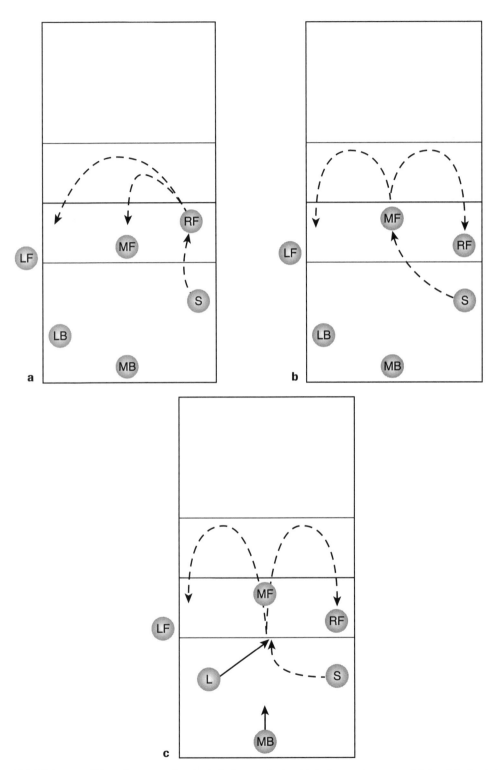

**FIGURE 4.16** When the setter digs the ball, the coach should designate the set to: *(a)* the right front, *(b)* the middle blocker, or *(c)* the libero (or whoever is left back).

right front is best if the player is a lefty or someone who can run a quick set. Having the middle blocker set allows the right- and left-side hitters to get a big approach, and there will likely be only two blockers. If the right front sets to the middle hitter, it is usually a higher set, which allows three blockers to be there together. Using the libero to bump-set removes the risk of a ball-handling error by one of the front-row hitters. The only problem with using the libero is that it is illegal for a hitter to attack the ball off a libero set if the libero is in front of the 3-meter (10 foot)line when he or she sets the ball. A set coming from the back row tends to create a harder angle for the front-row attacker to swing at, so he or she should be sure to get a wider approach. Each team must decide what strategy is best in light of the players it has. Early in my career, I had the right front player set; starting in 2005, I had the middle hitter do it. We've had more success getting kills off sets by the middle hitter. Next year, I may have the libero set if the setter cannot.

Each of these situations should be practiced on a regular basis so the team can react and adjust as needed. When they are mastered, your team will gain points; if, on the other hand, you don't practice solving them, your defense and offense will fall apart. Top teams make it look easy, but the key is that all six players are playing their roles to perfection. That is when six become one.

## Reading the Offense

Good individual and team defense can be improved by a team's ability to read the opponent's offenses and adjust accordingly. Top defensive teams seem like they're always in the right place at the right time. It's because they've learned the probabilities of what can happen in each situation and they play the odds. Teams need to read three aspects of the opponent's offense: the system, the situation, and the player.

Reading the system means knowing how many setters are being used and what type of patterns the hitters run. The 6-2 system involves two setters who are usually setting only out of the back row. When they come to the front row, either they become hitters or hitters substitute in for them. Knowing that the setter is always in the back row, the defensive wings don't have to be as concerned about him or her dumping the ball. This in turn means that they can start wider toward the sidelines and focus more on defending the hitter's attacks. Occasionally, you will find setters who keep the ball below the plane of the net and set the ball over on two. With an active setter, the defensive wings will have to be more alert, but they don't have to stay too close since the ball would still have to go up and over the net. It's a slower attack to defend than the dump, which is thrown straight down.

The 5-1 system poses different challenges for defenders, since the setter can tip, dump, and hit in the front row. The key to intelligent reading is knowing that when the setter is pulled off the net by a pass or dig, the blocker who was in charge of the setter can now focus on a different hitter. The defenders can either put two blockers on the middle hitter or let the left-side blocker take the middle hitter while the middle blocker kicks out to the right and doubles up on the outside hitter. The left-side blocker is usually in charge of the setter until the middle hitter goes behind the

Blockers must read situations and use the correct eye sequence—from the passer to the setter and then to the hitter's approach angle.

setter and changes zones. When that happens, the left-side blocker picks up the middle hitter, and the middle blocker takes the setter. If the middle hitter stays in front of the setter, then the left-side blocker stays with the setter even if it takes him or her to center court.

Reading the situation involves a combination of knowing the system and seeing the hitting patterns. The defending team should always identify what is happening with all of the opponent's available hitters as the ball is dug or passed to the setter. Blockers and defenders must visually follow the moves of the offensive players as each play develops and put themselves in the best position to defend the play. Better offensive teams move their hitters around in search of single or split blocks. There are a couple of maneuvers that right- and left-side blockers should learn to make. Right-side blockers should look to see if the opposing left-side hitter's pattern stays within the sideline or goes outside the court. If the hitter stays in the court, it is likely to be a gap set (a 32), and the blocker can come in off the antenna to block the ball. When the hitter goes outside of the court to approach, the blocker will probably have to protect more of the line. Left-side blockers can watch for similar movement. If the right-side hitter comes into the court to start the approach, the opponent may be running an X or stepping in to pull the block inside, only to run back out for a slide.

For both the right- and left-side blockers, communication is important. They need to verbalize what they are seeing to their middle blocker so he or she can adjust as needed. Middle blockers will also read situations, and this can simplify what could be a very difficult job. The most important thing for a middle to know is the accuracy of the pass. A poor pass limits the options for the offense, and the middle can kick out sooner to the outside hitter. Good passing can make it a tough night for the middle blocker because of all the options. Great middles are impressive because they have to be the hardest-working player on the court.

Reading the player helps both the front- and backcourt defense. Blockers should watch the approach patterns and the turn of the shoulders to know what direction the hitter will probably choose. Backcourt players must work around the perimeter of the block so they can see the hitter's attacking arm. If they can get themselves into a spot where they have a clean view of the hitting arm, then they have a good shot at digging the ball.

Reading the player's body language can also allow the defense to determine what velocity the ball will have. Some hitters show a tip early, and on a bad set you can see some hitters get cautious and passive. At such times, defenders should be ready to get mobile and play the off-speed shot. Knowing a hitter's situational tendencies can also help defenses gain points. For example, as mentioned earlier, if a hitter gets blocked a couple of times, he or she will likely come back with an off-speed shot in the near future. Smart, aggressive defenders pick up on such nuances and make the easy play.

## Choosing a Team Defense

There are numerous defenses to choose from, and it's important for a team to be good at two or three of them. Each defense has its strengths and weaknesses based on where players are aligned. If a team uses only one defensive alignment, it is predictable and more easily beaten, since a good opponent will figure out where the open or weak spots are and take advantage of them to score. A coach with an aggressive attitude toward team defense makes adjustments during the course of each game in order to put the players in their optimal positions. Here are four defensive alignments to choose from.

**Perimeter**   In this defense, the block is in charge of protecting the center of the court and the backcourt patrols the sidelines. When defending an outside hitter,

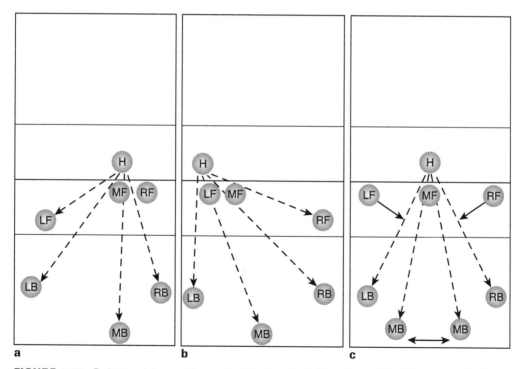

a                           b                           c

**FIGURE 4.17**   Perimeter defense: *(a)* against a left-side attack, *(b)* against a right-side attack, and *(c)* against a middle attack.

the block should leave a little line and channel the hitter to the line or crosscourt diggers. The off blocker is in charge of the off-speed shot to center court, and the middle back reads the seam of the block. The weakness lies in the big open area behind the block, so this is not a defense to run against a team that tips short. Figure 4.17a on page 91 shows this defense against a left-side attack, figure 4.17b shows it against a right-side attack, and figure 4.17c shows it against a middle attack. When defending the quick middle attack, if the right or left front blockers don't have time to help block, then they are in charge of off-speed shots behind the middle blocker.

**Rotation**    In a rotation defense, the block is in charge of sealing off the line shot from the outside hitters. The line digger rotates up behind the block for off-speed shots, the middle back rotates to the corner on the side of the hitter, and the off blocker comes off the net to the 3-meter (10 foot) line to dig. The player behind the block should be about 6 feet (1.8 meters) in from the sideline so that he or she is equidistant from a number of tipping spots. Some coaches like to start the rotated player up near the sideline so he or she can head into the court toward his or her teammates to make plays. I think that positioning puts the defender too far from some balls he or she will have to get. The weakness of the full rotation defense is the high seam shot to the middle back. You can play a "no-corner" variation of the rotation defense wherein the middle back stays in the middle to dig the seam shot. This ploy often works if you have a strong outside blocker who

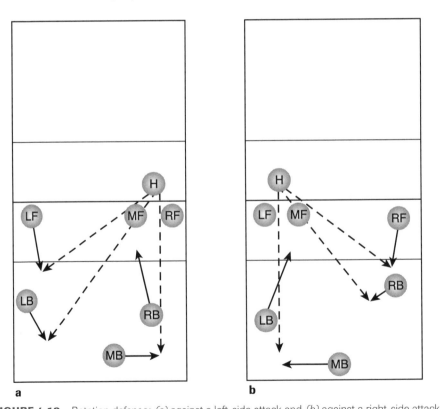

**FIGURE 4.18**    Rotation defense: *(a)* against a left-side attack and *(b)* against a right-side attack.

is good at sealing the line shot, thus preventing the hitter from attacking down the line to the corner. The weakness of the no-corner defense comes into play if an opponent is good at hitting an off-speed shot to the corner down the line. Figure 4.18*a* shows a rotation defense against a left-side attack, and figure 4.18*b* shows it against a right-side attack. There really isn't time to rotate against a quick attack.

**Roaming**    In this defensive scheme, the right back player roams behind the block and follows the set wherever it goes. The middle back player automatically goes to the right corner, and the left back player stays in the left corner. This is a great defense against teams trained to hit to the corners, since the defenders just have to pivot and face the attacker. They don't have to run anywhere, so they will be sitting and waiting for the corner shots. The off blocker drops off to dig the hard crosscourt shot from the outside hitter. The weakness of this defense involves defending setter dumps to the sidelines. Figure 4.19 shows the defense against right-side, left-side, and middle attacks.

**Single Block or Five Back**    This defense is great for smaller teams who really can't block. Such teams have a number of players who can't get their hands above the net, so trying to block doesn't make much sense. Put up a single block and have everyone else pick up tips and dig the hard-hit balls. The front-row player next to the blocker has tips, while everyone else is assigned an area to dig. This defense puts a lot of bodies in the hitting zones and can really frustrate attackers. Rather than

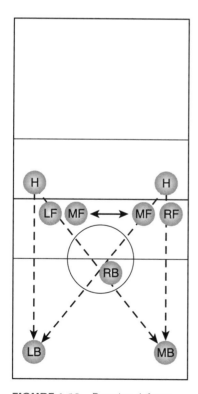

**FIGURE 4.19**    Roaming defense.

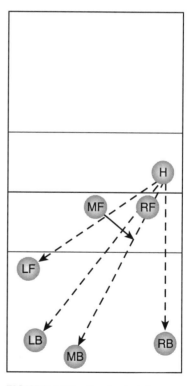

**FIGURE 4.20**    Five-back defense.

waste a player at the net who can't touch the ball, assign everyone a spot to defend behind the block. Playing this defense against teams who are very good offensively is difficult, but you may succeed with it against a team who is similar in size. Figure 4.20 on page 93 shows the five-back defense against the left-side attacker. The same defense against a right-side attack would use only the left front player to block. The middle blocker would be in charge of the short tip in both situations.

With each defense, players must perform certain skills in order for the team to be successful. The coach has to analyze each player and put him or her in the right situation within the defense in order to be as successful as possible. Players should be positioned according to their characteristics and talents—jump, speed, height, depth perception, ball-handling skills, and volleyball IQ.

In the front row, coaches often put the tallest player in the middle blocking position. Sometimes it's best to put the tallest player, or the biggest jumper, on the right side to block the opponent's best hitter. Most teams set the left-side hitter more often because bad passes dictate it and some setters aren't comfortable setting behind them. Putting your best blocker or tallest player on the right can really disrupt the opponent's offense and cause its players to set other areas they aren't as comfortable with.

In the backcourt, one area to look at is your setter's defensive base. If you use a perimeter defense, the setter needs to be back deep on the line before hitter contact, but you should answer the following questions before you put the setter back deep to dig: Is the setter a good defender? If the ball is hit to another defender, is the setter quick enough to get up to the net to set? If you answer no to one or both of these questions, then consider putting the setter in a better position. In a rotation defense, the setter would rotate up behind the block to pick up off-speed shots, which are probably the easier balls to handle. This system also puts the setter closer to the net so that the team can mount an effective transition offense. This position change works, however, only if you have a solid right-side blocker who can slow down or stop the line shots.

The middle back defender should be good at moving laterally. He or she must be able to sprint from corner to corner to defend the full length of the end line. This player might also have to sprint off the back side of the court to chase down a ball hit hard off the top of the block. Therefore, putting someone who is immobile in this position will cost your defense points on a regular basis. Right-side blockers often channel the opposition's left-side hitter to the crosscourt shots, so the left back defender should be a player who can dig hard-hit balls at close range. The left back player should also be quick enough to swarm the center of the court for off-speed shots and setter dumps. Over the course of scrimmages and matches, the coach has to look for ways to make the defense more efficient and effective. Randomly putting players in positions because "that's where they always play" is like putting a square peg in a round hole. Find the right fit for your players' talents and your defense can improve dramatically.

# Defensive Drills

## BLOCK AND TRAVEL TO SCORE

**Purpose**    For blockers to sprint from spot to spot alone in order to block balls. They will have to fight to get their hands across the net to block (or deflect) each ball in order to score points and get out.

**Goal**    To block or (for shorter players) deflect three balls hit by two coaches or by players on boxes.

**Equipment Needed**    Balls; two coaching boxes.

**Explanation**

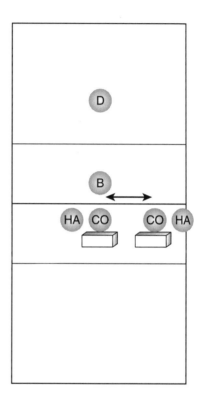

- Position two coaching boxes 8 to 10 feet (2.4 to 3 meters) apart on the same side of the net. Coaches self-toss and alternate hitting into the area of the blocker.

- The blocker must move from coach to coach with correct footwork and attempt to block every ball the coaches hit. Blockers need three stuff blocks or good deflections to complete a round, and each player does three rounds. Coaches should start slower in early rounds and increase the speed between hits in the second and third rounds.

- In order to earn the points, the blocker should have to fight to get his or her hands across the net before the coach swings at the ball. For shorter blockers, put a defender behind them for the drill and require the blockers to touch or deflect three balls in such a way that they can be played up by the defender.

## DEFENDER HEAVEN

**Purpose**   To teach defenders to stay calm and focused while performing high-quality, back-to-back digs.

**Goal**   To score 10 big points (1 big point is earned for two consecutive digs on target). If using setters, they need 10 good sets to the left-side and right-side target spots combined.

**Equipment Needed**   Balls.

**Explanation**

- One defender starts in his or her base position while teammates are ready to come in. Two coaches (or players) are on boxes, ready to hit. The first coach hits at the defender, and as soon as the defender plays the first ball the other coach hits at the same defender. Players must finish the first dig and immediately shift their body and focus to the second hitter to make a good play.

- Each defender needs both digs to go to the target area to count as 1 big point, and 10 big points are needed for a player to rotate out.

- An advanced version adds a setter or two who need 10 sets to the left-side and right-side target areas for the defenders to get out. Nonsetters should be used as well in order to improve their setting.

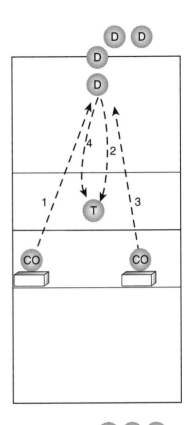

## DIG-AND-RUN-DOWN CONTROL

**Purpose**   For defenders to make two consecutive good plays to the setter that require different skills (a hard-hit ball to dig and an off-speed ball to run down). The setter must prove his or her consistency by setting two balls in a row to a designated target area.

**Goal**   To score 15 big points as a group (1 big point is earned when both balls are set on target).

**Equipment Needed**   Balls; one coaching box.

**Explanation**

- Start with three or four defenders, a setter, and two targets. The coach hits from a box at a single defender, who digs the ball to the setter. Immedi-

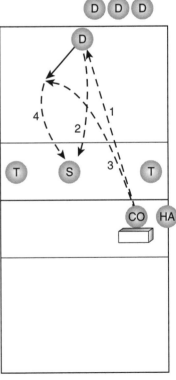

ately after the ball is dug, a second ball is tossed for the same defender to run down. The setter must set both balls on target for 1 big point. Eventually, you can change the sequence to give the off-speed ball first, then the hard-hit ball.

- If the defender scores a big point, he or she can stay in and attempt to score another one. Once the defender fails to score back-to-back small points, he or she rotates out and a new defender enters. The setter stays in for the whole group.

- This drill promotes high-quality defensive plays and consistent setting. Nonsetters can also rotate in to set in order to improve their skills.

## DUMP COVERAGE

**Purpose**    To teach defenders how to read an attacking setter and to teach setters how to dump (attack) a wide range of locations.

**Goal**    Offense competes against defense to reach 15 points. A dig in-target earns 2 points, and a settable dig earns 1 point. If neither occurs, the offense earns 1 point.

**Equipment Needed**    Balls; floor tape or discs to designate the target area.

**Explanation**

- Start with the coach hitting a down ball to two passers.

- The setter attacks to score in any area, and the blocker and defenders try to prevent the score. If the setter doesn't score off the pass, the passer who set the ball rotates out.

- The defenders attempt to play the ball into the marked-off area to score 2 points. If a defender doesn't make a play that earns a point, he or she rotates off.

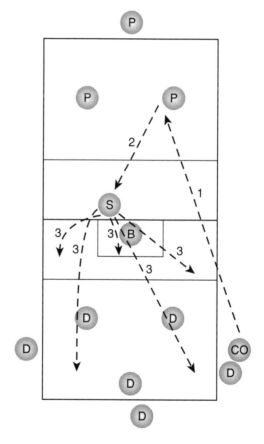

## PIT BONUS

**Purpose**    To teach defenders how to make great plays in difficult situations. Here are two drills based on the old "Pit" format, where the coach is banging balls at the player or tossing balls around the court.

**Goal**    One person in the pit goes for 60 seconds, but each dig back on target subtracts 5 seconds off the total time remaining. Alternatively, two people in the pit go together until they set 10 hittable balls to the right- or left-side target areas. This is a good drill for improving the quality of dug balls and testing players' toughness. It is not so good for involving a large number of players, since only one or two go at a time.

**Equipment Needed**    Balls.

**Explanation**
- One defender starts in the base position while a coach hits at him or her or tosses balls around the court (figure *a*). To make it more realistic, the coach could be positioned on a box on the other side of the net. The defender is in for 60 seconds, but for every ball played into the target area, he or she gets 5 seconds removed from the time remaining. The emphasis is on high-quality plays and getting done as soon as possible.
- Two players are on the court, but the coach hits only at one defender. The defender digs to center court, whereupon the partner must set the ball to one of the outside hitter target spots (figure *b*). Each set on target earns 1 point, and the pair must score 10 points to end the drill. Teamwork plays a big part in this drill because the player who is setting needs to make high-quality plays to help his or her partner finish before becoming exhausted. The drill can also be done by alternating hits to each player.

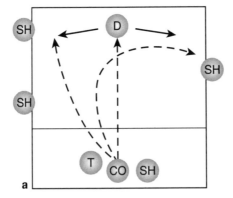

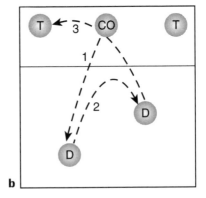

## POSITION-VERSUS-POSITION DEFENSE

**Purpose**   To promote competitive defensive attitudes and improve focus within chaos.

**Goal**   To dig 10 balls into the target area before your opponents do.

**Equipment Needed**   Balls; coaching boxes.

**Explanation**

- This drill involves three groups of three or four players; one player is on the court at a time, and the others are ready to rotate in. Two groups dig from their normal defensive bases while the third group is in the target spot for the defenders. The other players hand balls to the coaches. Coaches (or players) alternate hits as diggers work toward 10 digs into the target area.

- Whichever group gets 10 digs to target first gets to stay in the drill, and the target-and-handing group comes on to challenge the winning group. In the example diagrammed, the group entering for the second round would be the middle back defenders.

- Each time a group wins, change what they are digging. For example, first have them dig crosscourt, then down the line (from the other coach), and finally crosscourt with two players (add a blocker dropping off the net to dig). Middle backs can go crosscourt or rotate to the line.

- Keep target players near the net to be safe so they don't get hit by the coach's sharp crosscourt shot.

## 10-TOUCH PANCAKE

**Purpose**    For defenders to learn how to use the pancake technique.

**Goal**    To make 10 good ups as a group. To count as a good up, the ball must come up 4 to 5 feet (1.2 to 1.5 meters) off the ground and be considered playable by another defender.

**Equipment Needed**    Balls.

### Explanation

- Before attempting this drill, be sure to take the time to teach everyone the pancake technique so that no one is injured while attempting the drill.

- Start with three to six defenders on the end line. The coach is positioned at midcourt on the same side of the net as the defenders and tosses balls. The sequence of tosses is left, middle, right. Each toss should challenge the defenders to sprint and extend to play the ball.

- After each attempt, the defender sprints back to the end line to prepare to go again.

- This is a fast-paced drill that should encourage defenders to work hard, make good plays, and get out of the drill before it becomes too exhausting.

- The defender should put a strong, flat hand on the ground under the ball and let the ball bounce up off the hand.

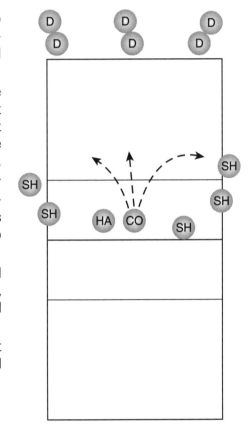

## TWO-ACROSS-THE-BACK DEFENSE

**Purpose**    To work on defensive shuffle moves, balancing the court, and hitter control.

**Goal**    The group needs 10 good digs to the setter before rotating clockwise and getting a new setter in.

**Equipment Needed**    Balls.

**Explanation**

- Starting positions are shown in figure *a*—two defenders across the back, a setter, and two hitters.

- A coach or extra player can initiate the first ball from off the court, whereupon the digger plays the ball to the setter. The setter sets to either hitter positioned at the net, and the appropriate hitter then hits the ball to any of the three defenders on his or her own side of the net (figure *b*). The diggers play the ball to the setter, and then the setter sets either hitter to continue. The hitter who does not get set shifts to dig crosscourt shots. The other defenders shift in the direction of the set to new bases.

- Each time the ball is set, the defense shifts according to which hitter is set. This is a continuous pepper drill off each dig. Rotate one position every 10 sets.

- Keep the ball in play as players rotate.

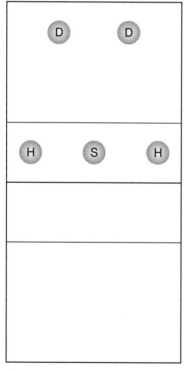

a

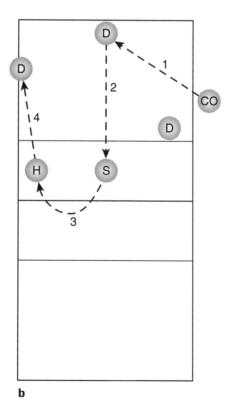

b

## TWO-PAIR DEFENSE

**Purpose**   To work on defensive shuffle moves, digging seams, and communication between defenders.

**Goal**   The group needs 10 good digs into the target area.

**Equipment Needed**   Balls; floor tape or discs to designate the target area.

### Explanation

- Starting positions are shown in the diagram; there are two pairs of defenders—one on the right half of the court and the other on the left half. A coach initiates the first ball by hitting to either the right or left half of the court. A second coach could run the same drill on the other half of the court.

- Each time the ball is dug, the two players in the pair who dug the ball switch positions with each other before the next ball is contacted. That is, the player closer to the net shuffles behind, and the player in back shuffles to the front. The players in the pair that did not dig the ball stay as they are.

- The coach can hit at the same pair right away or switch and hit at the other pair. Coaches should begin by hitting right at the players; as the players improve, the coach can begin to hit at the seam between them. For overpasses, subtract 1 point.

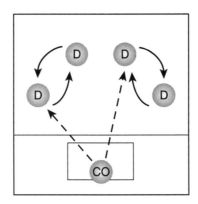

# 5

# Out-of-System and Transition Play

Offensive plays starting from serve receive are similar to plays in football. You have a little time to look over the defense and call your offensive set, and the play often goes as planned. In football, of course, the play ends and the offense has the chance to get together again and call another play. In volleyball, play often continues, as the ball is volleyed across the net a number of times. That's part of what makes volleyball great—transitioning from offense to defense and back again. It takes a well-trained team to keep the ball in play and think on the fly. Successful transition and out-of-system play is essential to the best teams, who rise above the rest, whether during a match or over the course of a season. "In-system" transition means that the ball was passed or dug near the setting target and the setter has a variety of good options under nearly ideal conditions. "Out-of-system" transition means that the ball was passed or dug far from the net or sprayed to one of a number of places around the court. These are the plays in which the setter is scrambling just to get to the ball and the options for setting are limited. In some situations, the setter may not even be able to set the ball, and a nonsetter will have to step in.

A team can succeed in a variety of ways with both in-system and out-of-system plays, but as with everything else, these scenarios must be practiced and trained for with an aggressive attitude. Most teams can master the basics of in-system volleyball, but championship teams also excel in out-of-system play. The difference is that the best teams consistently play aggressive volleyball regardless of whether they are in system or out, whereas weaker teams give way to the chaos when they are out of system. This chapter covers defensive goals, transition footwork for attackers, setter transition, play calling, and strategies for certain situations that will arise.

## Defensive Goals

As your opponent attacks, your team will set up its best defense in hopes of blocking the ball to end the play or causing the other team to make an error. If the opponent gets the ball by your block, your next goal is to dig it in a way that allows your setter to be near center court and within 3 to 4 feet (0.9 to 1.2 meters) of the net. It's important that defenders know what they are striving for in terms of the height and location of the dig. Placing the ball anywhere from 10 feet (3 meters) in from the right sideline to center court gives the setter an opportunity to move forward along the net, whereas digging the ball too far to the right or left limits the setter's options and makes it easier for the opponent to block. Any off-speed or three-quarter-speed shots that defenders can take in an upright position should be sent to the target area within a 3-foot (0.9 meter) channel along the net, which is an ideal setting zone.

When possible, defenders should try to put the ball right about at center court so that opposing blockers will have to travel equally far to the right- or left-side hitters. If the ball is passed to the left half of the court, the block will have an easy time getting to the left-side hitter. If the ball is dug too far to the right, the setter may have trouble pushing the ball all the way out to the left sideline. If the set to the outside drops short of the sideline, it can force the outside attacker to hit crosscourt instead of having the option of a line shot. Too many teams send a majority of sets to the left-side hitters when they're already having to hit a lot of the out-of-system sets. Attack on the right side as often as possible; it's an area that most teams aren't as good at defending. The height of the easier digs should be no more than 3 or 4 feet (0.9 to 1.2 meters) above the antenna. If all the defenders can make plays at a consistent height, the hitters can get in a good rhythm when they transition and make their approaches to hit. One way to gauge the tempo of passes is to count out loud from the time of the defender's contact to the time when the ball reaches the setter's hands. It should be close to a two-count from beginning to end (e.g., "one one thousand, two one thousand"). Another way to gauge tempo is to make sure a setter could run from the right back as the ball is being dug and still make a comfortable play.

When the opponent takes a full swing at the ball, the defender's goal changes. The tougher the play, the higher the ball should be dug and the more off the net it should come. A faster ball must be slowed down by the defender in order to keep it on his or her own side of the net. Some players still try to dig an extremely hard-hit ball right on top of the net, and this move often results in an overpass to the opposing blockers. Defending setters who happen to be in the back row will have trouble releasing to the really tight dig because they have to wait until they know the attack isn't coming to them. Defenders must learn the difference between a "good error" and a "bad error." A bad error is a dig that results in an overpass and a missed opportunity to start your offense. A good error is a dig that doesn't go right to the target area but is kept in play and allows your offense to begin. Many players try too hard to make the perfect play on a dig, thinking that they must make a pinpoint pass every time. Top teams are just as aggressive on defense, but their priority is to make every dig settable so that the team has a chance to attack and score. The harder the ball is attacked, the more the defender must keep the dig off the net.

# Transition Footwork for Attackers

As the defense is creating an opportunity for the team to stay in system, the attackers must get in position to attack while the ball is heading to target. All of the hitters need to work hard at getting off the net so that they can make a longer approach for hitting. The number of attackers moving away from the net as the ball goes to target will depend on whether the setter is front-row and whether the team is using any back-row hitters. The player who has to transition and react the fastest is the middle hitter, who must often jump to attack as the pass enters the setter's hands. The footwork for a middle coming off the net has three stages:

1. Land on two feet after the block. Landing in balance on both feet after the block is important because it's an indication that the hips and shoulders were parallel to the net during the block. If a blocker often lands on one leg, it is a sign that his or her hands are tilted as they reach sideways to close the block. Ideally, both of the blocker's hands should be at approximately the same height as they cross the plane of the net. Landing on two feet after the block also reduces the risk of ankle or knee injury.

2. Open up to the direction in which the ball is attacked and transition toward center court at the 3-meter (10 foot) line. It's important for middles to keep their eyes on the ball as it passes the block and track it back to where the setter will contact it next. If the ball passes them on their right, they should open up to the right; if it passes on the left, they should turn to their left. The goal is to get past the 3-meter line to begin their approach and prepare to hit a quick set.

3. Plant to initiate the approach angle. The approach angle depends on the strategy of attack spots used by each team. The attack spot is the location where a hitter stops moving away from the net and begins moving forward to attack. Most coaches have middles go to the 3-meter line at center court to begin their attack footwork. From there, the hitter's approach could be wide to the left for a 31, straight in for a 1, or running along the net and behind the setter for a slide.

When the setter is in the front row, the middle hitter should transition behind the setter (figure 5.1) for a slide attack (single-leg takeoff) as often as possible. Doing so makes the opposing middle and left-side blockers move to their left to track the hitter and gives the setter more opportunities to dump the ball since the opposing middle blocker must watch three different attackers.

The slide is used mostly in the women's game, but some men's teams are now using it as well. Coaches of women's teams realize the advantage of using the horizontal movement patterns to find gaps in the block. Men's teams used to rely on

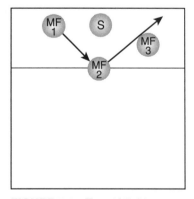

**FIGURE 5.1**   The middle hitter transition.

their outstanding jumping ability, but now they see how they can cause the block-ers even more problems by taking off on one leg. In the men's game, the middle normally transitions to first-tempo sets (quick sets) behind or in front of the setter (1s and 31s). In both the women's and men's games, keeping the middle in front of the front-row setter allows the opposing left-side blocker to come in and help with the setter and the middle hitter. That maneuver can create easy blocking situ-ations for the opponent if the setter gives the ball to the quick hitter right in front of the double block. By occasionally transitioning behind the front-row setter, the middle hitter will force the opposing blocker to stay behind the setter. To assure better hitting angles and options in front of the setter, the middle needs to be sure to stay far enough away from the net. Whether the pass is tight or off the net, the setter should keep the set off the net to avoid trapping the hitter and forcing him or her into the block. If the pass is tight to the net, the setter should still pull it off at least a foot (0.3 meter) to give the hitter some swinging room around the block to the sidelines and corners.

One way to loosen up the block and make them flinch is to use an active setter who can dump the ball. Just about the only bad time to dump is when the ball is passed right to the setting target, since this is usually the time when the blockers key in on the setter and expect him or her to attack on second contact. As mentioned in chapter 3, this one area of the net can be called the "No Dumping Zone." A better time to dump is when the setter is near the net and moving along it. The blocker will have to follow the setter and ball and will be slower getting his or her hands to the top of the tape. It's always tempting for setters to dump on the perfect pass, but that is not always the ideal area from which to score. Setters should practice dumping to all areas of the court (forward to the right sideline, toward center court, behind their head short, and deep to the right and left back corners) to keep both the blockers and defensive players off balance.

Transition footwork for left-side hitters is similar to that for middle hitters. Their goal is to get off the net as fast and as far as they can so that they can make an explosive approach. After landing on two feet following the block, the left-side hitter should turn and run at a 45-degree angle outside of the court. To be most efficient, the first step should be with the right foot and the stride should be as long as possible. The hitter should be sure to remain facing the court and never turn his or her back on the ball. The finish spot should be at least 11 meters (12 yards) off the net and outside of the court. The hitter must finish with a pivot in order to land facing the net again in a ready position from which to approach. How far the hitter can get from the net depends on the height of the dig. The hitter needs to stop his or her movement away from the net just before the setter is about to contact the ball. As soon as the setter releases the ball, the hitter decides the point of contact along the net and begins the forward approach.

Hitters on the right side go through a similar sequence, but since most passes are put slightly right of center court—meaning that the set to the right side arrives sooner—they usually won't have time to get as far off the net as left-side hitters do. There are two trains of thought for hitters' approach angles on the right side.

## A Tip From the Top

It was 1991, and Lloy Ball was a freshman. The game was at Ball State University. Three-thousand-plus fans attended as we played for the right to go to the NCAA tourney in Hawaii. It was the fifth set, and the score was 14-13 in our favor. (This was in the days before rally scoring.) We served, and Ball State attacked. We dug the ball, and Lloy set Fred Malcolm, our stud opposite. Ball State dug the ball and attacked, and we dug again. Lloy set Fred again, long distance, this time over his head. Fred killed the ball, and IPFW went to the first of six NCAA semifinals. Lloy made an aggressive decision to force a tough set, and it really paid off.

—Arnie Ball, Head Men's Coach, Indiana University–Purdue University Fort Wayne

Some favor transitioning off the court at a 45-degree angle so they can have the extreme cut shot and also get sets that go too wide past the antenna. Others prefer to transition straight back off the net along the right sideline. Doing so allows the hitter to more easily get to sets that drop inside and still hit a line shot but makes it harder to get to sets that go off the court to the right. It's best to analyze individual talents and see which approach angle works best for each hitter.

A team that uses hitters out of the back row will also need to train for transition patterns. Whether hitting from the left, center (pipe), or right side of the back row, each attacker needs to find the starting spot for his or her approach. In practice, hitters should locate the spot in the backcourt where they can begin their approach and always take off behind the 3-meter (10 foot) line. They should do so at full speed so that they can use the identical spot in matches. Some hitters go straight up on takeoff, whereas others fly forward over the line. To avoid a foot fault on the line, the hitter should always plant for takeoff at the same spot. This means that if the set is well in front of the line, the hitter should fly farther for it or come down below the height of the net before sending it over. In practice, hitters should find and memorize their ideal starting spot. Back-row teammates or the setter can also look at where the hitter plants for takeoff and warn them to not complete the attack if they are clearly on the line. Teammates should yell, "No, no!" so that the hitter can abort the attack and send the ball over from below the tape. It's not easy to stop in midjump, but it could save a point for your team. This is not, however, something you want to have to do on a regular basis, so hitters should memorize the exact starting point for their approach and get to it every time.

## Setter Transition

Setter transition from the front row is generally easy. Setters normally block on the right side and need only move a few steps to prepare to set the ball. The setter's transition from the back row is crucial to forging a successful offense and team. The setter is the only player who will run toward the net once a teammate digs the ball, since everyone else moves away from the net to prepare to hit. One major mistake made by many setters is to think about setting the ball instead of digging it. The best setters play defense first and take responsibility for protecting their area. A setter who doesn't defend creates a weak spot on the team, and opponents will take advantage of it. The setter needs to be determined to play great defense first and refuse to be caught off guard by a ball that comes in his or her direction. Here are some key points for a setter when defending and transitioning:

- Be in your assigned defensive spot and pause (stop moving) before the hitter contacts the ball.
- When the ball is attacked, make sure that you are in balance with your weight slightly forward. Being on your heels will cause a slow first step as you move to play the ball or release in transition.
- If the play is one you can make, play it in a controlled way so that a teammate can set the next ball. Once you make the dig, call out the name of the player who should set the ball (e.g., "Bobbi, set!").
- If the attacked ball is out of your area, or if your teammate has a better chance of playing it, immediately sprint for the target area in order to set. Sprint all the way to the net in case it is dug tight; you can always come off the net to get the ball.
- As you run to set, keep an eye on the direction of the dig in case you have to change your path to get to a ball dug off target.
- While transitioning to set, call the ball to clear the way if another player is in the area where the ball will come down. If that player is still in the way when you are about to set the ball, physically push him or her out of the way to claim the area.

How well the setter defends and transitions determines whether the team stays in system or gets forced out of system. A lazy setter who doesn't defend or work hard in transition can be the major reason that a team struggles to play at its highest level. It is critical for the setter to play defense *all the time*, fight hard to get his or her feet to the ball *all the time*, and cover his or her hitters *all the time*. The setter is the main cog on the wheel of the team. If he or she does not play aggressively, the team will not operate smoothly.

There will be times when the first ball comes to the setter and the team still has to make a seamless transition into the offense. Depending on the difficulty of the dig, the setter's teammates must quickly analyze the situation and determine who will set the next ball. The next decision to make is which setting technique the nonsetter should use. Beginning a few years ago, I asked my nonsetters to bump-set every ball from the backcourt. The reason was this: Too many times over the course of my career, I had watched (and cringed) as my nonsetters used their hands and got called for a mishandle. With rally scoring, that's one more point we don't want to give away, and having these players bump-set has worked very well for us. Just make sure that the middles are setting with their hands from the front row in drills

A great setter will always deliver a hittable ball no matter where the pass takes him.

and that everyone is learning to bump-set from the back row. Your players will all gain confidence in these skills, and they'll know how to adjust when the setter digs the ball. In the fall of 2008, the NCAA rules committee agreed to be more lenient in making the double-contact call. The new interpretation explains that if a player is making an "athletic move" to play the ball, he or she should be allowed to double-hit the ball without being called for double contact. As I write this, however, we are 3 weeks into the season, and nonsetters are still being whistled for mishandles. Thus, I will continue to have my nonsetters in the backcourt use their platforms to set the ball when our setter makes the first contact. It may take a season of following how the officials make the calls before I decide to change our strategy.

## Calling Plays

Offensive plays can be called in a variety of ways. In serve receive, setters have time to check out the opposition's block and give the hitters a hand or verbal signal. Sometimes, however, coaches prefer to send the play in from the sideline for young setters or those who (for other reasons) might be overwhelmed by the decision-making responsibility. Some coaches use placards with numbers or names of plays. That's all fine in serve receive, but calling plays in transition is a whole new challenge. There are two general ways to select plays during offensive transition. The first involves predetermined plays, and the second is the "middle audible."

Transitioning into predetermined plays means that each rotation of hitters knows that after the serve-receive play they will go into a specific offense. This is called a play set. Each hitter will stick with one type of set and location so that the setter has to think about only three or four basic things. The decision to select each play set will probably be determined by the ability, or inabilities, of the hitters. The coach should select plays with which each attacker is most successful so that the odds of scoring are better. One example of a basic play set with a back-row setter is 4-1-5, which involves a regular set to the antenna for the left-side hitter, a quick set for the middle hitter, and a high set behind to the right-side hitter. This is a basic play set for most high school teams and many college teams. If a team is very big and overpowering at each of these spots, it may be able to keep things basic and still win.

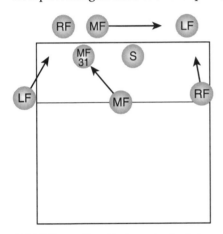

**FIGURE 5.2** Transitioning to the 31-5 play.

A slight variation is the 31, or shoot-quick, for the middle hitter. The 31 is a wide quick set approximately 3 to 5 feet (0.9 to 1.5 meters) in front of the setter and 1 to 2 feet (0.3 to 0.6 meter) above the net. Transitioning to the 31-5 play can really free up the right-side hitter by making the opposing middle blocker travel farther (figure 5.2). The 5 set is a high set behind the setter and out to the right-side antenna. As you can see in the diagram, this set forces the opposing middle blocker to move away from the right-side attacker, thus making it difficult for the blocker to fully close the block and usually providing a good scoring opportunity for the attacker hitting the 5. It's a simple play, but it's tough to defend. The 31 can also draw the attention of the opponent's right-side blocker, who is trying to protect the seam with the middle blocker. After running a few 31s, set over the top of the 31 to the left-side hitter and you might have an open net at which to hit. The key is to set the quick hitter on a fairly regular basis; otherwise, the blockers will kick out on the outsides. As mentioned earlier, when the setter is in the front row, the middle should get behind the setter as often as possible.

To actually use play sets, the coach will designate play set number 1 and play set number 2. For example, play set number 1 could be 4-1-5, and play set number 2 could be 4-31-back 2. Prior to the start of the game, the coach should tell the team what free-ball play they will be running. Before each serve, the setter can hold up a number 1 or a number 2 with his or her fingers. Using play sets makes decision making much easier for the setter.

The second type of transition play calling is the audible system or middle audible. In this system, the middle blocker calls out the desired set as he or she begins the approach. This tactic can be used by more advanced teams who can think on the fly and feature a setter who can stay composed when information is coming at the last second. After the middle calls his or her audible, the outside hitters call theirs.

If the setter is coming out of the back row, the right side and the middle can work off each other. If the middle calls a 31, the right side can call a high set to the antenna, a back 2, or a front 2 (a 2 is set about 2 feet [0.6 meter] in front of or behind the setter and about 3 to 5 feet [0.9 to 1.5 meters] above the net). It all depends on how athletic the right side is and whether he or she can think on the fly. If the middle calls a slide to the antenna, the right side would want to call a

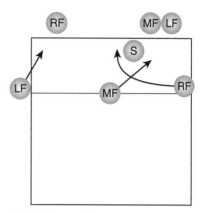

**FIGURE 5.3**  The X play.

front 2 and create a crossing pattern (figure 5.3) that forces the middle to move to the left following the slide and then possibly move back to the center to block the right side hitting the front 2. The left-side blocker might see the right side moving to center court to hit a front 2 but would be hindered by the middle blocker following the slide. If the setter is in the front row, the middle could call a quick set in front, and the outside would call a set to the antenna. That's the most basic play. If the middle audibles to go behind the setter, the outside can call a gap or what's called a 32—a lower and quicker second-tempo set which lands about 8 feet (2.4 meters) from the left antenna. It forces the right-side blocker to move in and block one-on-one with the left side, since the middle is following the slide hitter. The left side can then swing hard crosscourt, or if the block takes cross, then the left side can cut back to the left sideline. This play causes a lot of problems for the middle blocker, who must also keep track of the setter. If the setter is active (i.e., likes to dump), this play provides a great opportunity. Whether the middle runs a tight or wide slide, the setter will probably have a good chance to dump the ball. The middle blocker is usually leaning left and chasing the slide, so it's hard for him or her to get off the ground and block the setter dump.

## Transitioning for the Back-Row Attack

Whether the setter is front-row or back-row, it's always good to have a back-row attacker. This creates angles that are difficult to block and defend and thus helps keep the opponent off balance. Even when out of system, the back-row attack is a great outlet. It's a little easier for blockers to defend, though, because fewer options are available at that stage of the play. Coaches must identify which players on their team can attack consistently from beyond the 3-meter (10 foot) line. If they are making more errors than points, it's really not worth pursuing. In addition, players must also bring some defensive skills if they are going to stay in the backcourt at all. If they hurt the team defensively, it doesn't make sense to keep them in the game unless they're really putting up big numbers by hitting from the backcourt.

Once a player is given the role of backcourt attacker, a decision must be made about which area of the court he or she will run the pattern from. Many teams put that player in the middle back to provide an opportunity to hit at wide angles to the left and right. This play is often called hitting the pipe, and it can be very effective. The downside is that two and sometimes three blockers can converge back to center court to put up a block. The back-row attack from the left third of the court seems to be the most seldom used. For some teams, this area is the defensive spot reserved for the libero, since it positions him or her to dig the hard crosscourt shots from the opponent's left-side hitters. One of the more effective spots to attack from the back row is the right side. When a team digs the ball off the net and seems to be out of system, the opponent's blockers often kick out early to prepare to block the left-side hitter. Since the setter is probably not a threat to dump or attack from off the net, the odds are good that the left-side blocker can handle the middle hitter one-on-one. That's when the team with a good back-row attacker can benefit from having him or her on the right third of the court. It may be possible to attack with no blocker, and the opponent's left-side blocker may have to move from the middle of the court. This gives the back-row attacker the advantage since the blocker will have very little time to get in position. Again, the key is to use a player who can attack from the back row and play defense, too, so that he or she is not a liability.

# Attacking on First Contact

There is one aspect of transition play that most people would never consider to be part of the offense—the first play coming over the net inside the 3-meter (10 foot) line. Envision this scenario as if you are part of the defending team, and one of two things happens. Either your team is in a rotation defense (one player is waiting for off-speed shots right behind the block) and the opponent hits an off-speed shot that can easily be played by your defender standing inside the 3-meter line, or one of the opposing attackers swings the ball off the block, where, again, it can be played by one of your defenders inside 3 meters. Usually what happens next is that the defender passes the ball to his or her own setter in the center-court target area in order to begin the offense. This sequence happens many times during the course of each match, and it almost becomes rhythmical. The team that has just attacked moves to its defensive bases, and the defending team prepares to begin its transition offense. Alert players can take advantage of teams who do not balance the court as they are covering their hitters. In most ideal coverage situations, three players come in close to the hitter and balance the court inside the 3-meter line, and two players stay farther back and balance the deep court. However, some teams work so hard to cover their hitters that they all end up bunched together inside the 3-meter line, and an alert player can take a ball in the frontcourt and set it to the opponent's deep corner. This can't be used every time in this situation because opponents will be ready for it, but when used occasionally it can really catch a team off guard. It also gives players who normally don't get any kills the opportunity to put some points on the board, and it is often the fast-thinking defensive specialist who can use this play to get a quick point for the team. As soon as players have tried it once, you'll see them get excited about trying it again. They'll start looking for the right situation and will get stoked about the chance to score. Again, it's not a play that you can use often, but it's a fun wrinkle that also makes sense.

# Winning the Out-of-System Game

Much of what has been discussed in this chapter relates to transitioning from defense to offense and how your team must be driven to stay in system as often as possible. Great teams have the ability to take balls that are not ideal and still find a way to stay in system on the attack. Most championship teams excel in scoring when out of system, or at least attacking aggressively enough to force the opponent into an out-of-system situation of its own. Here are some keys to learning to be great when out of system:

• Train all of your nonsetters to set the ball. Give them opportunities in practice to set from every spot and in every situation that might come up in a match. They should all be confident with their hands and platforms, knowing that the attacker is depending on a hittable ball. Also be sure to train your setters to bump-set accurately if they can't get their hands on the ball. Too many coaches train their setters' hands but rarely force them to bump-set. Train them for the worst-case scenario so they can get you out of jams.

• Train your attackers to be patient. Setters deliver the ball in a consistently quicker tempo because they are the best players for the job. Nonsetters usually set the ball higher, meaning that attackers must gauge the height and location of the set before beginning their approach. If they are patient and still bring a dynamic approach, they can be just as successful off nonsetters. Setters will often launch out-of-system sets a little higher, too, so attackers should wait to analyze these sets as well.

• Teach your hitters to make shots from and to all spots. Many coaches give their hitters nothing but perfect reps in practice, either from a toss or from a setter who is not under stress. Use drills that mimic difficult situations for hitters so that they learn to adjust to sets that are not in their ideal attack zone. Also have hitters work on attacking those balls off the edges of the block and into the deep perimeter of the court. Some attackers try to hit an out-of-system ball straight down and find that the block is right there to greet them.

• Preach great coverage. A team that is out of system can quickly get back into system with a good coverage play. Teammates who cover with the true intent of keeping the blocked ball in play can turn the tables on the defense by putting the ball in the setter's target area. As soon as the attackers see that the ball is back in an area where they can run an in-system play, their odds of scoring on the next swing improve dramatically. Defending blockers can often be caught out of position, and the offense can regain the advantage and create a split-block opportunity.

- Stay aggressive. Many players and teams become cautious when they are out of system—and the moment they think they are in trouble, they probably are. The mind is a mysterious thing, and when the caution light goes on inside the brain, it's very common to make unforced errors. Players have to stay aggressive and fight to score in out-of-system situations; if they don't, they will be handing points over to the opponent on a regular basis.

The entire premise of being great when out of system is based on being ready to adjust and transitioning into aggressive positions. In-system play is generally considered normal, and out-of-system play takes many more adjustments. Every player must be trained for every out-of-system situation that will arise so that being out of system eventually feels normal and comfortable. Transitioning into aggressive positions means that every player has a role to prepare for so that the team can execute an offensive play that will score. Hitters must transition into aggressive attack positions, setters must transition into aggressive setting posture and preparedness, and defenders must transition into aggressive coverage positions. Being great when out of system requires bringing an aggressive mentality so that your team has a good chance to score. It comes down to feeling an urgency to win. Never miss a chance to be aggressive and score. You will want that point when both teams are battling it out to win the match.

# Transition Drills

## BOX FOR OUT-OF-SYSTEM

**Purpose**   To improve out-of-system play with the focus on defending, setting, and transitioning to attack.

**Goal**   To win one 15-point rally-scoring game, playing each point to completion.

**Equipment Needed**   Balls.

**Explanation**

- Both sides have a right back and left back playing defense and setting, and a right front and left front hitting and blocking.

- The coach initiates play by hitting at the right or left back. The other back-row player sets a front-row hitter. The hitter transitions from off the net to attack the ball that is being set from the back row.

- Defenders should dig the ball to center court 15 feet (4.5 meters) off the net. The players setting from the back row should set crosscourt so that the set isn't coming directly over the hitter's head. If you are concerned about mishandles, have them always bump-set.

- The coach can go under the net and alternate sides until one team gets 15 points. The drill can also be done on just one side to 10 points.

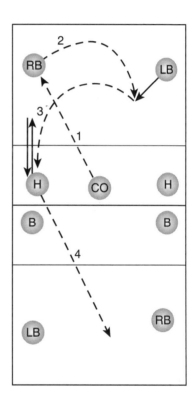

## DEEP-COURT FIVES

**Purpose**  To improve out-of-system play with the focus on attacking from the back row.

**Goal**  To win 15-point games with a setter dump and middle-hitter kills counting as 2 points.

**Equipment Needed**  Balls.

### Explanation

- Each side has five players with a middle hitter and setter playing in the front row.
- After the serve, the setter can dump, set the middle hitter (in front or behind), or set the back-row players.
- The opponents try to defend the play and run one of their own. Ideally, they dig the ball so that the setter can dump or set the middle, since either counts for 2 points. If they can't set the middle, they can set the back row and work on out-of-system offense.
- This can be a hard drill for the middle, and the total number of points needed can be reduced for lower-level teams.
- Defenders will have to read hitters better because there will often be a split block. The back-row players will have to set some balls if the setter can't get there.

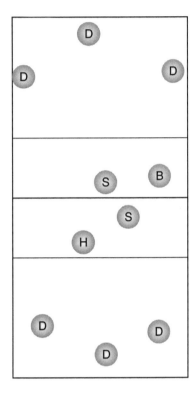

## DIG-TO-ATTACK TRIPLES

**Purpose**   To promote defensive ball control and improve transition footwork off passes and digs.

**Goal**   To score 10 big points (winning one rally-scoring game to 3 points earns 1 big point).

**Equipment Needed**   Balls.

**Explanation**

- Three groups of three play rally-scoring minigames to 3 points. Team 1 receives serve, team 2 serves, and team 3 provides the server and a setter on each side.
- Playing in the deep court, *the setter must set the player who passed or dug the last ball.*
- After each 3-point minigame, the winning team moves to the far court to receive the next serve. The team that was providing the setters and server moves to the challenger court, and the losing team then provides the next server and setters.
- Another version of the drill is to allow the attackers to hit from in front of the 3-meter (10 foot) line.
- This is a very good drill for improving hitter mobility.

## FULL D VERSUS 3 C

**Purpose**    To challenge a team to stop the ball with the block or improve its out-of-system offense.

**Goal**    For the defending team to score five times by either stuff-blocking the ball or transitioning and scoring.

**Equipment Needed**    Balls; three coaching boxes.

### Explanation

- One team of six players get in their base defensive positions, ready to defend against three coaches (or players) on boxes. Other players who are not in the drill are handing and shagging balls.

- Coaches hit from middle, left, middle, right, middle, left, middle, and so on at a quick pace (each ball is hit as soon as the previous ball is down). Blockers put up double blocks as each coach hits. The team has to finish quickly before the middle blocker starts fading.

- The defensive group rotates out after transitioning and/or blocking to score five times. Hits from coaches should be gamelike, including off-speed shots and balls thrown deep off the court. Make the pace quick, occasionally tossing the ball over before hitting to prevent the wings from releasing early.

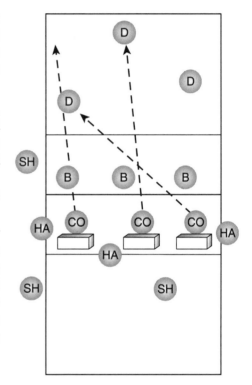

## TOOL TIME

**Purpose**    To teach offensive players to be comfortable scoring off the block and teach defenders to transition from a deflection block into a scoring situation.

**Goal**    To be the first team to reach 25 points.

**Equipment Needed**    Balls.

**Explanation**
- This 6v6 drill starts with a player serve. Rotate normally after winning a rally.
- Points can be scored only as follows:
    - Tool off the block to score earns 1 point.
    - Stuff block earns 2 points.
    - Deflection block and score on first attack attempt earns 1 point.
    - Coverage play and score on first attack attempt earns 1 point.
    - Service ace earns 1 point.
    - Service error means 1 point is subtracted.
- This drill puts players' focus on the block and on how they can use it to their advantage.

## TWO SIDES AND A SERVE

**Purpose**    To improve the team's ability to score in sideout situations, then follow it up with a strong serve.

**Goal**    Side 1 needs to score on serve receive, score off an opponent's attack, and serve a tough ball to earn a rotation. Six rotations are needed in order to finish the drill. The drill can also be done on both sides by alternating receiving teams whenever the serving team stops the receiving team. If a team earns a rotation, it gets to receive again.

**Equipment Needed**    Balls; coaching box.

**Explanation**

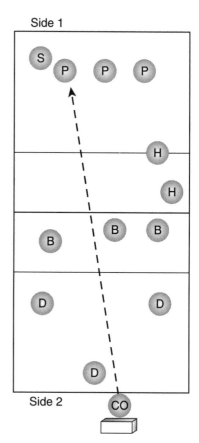

Side 1

- Six players (side 1) receive a served ball from a coach (or player) positioned on a box to mimic a jump serve.
- Six defenders (side 2) block and dig to stop the receiving team. If side 1 scores on its first attempt, it gets a ball to defend coming from live hitters on side 2. (Side 1 must score on the first swing.) The coach can toss ball 2 in from the end line for the setter to set.
- If side 1 blocks the ball or transitions out for a score, it earns a serve.
- The right front goes to serve and must keep side 2 passers from passing a 3.
- If successful scoring occurs on both sides and a serve is achieved, side 1 rotates and the coach serves again.
- Six rotations reaches the goal. Continue as desired.

Side 2

## VIRUS

**Purpose**    To improve team scoring when out of system.

**Goal**    To win seven rallies before the opponent.

**Equipment Needed**    Balls.

### Explanation

- Six players are on each side with a coach (or multiple coaches) positioned on the sideline, ready to toss balls in.

- The coach tosses a ball in (70 percent of the time to a nonsetter). A player calls for the ball and shouts the name of the teammate to whom he or she plans to set the ball. The player sets the ball to an outside hitter or a back-row player. Players transition off the net and approach to attack. Rally continues until one team scores; the team that scores gets the next toss from the coach.

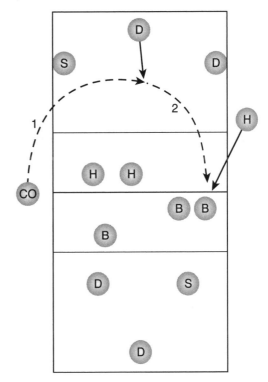

- Play continues until one side scores seven times, then each side flips its own front- and back-row players, and the drill continues. Play until one side wins four games.

- The coach should intentionally give a wide variety of tosses to prepare the team for any situation. Toss off the court, on and in the net, low and fast at a player, and soft into the open areas of the court.

# 6

# Cultivating Player Competitiveness

When you want your team to play aggressive volleyball, the key is competitiveness. Height, vertical jump, speed, and training repetitions are great, but your team can't go to the highest level without competitors. Many volleyball players think they are competitors simply because they pull on their kneepads, lace up their shoes, and play on a team. That's simply not the case, and you can see the separation as the top teams consistently move up through the playoff brackets. If you watch those teams, you'll see that they are able to play with more intensity and desire for longer periods of time. Think of the phrases commonly used for competitors: "They rise to the top," "they kicked it into gear," "they never back down," "they went for it," and so on. These people are risk takers; they aggressively pursue what they want and they don't stop until they get it. They love to compete and they love challenges. Whether it's a swimmer racing against the clock or a wrestler going head-to-head with an opponent, competitors thrive on opportunities to prove that they are the best. They so often come out on top because they never let up and they never give up. This chapter addresses how to instill aggressiveness, how to balance competitiveness with team chemistry, how to be a competitive coach, and how to sustain competitiveness. As your players learn individual and team concepts, these focuses will provide the bridge your team needs to make the move to the elite level.

## Instilling Aggressiveness in Players

People often ask me, "What do you look for in recruits?" The people who ask are usually parents or coaches who want to see if their kid has what it takes to play for us. What I really want is a player who is 6 feet 2 inches (1.9 meters) tall, athletic, able to touch a point 10 feet 6 inches (3.2 meters) above the ground, and confident. She should be academically solid (GPA of 2.8 or above on a 4-point scale) and should be well trained by her previous coaches. High-level experience helps, but I want her to still be eager and fresh, so she can't have played too much during the high school years. Ideally, she'll also have a great topspin serve with some movement, as well as excellent ball-handling and defensive skills. If she's a good citizen and a great leader to boot, I'd be in heaven. She should be mentally and emotionally stable, be strong, and possess a true passion for playing the game. Last, but certainly not least, she has to be a competitor.

Now, can I get all of those attributes in every recruit? Of course not, but I'll try to get as close as I can. If two recruits are comparable in most categories, the most competitive one will usually win out, and sometimes the most competitive players come in the smallest packages. It may be the 5-foot-5-inch (1.7 meter) defensive specialist or the undersized middle who brings the competitiveness that takes your team to the top. One of my favorite quotes is, "It's not the size of the dog in the fight; it's the size of the fight in the dog!" That's an important statement to remember when building a championship team.

When I talk to recruits, I want to find out what they can bring to my team. Their actions may say something different from what their coach, parent, or bio says. These sources will all say that the player is competitive, but it depends on what you are comparing the player with. Some players are naturally competitive and probably showed signs of it in kindergarten. My question to the recruit is this: "Do you hate to lose, or do you love to win?" Almost everybody loves to win. Why wouldn't they? What a great feeling it is when everybody is jumping up and down and feeling proud of themselves! It's one of the reasons that people play games. But over the course of my 20 years in coaching, I've noticed that some of the greatest competitors are the ones who hate to lose more than they love to win. The feeling after a win is often temporary; it's something you enjoy for a while, and then it's gone. Losing, on the other hand, seems to stay with you a lot longer. It's like a kick in the gut, and it can even hurt physically. Some people hate losing so much that they will compete extra hard to avoid that lousy feeling. You'll even hear them say it out loud at times: "I hate to lose!" Whether it's cards, rock-paper-scissors, or volleyball, they truly *hate* to lose.

I recall a great example from when I was coaching one of my early teams in the championship match of the conference tournament. We were up two games to one and were leading 11-0 in the fourth game. This was during the days of sideout scoring, and the games went to 15 points. This type of blowout score was unheard of in a championship match, but our players were performing flawlessly. As our opponent, the host school, took its last time-out, my team came to the bench. I was impressed when my setter and captain said to her teammates, "You guys, they

## A Tip From the Top

During the last week of 2007 Big 12 conference play, Iowa State faced a must-win match at the University of Kansas. Unfortunately for the Cyclones, nothing was clicking, and we found ourselves down 1-2 in games and behind 3-11 in the fourth game. Just as it looked like we were going to lose, senior captain Erin Boeve began to take over. Her whole court demeanor changed. Her approach was more aggressive, she hit the ball harder, and she celebrated each play with more enthusiasm. It wasn't long before the rest of the team caught on, and soon the Cyclones were back in it. We battled back to win games four and five, keeping our NCAA tournament hopes alive. Boeve finished the match with 19 kills and 7 blocks; more important, she inspired her team to make a great comeback.

—Christy Johnson, Head Women's Coach, Iowa State University

can come back! We gotta finish 'em off! We are *not* losing this game!" Two things struck me right then. One, we were up 11-0 and she thought the other team could come back. Two, she didn't say, "Come on, you guys, we can win it!" She said, "We are *not* losing!" She hated losing so much that she willed that team to a 15-0 win and the tournament championship. That kind of score just doesn't happen when two top teams collide in a final game. I had never seen it before and haven't since. That player taught me that true competitors can drive their teammates on to victory; in fact, they are usually the main reason teams win or lose.

If you are lucky to have a few real competitors on your team, you'll likely enjoy many more wins than losses during those players' tenure. If you don't have as many as you would like, you will have to cultivate your players' competitiveness through what you say and do on the court. There are times when coaches have to be creative and think outside the box to solve problems. Coaches need to find what motivates each team. The following sections present two unique ways to develop players' aggressiveness while helping the team become a stronger unit.

## Fifty Motivational Words

One system that has worked for me is called 50 Motivational Words. My intent in creating it was to change the mind-set of the team and spur the players to think more aggressive and competitive thoughts. I wanted them to come to practice in a frame of mind that led them to become mentally stronger each day. This system gave them ownership of the outcome I was looking for.

I began by writing down the most powerful words or short phrases I could think of. Each conveyed an attribute of elite athletes from any sport—qualities that give them the edge over average competitors. I came up with about 30 and left room for the players to come up with 20 on their own. We then held a team meeting at which I handed out paper and pen to each player; their assignment was to write down 10 of the most powerful words or phrases they could think of. After 5 minutes, I had the team write the results on a dry erase board where we could all see them. Having the players do this rather than writing the words on the board myself gave them their first chance to gain ownership in the process. As the words went up, we saw some overlap from player to player. As they filled the board, I checked the duplicates off my list. They also came up with some that I hadn't thought of. When they were done with their list, I gave them my suggestions and those of my assistants. By the end, we had built our team list of 50 Motivational Words (it included a few two- or three-word phrases where they were needed to make a point). Here it is:

| | | |
|---|---|---|
| Aggressiveness | Confidence | Discipline |
| Ambition | Consistency | Drive |
| Commitment | Dedication | Emotion |
| Communication | Desire | Energy |
| Competitive drive | Desire to improve | Enthusiasm |
| Competitive mind-set | Determination | Excitement |

| | | |
|---|---|---|
| Extra effort | Hunger | Positive attitude |
| Fearlessness | Hustle | Shake off mistakes |
| Fight | Improve others | Stamina |
| Fire | Intensity | Steadiness |
| Focus | Leadership | Strength |
| Gumption | Love of the game | Team player |
| Guts | Mental toughness | Tenacity |
| Hard work ethic | Need to win | Trust |
| Hate to lose | Passion | Urgency to win |
| Health | Perseverance | Will to win |
| Heart | Physical toughness | |

After the list was complete, I had players each give an example or definition of every word as it related to our team. When they were done, we ended the meeting and headed up to practice. The next part of the process—putting these words in a form that players could relate to every day—was in my hands. I typed the words into the computer, rendered them in a strong font and color, and printed them up on cardstock at about 1 by 3 inches (2.5 by 7.5 centimeters). Then I had them laminated and cut them apart so that we had 50 separate words and short phrases. The next step was to attach a magnetic strip to the back of each word or phrase (we used magnets that could be cut to length and that had their own adhesive backing). Finally, we made an 8.5-by-11-inch (21.5 by 28 centimeter) sign that said, "What are *you* bringing to the court?"

There is a metal door just outside our team's locker room. This is where we posted the sign and attached all of our 50 Motivational Words. Before practice the next day, the players were told to select one word that was important to them personally or to the team. We took time before practice that day to have all the players briefly say why they selected their word. The reasons ranged from identifying something they needed to improve on to highlighting something they felt they could bring to make the team better. It was important to let each person explain her reasoning because it gave everyone more insight into that player's view of herself and of the needs of the team. So often, the older players are the only ones to speak up in group situations, but this exercise allowed quieter players to have a voice and begin to gain confidence in themselves. When they were all done, the players attached their words to a handrail located just off our court. At the end of practice, one person took all of the words back to the door next to the locker room.

Each day for the next week, the players selected different words and explained their choices to their teammates before practice. We started to see a noticeable improvement in the focus of the players as they began practice; they seemed to have a more powerful intent in everything they did. As the next week began, the players continued to select words, but I didn't ask for their reasoning before practice. Every once in a while I would check the words they brought up, and on occasion I'd ask them why. The random requests kept them on their toes but didn't take time from practice every day. After the first season of use ended, I kept the words on the door until the next preseason began. On the first day of practice, without my asking, the players each chose a word to bring up. I was impressed by the fact that this was a system the players enjoyed and wanted to continue.

In the second season, I added some powerful skills to the word group to plant more aggressive thoughts in their minds: *dominating blocking, prolific dumping, undeniable offense, relentless drive, attacking serve,* and *swarming defense.* I put up two or three copies of each so that a couple of players could choose the same one if their preferences worked out that way. The system served as a good way to plant aggressive thoughts in players' minds and give them ownership in the season's outcome. At the start of the third season, I did not put the words on the door for the first day of practice; rather, I put them away because I didn't want to force the exercise on the players. Sometimes, attempts at motivation can grow old and the effect can wear off, and I didn't want that to happen. Within the first week, however, one of the players asked where the words were and said that she liked to have them there. That was my signal to pull them out again, and we continued for the rest of the season. The motivational words have served the purpose we had in mind, and they've helped us stage more intense and purposeful practices. As the players' intentional mind-set became habit, the attitudes carried over to matches and the team became much more independent.

## Competing for Grades

Some will say that there are differences in the competitiveness of men and women, but there are also similarities. We've all seen the 7-foot (2.1 meter) men's basketball player who won't dunk or the huge football lineman who is really a teddy bear. They lack the competitiveness that their coaches want them to have, yet they participate in sports that are very competitive by nature. In my many years of coaching and talking to coaches of males, I definitely see some trends in how male and female athletes relate to their teammates and to competitive situations. Women seem to be more social by nature and have been trained not to be competitive. Years ago, I heard Kathy DeBoer speak on differences between men and women. At the time, Kathy was a very successful volleyball coach at the University of Kentucky after having had a great college career. Kathy's view of male athletes is that they see life as a mountain and their main goal is to get to the top first. On the trek up, they will fight for position, and they're always trying to prove where they fit in. If men are golfing, they'll not only keep their scores on each hole; they'll also play games within the game just to compete even more. Conversely, she feels that women are much more social and prefer to be part of a web, connected to every other part of the web (their team) and not standing out more than anyone else. For women, she says, life is more like an extended family reunion, where they always want to know what's going on with Aunt Sally and Uncle Charlie. I've seen this theory come into play with the women's teams I've coached. If I have 14 players, player 1 is happy only if player 14 is happy. Even though player 14 may not have the skills to hang with the top group, the best players don't want to see player 14 get emotionally hurt.

Taking these differences into account, one way to cultivate player competitiveness that works particularly well for women's teams is to relate what they do on the court to how they compete for grades. Girls and women seem to be much more motivated academically than most men. In my experience, women really want to work hard to improve their grades, whereas male players tend to focus more on what they do on the court. Thus, if your team is really struggling with most areas of the game, you can break it down like a report card and ask them to work for straight As instead of wins. If academics are important to the group, then they may be able to relate to this method of competing to improve. This system allows individuals to blend into the team as a whole yet still feel individual pride if they help raise the level of the team. The team starts competing to achieve a team goal, and to reach that goal they each have to be more competitive individually. The reason this works so well with women's teams is that no one is singled out for being the cause of the problem. Everyone's individual play is blended with that of the entire team, and the outcome depends on having the whole team raise the level of play. This approach gives the group a kick start, and once the players know how to compete for a team goal, they will also gain the confidence to be more competitive as individuals.

To begin with, make a list of the areas in which you would like to see your team improve. Limit it to about 10 categories so that it doesn't overwhelm the team. Most coaches could probably find 20 areas to improve, but 5 to 10 will do the job. Next, create a grid that allows you to record grades for the team in each category for each game on your schedule (figure 6.1). You may want to separate the matches into groups based on preconference, conference, and playoff schedules. In any case, format the grid to look as much like a report card as possible in order to help players relate to it.

| | | | | | | | | | |
|---|---|---|---|---|---|---|---|---|---|
| 1. Intensity | | | | | | | | | |
| 2. Consistency | | | | | | | | | |
| 3. Passing | | | | | | | | | |
| 4. Serving | | | | | | | | | |
| 5. Blocking | | | | | | | | | |
| 6. Defense | | | | | | | | | |
| 7. Setting | | | | | | | | | |
| 8. Coverage | | | | | | | | | |
| 9. Back-row attack | | | | | | | | | |
| 10. Free- and down-ball efficiency | | | | | | | | | |
| 11. Mental toughness | | | | | | | | | |
| Average grade | | | | | | | | | |

**FIGURE 6.1** Sample blank report card.

Before you use the report card for the first time, explain the categories and the plan to the team. Let the players know that if they improve in these areas, they'll start being more competitive and winning more matches. At practice on the day after a match, have the players grade the team's performance in each category. The coach's opinion can be integrated into the conversation as well to ensure that the grade is realistic and that the players aren't too hard on the team. After grading themselves for the first few matches, the players should understand the system, and the coach can step back from the process. This is a great way for the team to take ownership, and individual players will begin to become more vocal during the grading. Keep it short—5 minutes is usually enough. Between matches, the report cards should be posted in or near the locker room so that players can start seeing their overall progress. They'll begin taking more pride in accomplishing the little things in each match, and they will compete for better grades every time they walk on the court. Players will want to improve each category and they will understand exactly what you want them to accomplish. Small improvements from game to game will lead to big changes in your team by the end of the season.

You will be able to use the report cards to track how the team improves as a group from the first intrasquad scrimmage to the final matches in postseason play. Figures 6.2 through 6.4 show examples of report cards in each phase of the season. In preconference play, players may realize that they are unfocused and inconsistent in their

| | Intrasquad scrimmage | Missouri, L 1-3 | Georgia Tech, W 3-2 | Denver, W 3-0 | Kansas, L 0-3 | Rhode Island, W 3-1 | Virginia, W 3-0 | Marshall, W 3-0 | Cincinnati, W 3-0 |
|---|---|---|---|---|---|---|---|---|---|
| **1. Intensity** | B | B | A- | B | B | C | A | A- | A |
| **2. Consistency** | C- | D | B | B- | C | C | A | B+ | A |
| **3. Passing** | C | C | B | B | B | B- | A- | A- | A |
| **4. Serving** | C | C+ | B- | C | C | C- | A | B | A |
| **5. Blocking** | B | B | B- | B- | C | B- | B+ | B | A+ |
| **6. Defense** | C- | C+ | B | B- | C- | C- | A | A- | A |
| **7. Setting** | C- | B- | B+ | B | B | B | A- | B+ | A |
| **8. Coverage** | C+ | B- | B- | B | C+ | B | B+ | B+ | A |
| **9. Back-row attack** | B- | C+ | C | C | C | C | C | B | B+ |
| **10. Free- and down-ball efficiency** | C- | C+ | B- | B- | B- | B- | B+ | A- | A- |
| **11. Mental toughness** | C | D | B+ | C | C | C | A | A | A |
| **Average grade** | C+ | C | B | B- | C+ | C+ | A- | A | A |

**FIGURE 6.2**   Sample preconference team play grades.

| | Iowa, W 3-0 | Minnesota, W 3-2 | Northwestern, W 3-0 | @ Illinois, L 0-3 | @ Penn St., L 0-3 | @ Ohio St., L 0-3 | Michigan, W 3-0 | Michigan St., W 3-1 | @ Purdue, L 1-3 | @ Indiana, W 3-1 |
|---|---|---|---|---|---|---|---|---|---|---|
| 1. Intensity | A | A | B+ | C | A- | C+ | A | B | C+ | B+ |
| 2. Consistency | A | A- | A- | C- | B- | C | A | B- | B- | C |
| 3. Passing | A- | A | A- | C- | A- | C | B- | B | B- | B+ |
| 4. Serving | B- | A+ | A | C+ | C | D | A | A- | B | A |
| 5. Blocking | B+ | A- | B+ | C- | A | C+ | B- | B- | B+ | B- |
| 6. Defense | B+ | A | A | B- | B- | B | B+ | B | C- | B+ |
| 7. Setting | A | A | A- | C | A- | B- | A- | B+ | C+ | B+ |
| 8. Coverage | A- | A | B+ | C | C | C | B+ | B | C | C |
| 9. Back-row attack | B | A | B+ | B- | A- | B+ | A- | B+ | C+ | A |
| 10. Free- an down-ball efficiency | A | A | A | B | B | B | A- | B | B- | A |
| 11. Mental toughness | A | A | A- | D | B- | C+ | A- | B+ | C- | B+ |
| Average grade | A- | A | A- | C | B- | C+ | A- | B | C+ | B+ |

**FIGURE 6.3** Sample regular-season team play grades.

| | Loyola, W 3-0 | Notre Dame, W 3-0 | Hawaii, W 3-2 | Stanford, L 0-3 |
|---|---|---|---|---|
| 1. Intensity | A- | A | A | B+ |
| 2. Consistency | A- | B | A- | B+ |
| 3. Passing | A- | A- | A- | B |
| 4. Serving | A- | A | B | B+ |
| 5. Blocking | A | A | A | B |
| 6. Defense | B | A- | A | A- |
| 7. Setting | B+ | A- | A | A- |
| 8. Coverage | A | A | A | B |
| 9. Back-row attack | B | B+ | A | B |
| 10. Free- and down-ball efficiency | A | A | A | B |
| 11. Mental toughness | A | A+ | A+ | B+ |
| Average grade | A- | A | A | B |

**FIGURE 6.4** Sample postseason NCAA team play grades.

skills and attitude. As the weeks go by, they make progress but still have off days. During the season, it is the coach's job to give players drills to improve their skills, and it is the team's job to execute them on game day. Players will learn that they can control the outcome of matches by simply improving in the categories listed on the report card. Since they are grading themselves, they will take full ownership in the process and will be able to track their improvement on the card. They will quickly make the connection between excelling on the report card and earning victories.

This tool for self-evaluation can be valuable for teams to get them to begin goal setting and improve teamwork. If some categories are effort related, teams don't have to be highly skilled to improve their grades. Young or inexperienced teams can really benefit from the process because it serves as a guide to help them find their way. As I write this, I'm using this tool again for the current season. We are an inexperienced team, and it's helping the players focus on making strides each week. Coaches should merely serve as the training wheels for their teams by finding ways to help them to continue moving forward without falling down. Once the players develop the strength and confidence to continue on their own, the coach can step back and watch them go.

## Channeling Aggressiveness Effectively

Many coaches think they want a full team of ultracompetitive players on the floor. Let me restate that: "Many coaches *think* they want a full team of ultracompetitive players on the floor." It's true that most championship teams include a high percentage of very competitive players; if they didn't, they would lose matches on the nights when their competitive members were not on their A-game. Having a full squad of ultracompetitors, however, requires a coach who is able to manage all of those personalities throughout the season. If they are going toe to toe every day in practice, it will definitely make them better, but you also risk emotional explosions between players. At some point, the team must find a balance that keeps such situations from igniting. It could be a level-headed player or a coach who senses when to tone things down and knows how to defuse situations. The 1984 U.S. Men's Olympic Team is a great example. This team was known to hold some of the most intense and competitive practices ever seen in any era of any sport. As the head coach, Doug Beal put together a team of supercompetitive players, including Dusty Dvorak, Tim Hovland, Karch Kiraly, Chris Marlowe, Pat Powers, Dave Saunders, Steve Timmons, and Marc Waldie. Dvorak may have been the most competitive, and Karch set his personal standards so high that it would raise the playing level of everyone around him. Beal had to know when to fuel their competitive fire and how to resolve any explosions that took place. This U.S. team won a gold medal because the players were ultracompetitive and Coach Beal did a great job of managing their blend of personalities. Any coach who wants his or her team to play aggressive volleyball must learn what drills and situations create competition and must make sure not to stifle the intensity with too much talk during the most intense times.

Courtesy of University of Wisconsin Athletic Communications

Truly competitive players have a pure passion and love for the game.

Another example is Michael Jordan of the Chicago Bulls. His competitiveness would intimidate new players, and Phil Jackson realized that Jordan would tear apart the rookies and break their will. Jordan was just doing what he did best—playing to win—but these were his teammates, and they wouldn't be any good to the team if he took away their confidence. Jackson managed the situation by keeping Jordan from guarding the rookies and by letting him know that he had to build them up instead of breaking them down. If any player could stand up to Jordan, he could stand up to anyone in the league. Jordan was such an elite competitor that no other could match his fire over the course of a season. Every team includes players of varying degrees of competitiveness, and the coach must know how to handle each one of them.

Problems can arise when you have too many ultracompetitive players—or when they are too vocal. An ultracompetitive player's ability to be effective depends on the personalities of the players around him or her. As with packs in the animal kingdom, teams always have an alpha personality. This player is literally the leader of the pack, and his or her attitude, confidence, and leadership guides the team. If there are two ultrastrong personalities, the team will succeed only if they both understand the need to share the top spot. This is where leadership style can come into play. One might be an angry and intense leader, whereas the other is emotional and positive. Both are strong leaders, and it's possible that when a match gets tight and stressful, these two personalities will clash and explode. If they find a way to coexist, they can take their team to the championship levels; if they don't, the whole group could implode around them.

You can also face problems when you have a few competitive players and a couple of quiet or passive ones. All will seem well when the game is flowing and the team is on track, but when players start faltering, the competitive ones may begin to bark. This is their way to wake people up and motivate them, but the quieter players may tense up. I've seen All-Americans who can take over games crumble when their own teammates push them out of their comfort zone. If players don't seem to be jelling on the court, it might be time to put the balls away and have a talk. Give each player the opportunity to tell teammates what motivates him or her. Players should honestly indicate what they like to hear from teammates and coaches—and what they don't like to hear. Some will say that they like it when people are always encouraging, even after mistakes are made. Some might say that they like it when a teammate challenges them and gets in their face, and others will say that they clam up when this happens.

One constant is that it matters *how* comments are made. Not many players want to hear, "C'mon you gotta get that!" after a mistake, especially if it's delivered in a whiny or harsh voice. Unless all the players are strong both emotionally and mentally, they'll probably start separating when they hear such comments. A better approach is for teammates to encourage each other before plays to build up trust and confidence. In addition, showing pure joy after great plays creates a positive attitude that feeds off itself. At the same time, there is no doubt that some players play great when they are mad and filled with unbridled intensity. Teammates must know what makes each other tick. All players have a trigger—something that sets them off to do great things or shuts them off and causes them to lose focus. Sharing this personal information enables players to begin blending together in a productive way. Teammates must also understand that if the goal is to play volleyball aggressively, then there will be some emotionally charged situations with which they need to be comfortable. As they say, if you can't stand the heat, get out of the kitchen. Teammates must be willing to bring the right type of motivation for each person on the team in order for each player to play his or her best.

If your players are barking at each other, it is hard to win a match because their focus is on each other instead of on the opponent. Then suddenly they stop talking, and they don't want to play for or with each other. But if your players learn each other's triggers, they can be on the same page and focus on the opposition. Great teams put their aggressiveness into attacking the team across the net. They call out hitters, point out patterns, and channel their energy into a single focus. Players aren't allowed to yell across the net at opponents, but it definitely happens. Internationally, it's much more widely accepted than it is in the United States, and you can hear the chatter intensify as the match gets tighter. Officials may give some warnings about taunting, but some players definitely do their best when throwing verbal jabs and insults across the net. One word of caution, however: Smack talk sometimes motivates opponents to play even better; it may help them bring out an energizing anger they hadn't been playing with. In the end, every type of competitiveness carries associated risks, and that's one of the exciting parts of high-level volleyball.

# Competitiveness in Coaches

Most people who coach do so because they enjoy being in the competitive arena in some way or another. Some enjoy the teaching and training involved in practices, and others do it for the chance to be part of the competition on game day. This section discusses the characteristics of competitive coaches, how a coach can alter his or her competitive style, and how to adapt a coaching style based on the team's personnel.

## Characteristics of Competitive Coaches

Coaches must be competitive in order to be successful; if they aren't competitive, they probably won't be coaching very long. Competitive coaches seem to share certain characteristics:

- They hate to lose. Of course they love to win, but they probably hate to lose even more. Just like competitive players, they will fight with every weapon they have to avoid losing. They may even feel the effects of a loss physically, and winning may seem like more of a relief than a positive in itself.

- They have a vision. Their minds are always filled with ideas of how to improve players' skills, attitudes, and fitness while also seeking the best systems, lineups, and strategies. They know what the players need in order to become a team—and what the team needs in order to become a winner.

- They are creative. In order to improve the team every week, they are able to use various methods and styles to teach their players to be competitive and skillful. If one approach isn't getting through to a player or to the team, they will find a new way.

- They will risk relationships. They understand that they can't make everyone on the team happy, so they will make decisions based on what gives the team its best chance to win. They make tough personnel decisions that might upset players, parents, and fans for the sole purpose of putting the team in a competitive position. This could mean benching an all-star or a senior who usually plays all the time.

If you watch coaches on the sideline, you will see some very different competitive styles. Novice coaches are still learning which style suits them best, whereas experienced coaches have found out how to pass their competitiveness on to their players. Some coaches stand up all the time and talk regularly to their team and to the officials. Others who are very competitive sit on the sideline and remain very calm and quiet. Don't be fooled into thinking that these coaches aren't as competitive as those who stand and yell during the whole match. Some of the most competitive coaches are very composed during matches. They feel they have prepared their team well enough during practice and that the match is a time to show confidence in the players. Of course, as with most things, some coaches use a combination of both styles and will display whatever type of personality they feel their team needs at the time.

## Competitive Coaching Styles

There are probably dozens of different coaching styles, but I'm going to focus on seven that I've seen as a player, a coach, and even a spectator. Some styles tend to be more effective than others, but it's amazing how many different styles can be used to create championship programs. The styles I'll be describing are passive, analytical or mathematical, high-energy, informational, combative or negative, purely positive, and sensing. Most coaches are a combination of a couple of categories, and the top coaches know when to best be a little of each.

**Passive**    Quiet, passive coaches never raise their voice and don't take many chances. They may be positive to the point that they are unwilling to criticize players and risk the relationship, but there are times when a team needs energy from the coach, or at least strong, confident leadership. Other coaches are passive because they lack the knowledge to analyze situations and give their team a plan of attack. Sometimes these coaches wait until it's too late to call a time-out (e.g., when down 9 points with the opponent 2 points from victory), and when they do call a time-out they may not have anything constructive to say. In practices, they may be so passive that the players realize they need to take charge and run drills. In a strange way, this can help some players step up and take on leadership roles. If the entire team can see that the coach won't be bringing any energy or assertiveness, then the players might fill those roles themselves and be successful. The downside is that certain players who try to step up may end up trying to coach their peers. This doesn't usually work in the long term, and it can lead to arguments between players because they aren't getting direction from the coach. Very few passive coaches are successful over the course of time.

**Analytical or Mathematical**    These coaches are very good at working with numbers, statistics, and probabilities. They know the sideout percentages in each rotation and see the strengths and weaknesses of their team through numbers. They may also use numbers to create competition between players in practice by taking statistics and posting them for players to see. This can be a great way to motivate players without having to do much coaching or talking. Using the dry erase board right next to the court every day can get players in the habit of checking where they stand in each category. If you post the top three names in kills, digs, aces, blocks, and so on, your players will want to improve their numbers to get their name on the list. Be aware that posting all of the names can really shake the confidence of those in the last slots, so the top three or four will do. This is a great tool to use in preseason practices to help you start forming your lineup; it creates competition and gives you clear-cut reasons for starting one player over another. However, overusing statistics can also have a downside. It may confuse or bore the players as well as make them focus too much on their individual numbers rather than those of the team as a whole.

**High-Energy**  Some coaches seem to be in constant motion—they never sit down and they never stop talking. They may have trouble sitting still during matches and practices, and they may be the ones who pace the sideline while the match is in progress. Some coaches seem to have a constantly high level of energy, and they pass that on to their team. In the right doses, this can be a great thing because it will help more subdued players compete with more intensity. In extreme cases, if the coach is constantly demanding players' attention and feeding them information, this style can be very distracting for a team. When high energy is coming at a team all the time, they may become dulled by it and always rely on the coach to create the intense atmosphere on the court. This dependence can prevent the team from learning how to bring it on their own, and if they aren't up and on their A-game, they may have a tendency to sink to lower lows. High energy should always be combined with good skill training. Without a good base of skills, the energy and intensity of the coach won't be able to keep the team in the game.

**Informational**  Some coaches know a lot about the sport and enjoy passing the information on to their players. In the right amount, this can make for a great team, because the players understand every aspect of the game. But when coaches ramble on in the middle of a drill, players lose concentration and drift off. Similarly, if information is constantly coming from one coach (or all of the coaches at once) during a match, players experience information overload. They try to focus on all of the information, and their minds and bodies can lock up as a result. They simply can't absorb all of it; in fact, their heads may be spinning. The human brain can accept only so much information at one time and still function. Thus, to make good use of the learning process that happens during practices, it's important to give a player only one or two concepts to work on at a time. As with a golfer taking lessons, it's important to keep the brain out of the way of the body. If a golfer is working on the backswing and is told to keep the left arm straight and the head down through the swing, he or she can master those techniques before adding another concept to work on. If, on the other hand, the golf pro tells the student to bend at the waist, flex the knees (but don't shift sideways), keep a slow tempo, loosen the grip, and follow through high, that golfer will likely be a wreck. Volleyball coaches need to remember the same principle: Constantly talking to players denies them the chance to think on their own. Keep it simple and allow them to master one concept at a time.

**Combative or Negative**  Some coaches prefer to use the combative style, and they regularly get on their team in a negative way. They may yell, swear, and downgrade their players to try to make them tougher and well prepared for the hardest battles.

When a coach uses this style on a regular basis, two things can happen. Some players may become very passive and lose their self-confidence. In this case, they look like a dog that's been kicked, and their body language is that of a puppy with its tail between its legs. Other players may become immune to the yelling and end up being mentally strong. Nothing can phase them, and stressful match situations seem commonplace to them. They are not distracted by hostile crowds, and they learn to listen to what the coach says instead of how the message is delivered. Bobby Knight is an extreme example of a coach who used this approach, and his teams were known for their mental toughness and tenacity.

**Purely Positive**    When a coach is positive all the time, he or she is trying to build the confidence of every member of the team. Volleyball is a game of mistakes, and it's very easy for players to get down on themselves. These coaches rarely raise their voice except in an excited way, and they are always trying to encourage their players through positive reinforcement. In theory, this sounds like the ideal way to coach, because everybody feels good about what they are doing. In reality, however, I've seen some coaches of this type struggle to get their teams to win on a regular basis. I've watched both volleyball and basketball coaches who use this approach and field teams that tend to be soft when the intensity escalates. These coaches also tend to get good results early in the season, but those results fade as each month passes. Players even seem to realize when being nice all the time just isn't enough. Coaches who can use this style and consistently produce winning teams have a unique demeanor about them; it's a gift that is very hard to teach.

**Sensing**    These coaches are not necessarily just sensitive people; they have the ability to sense what each situation needs. They closely monitor the members of both teams and create a lineup and a game plan according to what they see happening. These coaches watch for body language, mood swings, communication between players, and reactions to situations. They are good at identifying the flow of the game and realizing how they can help their team by doing whatever is needed. They might insert a player, lay out a new strategy, or inject a shot of energy. They have a good sense for the tempo of the match and are good at managing situations as they arise. They are always finding ways to help their team. They can sense when the team needs more energy or needs to be calmed; in contrast, coaches who are *not* good at sensing what their team needs may miss important signals that players are sending. Over the course of a long season, a sensing coach will know when the team is flat and needs a day off to recharge, whereas coaches who can't sense such a need will continue to train their players into the ground and may take some losses as a result.

These are just seven kinds of coaching styles, and there are many more. When learning how to cultivate competitiveness, a coach must use a combination of styles. As with anything in life and sport, it's all about balance. If you pick any one of these categories and coach only in that style, you will probably lose matches that you could have won if you had brought more variety to the table. Any good teacher or coach should be willing to use different styles as situations dictate.

Players may call it playing head games, but coaches call it pushing buttons. The challenge is to improve the team as the season goes on, and sometimes doing that requires taking players out of their comfort zones. Cultivating the soil means working through it and moving it around in preparation for the growth of a plant. Cultivating competitiveness within a team means manipulating situations to spur growth in the athletes. Coaches should try to learn what motivates each player to be more competitive and then provide drills to prepare players for the most competitive teams they will face.

## Sustaining Team Competitiveness

Surges, lulls, roller coasters, and runs—all of these come into play as a team goes through a match. It is important for a team to be able to sustain a high level of competitiveness from the first whistle to the last point.

Volleyball is a game of mistakes, and the team that makes the fewest generally wins. When you watch a match, you will see mini-celebrations when a team does something well, and this ritual is an important part of maintaining players' confidence. But here is what I've come to believe about celebrations. The teams with the loudest cheers and largest celebrations over any good play are usually the worst teams (or are the ones that can't sustain good play). You see this most often at the high school level. They go nuts because they know they don't make great plays very often. They have some awesome cheers because they've worked more on those than on their skills. The teams at the next level up still celebrate, but it's more subdued. They bring energy when it's needed, and they enjoy the good plays before moving on to the next. As the match gets more intense, these teams can increase their intensity and focus. Sport psychologists call this "playing in the zone," and the top players and teams stay in that zone for longer periods of time. If players increase their intensity too much, they can actually pass their ideal playing level, and playing "past" the zone leads to more errors because players are overstimulated. Afterward, they generally suffer a drop in performance because they can't sustain the extremely high level of intensity. The best teams, however, can stay in the zone longer and avoid extreme highs and lows.

In order to sustain team competitiveness, players should experience competitive situations during practices in drills that mimic the intensity of a match. If practices are slow or fail to challenge players, it will be hard for the team to sustain competitiveness during matches. If a rally in a match would last for 5 to 15 seconds, then the players should train in drills that force them to sustain their focus and drive for 20 to 30 seconds or more. One way to do so during scrimmage situations is to toss extra balls in after the first play ends. This challenges players to remain focused and stay competitive for a longer period.

Some coaches say that they want their practices to be harder for their team than the matches will ever be. The concept of overtraining is used in many sports, and all of the coaches are doing it for the same reason. Swimmers and track athletes log many more miles or kilometers than their race involves, and they do it so they will be stronger physically, mentally, and emotionally. On race day, they can give their maximum effort and know that their technique will remain correct throughout the race. In volleyball, players who are put through taxing training sessions will be able to remain sharp in the toughest of matches. Teams who are not as well prepared will have great competitive spurts, but as their physical conditioning wanes their skills will falter and their competitiveness will fade. Many teams can play aggressive volleyball, but only the top teams can sustain their competitiveness from set to set, match to match, and week to week. Keeping practices challenging and interesting helps players develop the desire they need for matches. Drills geared to specific goals force players to compete, and longer competitive drills help them learn how to sustain their aggressive

Compete on every point like it is the last point to win the match.

mind-set. Players should feel an urgency to win that makes them want to race to the final point of the set.

In order to sustain that competitiveness over the course of a season, coaches must find a way to break the season up into smaller sections. For most teams, the season consists of three basic parts: preconference play, conference play, and tournament play. If players begin a season by trying to think about the playoffs right away, they are likely to overlook some opponents that will take them by surprise. The season is a journey that involves many steps along the way. If you ask a coach who the team plays in 3 weeks, he or she might not be able to tell you. Coaches know that you have to build the team and the enthusiasm as the season continues. Take care of one section of the season at a time and sustain the competitiveness throughout that section.

Players must be motivated every time they step onto the court or they will lose their mental edge. Motivational quotes, stories, and speakers can keep the team mentally sharp and eager to compete every day. On the flip side, beating down a team physically, mentally, or emotionally is the fastest way to dull its competitive nature and ruin a season. A team that is healthy and happy can go a long way because the players are enjoying what they are doing. Teams also need to have the technical and mental skills to sustain their competitiveness. It's hard to compete when you can't keep up with the opponent's speed or ball control skills. Coaches who want their teams to play aggressively throughout the season must give their players a competitive environment in practice. Once they do that, the team will learn how to sustain its competitiveness all the way to the conference, state, or national championship match.

# Competitiveness Drills

## HITTER'S SOLO FIGHT

**Purpose**    To improve competitiveness by forcing a hitter to score against a full defense.

**Goal**    One hitter must score five times against the full defense before being stopped five times.

**Equipment Needed**    Balls.

**Explanation**

- This is a 3v6 drill with a passer, a setter, and one hitter on one side and a full six-person defense on the other.

- The coach initiates the ball to one passer, who passes to the setter. The setter sets whatever play the hitter calls for, and the hitter tries to score in any way possible. If the hit is blocked, teammates can cover the hitter and keep the ball in play.

- If the hitter scores five times before the defense scores five times, then the hitter wins, the round is over, and a new hitter and passer come in to start the next round. If multiple setters are available, they can rotate through after each hitter. If a hitter loses a round, he or she sits out one round, then tries again.

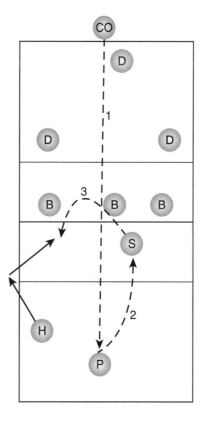

## MIDDLE VERSUS MIDDLE

**Purpose**    To teach attackers to score in one-on-one situations, to front the hitter when blocking, and to compete hard for each win.

**Goal**    One hitter must score four times off a setter against a single blocker.

**Equipment Needed**    Balls.

**Explanation**

- Two middle blockers go head-to-head to see who is the best attacker and blocker. Coach 1 and coach 2 alternate tosses; the middle blockers transition off, call for a set, and attack. They can call a 31, a 1 in front of the setter, or a 1 behind the setter; no tips count.

- Each kill counts for 1 point, and the middles race to 4 points for the win. If middle blocker 1 scores a fourth point, middle blocker 2 gets one more toss to tie (if he or she was at 3 points). If they tie at 4, each hitter gets the same number of tosses until someone wins by 1 point.

- This is a great drill for middle blocker transition, setter connection with middles, aggressive blocking, and learning to push hard.

- The drill can also pit left front hitters against right front hitters.

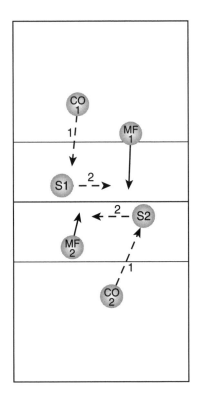

## ONE PLUS TWO

**Purpose**    To teach teams to be focused for consecutive plays and to become more competitive.

**Goal**    To win a rotation, the team must win a serve-receive ball and two free balls. The first side to win six rotations wins the drill.

**Equipment Needed**    Balls.

**Explanation**

- This is a 6v6 drill with a coach on the side, ready to toss in two free balls after the previous play ends.
- One side receives a served ball and gets two free balls tossed to random spots. Over time, make every player handle a free ball to see how the team adjusts and reacts to different situations.
- Lower-level teams need to win just two of three to rotate; higher-level teams must earn all three. If a team does not win a rotation in three tries, it moves to the next rotation; eventually, it must go back and win the ones it skipped.
- One variation is to require that the team serve, win the rally, and then win two free balls; you could also make it three free balls to force the team to sustain focus longer.

## SERVING CHAIR KNOCKDOWN

**Purpose**   To teach players to serve strongly and aggressively and to compete as a team.

**Goal**   To score more points than the opposing team does during a 2-minute game. Servers get 1 point for hitting a chair (even on the first bounce) and 5 points for knocking a chair down.

**Equipment Needed**   Balls; chairs.

**Explanation**

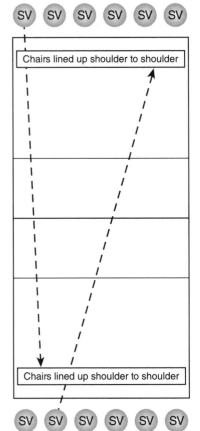

- Line up the chairs side by side across the end of the court. Place them 5 feet (1.5 meters) in from the end line to promote deep serves at the passers' shoulders. The chairs should be light enough to get knocked over when hit but not so heavy that they will damage the floor when they go down.

- On the whistle, all players on both sides serve at once and race to hit the most chairs in the allotted time. A coach or manager can be positioned at each end line to count the points earned. This drill promotes strong serving, and the teams become competitive as the clock is counting down.

- One variation is to put chairs or boxes where passers would be. The goal in this case is to *not* hit the chairs. One point is given for each chair hit, and the lower-scoring team wins.

## SIDEOUT TO WIN

**Purpose**   To improve as a sideout (receive a serve and score) team and become efficient scorers.

**Goal**   A team must win five of eight rallies from serve receive. Once this goal is achieved, the team rotates. All six rotations must be completed to finish the drill.

**Equipment Needed**   Balls.

### Explanation

- This is a 6v6 drill geared toward scoring a high percentage of the time out of serve receive.
- The starting team receives eight serves and must score on five (62.5 percent) of them in order to win. Play each rally to the end, but if one side reaches its target number (servers need four wins, receivers need five), then stop and begin again.
- The passing team gets three chances to win each rotation. If it misses one along the way, it must go back when done with the others.
- Targeting a specific percentage as a goal teaches players the numbers they need to achieve in order to win matches; it also creates an extremely competitive environment.

## TRIANGLE TRANSITION

**Purpose**　To teach players how to attack, transition back, and attack again.

**Goal**　Each hitter gets two balls and must score on both to earn 1 big point. The first hitter to earn 4 big points wins, and all hitters are then replaced by new hitters.

**Equipment Needed**　Balls.

### Explanation

- The coach hits a down ball to the passer, the setter releases to set, and hitter 1 transitions off the net.

- If hitter 1 scores on the first attempt, the coach initiates the second ball. If hitter 1 scores again, he or she earns a big point. If hitter 1 is dug, the defense sends the ball over on the second contact for hitter 1 to try again. If hitter 1 makes an error, the coach initiates another ball, and hitter 2 begins the same sequence. If hitter 2 makes an error, then hitter 3's turn begins.

- After every set, the passer and setter should cover. If they pop the ball up, the hitter should transition off, and they can try to score again. Hitters will learn that it is OK to hit a three-quarter-speed shot into the block knowing that their teammates are covering them.

- You can add back-row attack and setter dump; they need six kills to win.

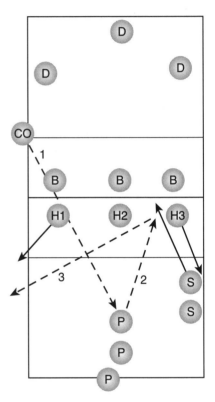

# WIN

**Purpose**    To increase aggressiveness and competitiveness in out-of-system situations.

**Goal**    To win three rallies in a row in order to earn a rotation. First team to complete all six rotations wins.

**Equipment Needed**    Balls.

## Explanation

- This is a 6v6 drill with a coach on the side, ready to toss a ball in to the team that won the last rally.

- A team earns a W for its first rally win, an I if it wins the next rally, and an N (and the win for the rotation) if it wins three rallies in a row. If one team wins a W and an I but the opposition wins the next rally, then the opposition has earned its W. Play continues until one team has won all three letters.

- When a team wins a rotation, it moves on to the next.

- The coach can initiate each play by hitting the ball hard at a player or tossing it anywhere. The coach should put the ball in play in difficult spots so that the teams learn to adjust. This is a very competitive drill.

# 7

# Communicating Effectively

Since volleyball is a team sport, good communication is vital to winning at any level. The clearest example is found in watching lower-level volleyball. Whether they are in the sixth grade or are adults, many novice players don't say a word or even move during a play. That's usually because they are neither confident in their skills nor sure what to do. On occasion, they may try to play the ball when it's hit right to them, but a ball heading between teammates usually causes both players to freeze, since each is afraid of making a mistake. With a little coaching in the technique of communication, however, most people start to enjoy the game and keep getting more confident and aggressive. Teams who communicate well flow together and play as one.

To play truly aggressive volleyball, teammates must learn the art of communication. This chapter addresses communication between teammates, communication during practices and matches, and communication between coaches and players. Each of these skills contributes to the overall goal of building a team that works and thinks as one. Teams who don't communicate well can fall apart on many levels, and it doesn't matter how much physical talent they have. Championship teams work on their communication skills as much as they do on any other skill, and their results prove just how important communication is.

## Communication Between Players

Communication may be more important in volleyball than in any other sport. How many sports have six players moving together in such a small area in pursuit of a fast-moving ball that they are prevented by rule from holding or letting touch the ground? Volleyball players must also solve the opponent's tactics and work together as a tight unit. They need to become good listeners toward their teammates and coaches along with learning how to provide information clearly to others. Good communication is a major component of playing aggressive volleyball, and it's truly an art that everyone involved in the game must learn. The following sections discuss some general rules of verbal and nonverbal communication. If you are working with a young or inexperienced team, these guidelines should be conveyed clearly and *over*emphasized until every player uses them correctly. Once ingrained in the team, these skills will often make the difference between winning and losing a match.

# Verbal Communication

The goal of verbal communication is to communicate clearly, regardless of whether the match is just starting or the score is 14-14 in the fifth. To avoid confusion, it is best to use words that are short, clear, and loud. Repeating the same word multiple times is better than saying three different words. For example, "Mine, mine!" is preferred over "I got it, I got it!" If you lose even 1 point in a match due to confusion, it is worth taking time to correct the problem as soon as possible. Here are some tips for effective verbal communication:

- Call "Mine!" on all balls you plan to play. Call it well ahead of time so your teammates can clear out of the way. If the ball is heading to a seam between players, call the ball two or three times and increase the volume with each word if the other player doesn't stay away: "Mine, MINE, *MINE!*"

- If the setter is heading to the ball and another player is thinking about setting it, the setter needs to call out a quick, "Mine, *Mine!*"

- When the ball is near the sidelines or end lines, give a clear call: "Good, Good, *Good*" or "Out, Out, *Out!*" to help the teammate making the play.

- If there could be any question about who you're addressing, use the intended person's name.

- On a free ball, everyone should call "Free!" as soon as they recognize the situation.

- Front-row players are in charge of locating the opposing hitters and calling out if the setter is front-row.

- While covering, defensive players should glance at the opposition's defense after the attack to identify holes; then, between plays, they should share any information gained with the setter and hitters.

- Players on the bench should help by calling balls in or out and by giving positive reinforcement to those on the court.

- There should be no negative emotional outbursts. The team will better control momentum swings if players stay focused on the task at hand and use intense situations to raise their level of play.

- Keep words with the officials or line judges to a minimum. Let the coaches and captain worry about the officials.

Just as all players join the team needing to work on certain physical skills, many players have to be taught how to communicate. If a quiet or passive player becomes an issue during play, coaches should address the situation right away. The first thing to do is simply ask the player to be more vocal; in some cases, being vocal just isn't something that was done where the player grew up. If that doesn't work, you have to give the player opportunities to practice being loud. For example, I've seen players who are so quiet that they won't call "Mine" loud enough to avoid confusion between players. Here's one solution: Anytime the player doesn't speak loudly and clearly enough for a ball in practice, send him or her off the court and out of view—50 to 75 feet (15 to 23 meters) away should do it. Then have the player yell, "Mine, Mine, Mine!" loud enough for everyone to hear it back on the court. Once the player has done this, bring him or her right back into the drill. If the player is quiet on the next relevant play, send him or her out to yell again. Pretty soon, this player will understand the concept and start using a loud gym voice when it's needed on the court. Some players think it's funny and are glad that someone is telling them it's good to be loud. Others will feel stressed and embarrassed because being loud is something they've never been comfortable with. Like anything else, it takes practice. Each time they do it, they'll move closer to making it a good habit.

Another way to help players become more comfortable with speaking in front of the group is to have them call out the score before every play during scrimmages. Ask a quiet person to be the scorekeeper for the whole scrimmage; he or she should be the only person to call out the score. Hide the scoreboard so the individual has to keep track of the score, and make sure he or she calls it out loud enough for people to hear it on the far end line. As each day goes by, this player will understand that he or she is responsible for calling out the score if the scrimmage is to continue. Most quiet players will find it much easier to speak up after using this method.

## Physical Communication

When spectators watch volleyball, they notice a couple of things. They see that the court is much smaller than a basketball court, that players from the same team stay on one side of the net, and that when it's played right it is a very fast game. When people watch volleyball for the first time, they often ask the same question: "Why are they always touching each other between plays?" It seems that, over the years, volleyball players have found it important not only to connect verbally between plays but also to stay connected by touching each other. Watch good teams between plays. They slap hands almost every time they pass a teammate while heading to their positions for the next play. Why all this contact? Every time they touch, they are saying something to each other. The touch can range from an excited high five or chest bump after a huge block to reaching out and lightly touching the hand of the passer. Sometimes players are saying, "Great job!" At other times, the touch means, "It's OK, you'll get the next one."

Another thing to watch for is the dysfunctional player who doesn't connect with teammates. This player may be mad at him- or herself after a play and walk away from everyone. Unfortunately, teammates don't always know who the player is mad at. Before long, they may begin to think the player is mad at them, and suddenly the team isn't thinking about the game or the opponent. Some players will reach out to a teammate to get the normal confirmation that everything is OK but will be snubbed or ignored. Coaches need to keep a close eye on how their players communicate and whether their communication brings them together or splits them apart. The coach who notices communication issues within the team must find ways to fix them in practice before they cause problems in a match.

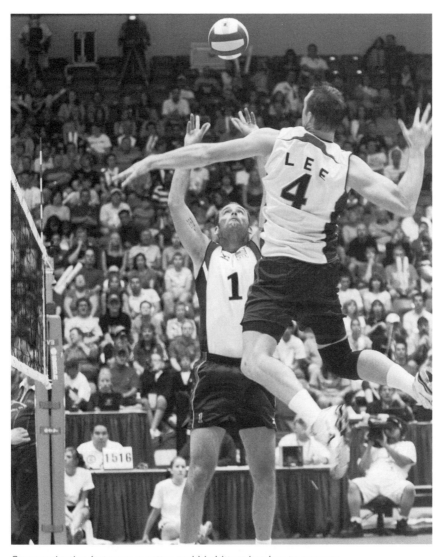

Communication between a setter and his hitters is a key to success.

The following examples of communication explain a wide variety of ways in which individual players can form a tighter connection with their teammates, create good team chemistry, and become a coherent unit.

• Passers should claim the area physically. As the serve is crossing the net, the passer should move as soon as possible to the area where the ball will land. Once there, the passer should center him- or herself on the ball and be ready to make another move if the ball floats. If another player is heading to the same area, the passer who arrives first should claim the spot like a basketball player boxes out for a rebound. Players who arrive for a pass in passive fashion run the risk of confusion or even a collision with a teammate.

• Setters may need to physically clear the way so they have room to set. If a teammate is hindering the setter from getting to or actually setting the ball, the setter should first verbally clear the way and then, if necessary, physically make space to set. Without harming the teammate, the setter may need to put his or her hands out and shove the other player out of the way in order to get in position to set. Middle blockers often get in the way as they transition off the net, and the setter needs to make it clear that he or she intends to set every second ball whenever possible.

• Open lanes on serve receive and look at the passer and the ball. Turn and face the person passing the ball and establish good balance with knees flexed. If the passer shanks the ball, you have to be ready to chase it off the court if needed.

• If you make a mistake, briefly analyze what went wrong, then move on to the next play. Errors are part of the sport, and the key to being a great player is to not let mistakes take you out of the game mentally. Showing disappointment physically (e.g., poor body language or facial expressions) can distract you and your teammates from focusing on the opponent. Reconnect with your teammates to let them know you're OK and ready for the next play.

• Practice good listening skills and posture. During practice or time-outs in matches, stand tall and look the speaker in the eye. It is distracting if, instead, you are talking to teammates, fidgeting, playing with your hair, or biting your nails. Whether it's a coach or a teammate, the speaker deserves your respect and needs to know that you're paying attention. It can make a big difference after a time-out if everyone remembers what play was called despite all the distractions around the court.

• Show enthusiasm after good plays. Take every opportunity to grab momentum and use that energy to play at a higher level. Negative feelings carry a heavy energy, whereas positive feelings are uplifting. Some beginning players are very quiet or serious, and they actually need to practice expressing their joy in order to release their inhibitions and play at a higher level.

With improved communication skills, players learn to listen to and trust each other. They can evolve from a set of dysfunctional individuals to a group that is truly a team. From the first time a coach meets with the team, he or she should observe how each player communicates both on and off the court. Some are shy. They stand on the fringe and observe everyone else. They're soaking everything in, but they rarely contribute to conversation. Some drop their heads and look to the ground when someone is speaking, and they always defer to older or more outgoing players. Some players are totally different on the court, where they have an aggressive, outgoing persona. That's one of the great things about sport; it can give players confidence they otherwise wouldn't have.

There are noticeable differences in the ways in which men and women communicate. Men generally aren't known to be overly talkative, but they find other ways to share information. They convey a good amount of information through looks and nods and don't feel the need to be close to their teammates all the time. They'll definitely call out hitters and strategize to find a way to beat the opponent, but communication tends to be based on a need for information rather than for closeness. Women, on the other hand, are more likely to seek continuous connection. You will often see women's teams meet in the middle of the floor after every play to make sure everyone is good to go for the next serve. Some of my top-level women's teams have said that to improve their competitive level they need to come together as a unit between every play. On the surface, this may not seem so important, but these players all want to know that they are OK with themselves and with each other before the next whistle. There's not much time to say a lot when they join in the middle, but they all seek the positive energy and reinforcement they get from each other. They may share information about the next play, but their main purpose is to connect, and if this makes them feel better and more confident, then I'm certainly not going to argue with it.

## Self-Talk

One of the challenges of teaching good communication is the presence of positive or negative self-talk. Positive self-talk is a trait of good players; they know how to treat themselves well so that they can move forward in the game. Most top players blow off bad plays—even laugh them off at times to protect their psyche.

On the other hand, one of the most harmful habits a player can have is negative self-talk. When players with this tendency make any kind of bad play, they hammer themselves with a tirade featuring words that can't be repeated in family settings. Some speak aloud, but most hold it in and turn the abuse on themselves. Only a small minority of players can use this method to motivate themselves to be better on the next play. Most will totally lose their focus and continue with a streak of bad plays.

In postmatch interviews, players and coaches of losing teams often say, "We just stopped talking out there." The worst thing that can happen when players make mistakes is that they get mad and withdraw into themselves. If they cut off communication with their teammates, a question arises as to who they're really mad at. Often, they are extremely mad at themselves and think the right thing to do is to show everyone how upset they are. Unfortunately, many teammates wonder if the upset player is mad at something *they* may have done. Bad set? Didn't cover well enough? Got in the player's way? Suddenly teammates are questioning their relationship with the person who made the error instead of focusing on the next play and on the opponent. Thus, one player's cutting off of communication with teammates can cause a downward spiral for the whole group.

Look at the face of a player who has been aced or stuffed straight down on an attack. If the player's face looks blank or the player turns away quietly from his or her teammates, it's likely that another bad play is coming very soon. If coaches can see their own teams behaving this way, you can bet the opposing players and coaches are watching for the same thing. Players who don't handle mistakes well must be taught how to use communication recovery techniques just as they learn any other skill, and the best time to do so is during practice, since it's hard to change a bad habit in the middle of a match.

One example is the passer who shanks a ball and becomes immediately, and obviously, disgusted with him- or herself. The body language may be dramatic or low-key, but either way it's clear that the player has tightened up, and you might hear him or her say something like, "Korie, what are you thinking?" or "Pass the ball, you idiot!" If you don't hear it out loud, you may see the player clench his or her fists and stomp away from the play. Either way, you know that what the player is thinking is not good. Try stepping up to the player and asking what he or she was saying or thinking. The player may be a little shy, because it may have been a string of vulgarities that he or she wouldn't normally say in front of a coach. If you don't mind hearing it, have the player say it out loud to you so you know exactly what you're dealing with. Then, the next time the player's passing partner makes a mistake, have the first player say the same words to the partner. The player you're trying to help will probably be shocked by your request, and if that player actually complies with it, he or she will realize how much it hurts the teammate. It's very likely, of course, that the player won't follow through and say it, but he or she may still gain understanding of the fact that negative self-talk can be extremely harmful to his or her game. In fact, I've seen players take their game to the next level once they learned how to be good to themselves. It may not happen overnight, but the hope is that they mature enough to remain composed and relaxed.

Besides learning how to laugh at their own mistakes and counter negative self-talk with positive self-talk, it's good for players to reconnect with their teammates after errors. Saying something as simple as, "Hey, I've got the next one," can go a long way toward solidifying the confidence of the person who says it, as well as that of his or her teammates. Many players will say, "My bad—I got it," meaning they'll take the blame for the last point and are ready for the next.

# Communication During Practices and Matches

Most coaches use practice time to work on the many physical techniques of volleyball, but some neglect the communication skills that are important to the team. If coaches expect their teams to communicate well during a match, they have to make sure that they work on it in practice. In matches, how many times have you heard coaches say, "Why aren't we talking out there?" When teams are playing well, it's very easy for them to communicate. The tough part comes when players are struggling or the team is losing. If teams can stay composed and communicate under duress, then they still have a great shot at winning the match. This section covers how to create energy and enthusiasm, communicate physically, communicate positively under stress, and give the team ownership through communication. Mastering these skills gives every player more confidence on the court and allows each to play more aggressively.

## Creating Energy and Enthusiasm

Two of the most powerful forms of communication are energy and enthusiasm. In fact, you could post the words *energy* and *enthusiasm* on the locker-room door to remind your team of their importance in the gym. Fist pumps, chest bumps, and high fives all communicate the excitement and intensity of the situation. Some teams, however, don't know how to raise their energy level when it's needed, and they lose matches because of their lack of enthusiasm. As coaches train their teams, they need to be aware of who is bringing the energy and who might be draining it from the team. Oftentimes, coaches are the ones doing the cheering and pushing as they prod the team to raise its intensity to the level needed for a match. That's a good strategy, as long as the players pick up on the plan and start doing it themselves. If the coach is the only one bringing the energy, however, the players won't know how to create it for themselves during a match. Every player should be able to tell when the team is showing signs of being flat—and be able to cure it.

One method that can help is based on the simple coach-on-three drill (also called "three back"), in which the coach, positioned at the net, hits balls at three players positioned in their defensive bases. The goal is for each defender to play the ball back to the coach so he or she can hit it right back to the defenders. It's a basic ball control drill that most teams use to improve their defense and warm up the team. First, run the drill for three rounds (1 minute each) to get the players going. Make sure a couple of players are designated to shag and toss balls in when needed. It's best to have a group going on each side of the net so that more players are involved in the drill; use a second coach, or a player if necessary, to hit on the other side of the net. This drill helps players improve their hand contact on the ball and their hitting control. You'll probably notice a couple of players encouraging their teammates, but many will be fairly quiet through the whole thing.

Afterward, assign a player to serve as motivator for each defender on the court and have the motivator stand next to the sideline or end line near the designated defender. The motivators' assignment is to energize their defenders during the 1-minute round. They should be yelling and clapping for the entire minute and should each focus entirely on the one person they are assigned to. You can also extend the drill by changing the 1-minute length to whatever time is required for the side to make 10 good digs back to the target in order to win. Adding this competitive aspect gets the players' competitive juices flowing as they work to beat the team on the other side of the net.

Go through the drill a couple of times, then take a break and ask the players if they noticed a difference in the level of their play. They'll likely realize that making a specific effort to bring more energy creates an exciting training environment and raises everyone's level of play. They'll also discover the fact that with a teammate pushing them they will give everything they have. If you have enough players, you could even assign a person to yell at the motivator cheering for the defender. The team might think this is funny, but anyone who is usually quiet will lose his or her inhibitions and learn how to communicate through energy.

While it's important to learn to create energy through enthusiasm, teams cannot constantly bring high-octane intensity. In fact, players who are the best leaders also know how to communicate quietly and one-on-one with a teammate. One example might be seen between plays when two defenders are standing side by side as they get ready to head to their defensive base. If one player calmly but intensely says to the other, "You and me, *nothing* hits the ground!" then suddenly those two have formed a specific bond and identified a short-term goal. The player who made the initial request will raise his or her own effort level upon asking the teammate to do so.

Another example involves a setter talking to a passer before the serve. Some setters just stand at the net and get ready for the serve; they often choose to look at the server and therefore don't really connect with their own team. The best setters, however, take more responsibility for keeping their teammates focused and on task. It doesn't need to happen on every play, but on occasion the setter should connect with passers before the play. The setter should use the passer's name and encourage him or her to put the next ball on target. Saying something like, "Here you go, Bobbi, you've got this one," helps the passer be a little more alert and feel like he or she is not just passing to a target area but is passing *for* the setter.

---

## A Tip From the Top

Each season seems to feature one moment that determines a team's destiny. This particular story comes from a time early in my career when I was head coach at the University of Texas at Arlington. One of my favorite memories involves a fiery defensive specialist from Uruguay who spearheaded a David-and-Goliath feat against the Texas Longhorns. In the second match of a home-and-away series, UT Arlington welcomed the Longhorns to Texas Hall. Just 2 days earlier, Texas had beaten us 15-2 in a disappointing fifth game. After reliving the experience via videotape and watching Quandalyn Harrell, a 10-foot-7-inch (3.2 meter) skywalker, crush ball after ball, we knew we would need a courageous effort in order to produce a different outcome in the return match. Before leaving our locker room for pregame warm-ups, Adriana Campon, a 5-foot-4-inch (1.6 meter) senior, asked me if she could read a story to the team. It went like this:

> This is a little story about four people named Everybody, Somebody, Anybody, and Nobody. There was an important job to be done, and Everybody was sure that Somebody would do it. Anybody could have done it, but Nobody did it. Somebody got angry about that because it was Everybody's job. Everybody thought that Anybody could do it, but Nobody realized that Everybody wouldn't do it. It ended up that Everybody blamed Somebody when Nobody did what Anybody could have done.

Impassioned, Adriana urged the players to give everything they had and to unite in pursuing their goal. Her plea's impact was impressive, and the team responded well, but Adriana's play in particular spoke volumes of her determination as we secured a five-game victory. It is this type of moment that makes me smile, even 20 years later, as I replay the scene in my mind. Players like Adriana are special, and you need to have at least one or two on every team if you are going to reach for new heights.

—Cathy George, Head Women's Coach, Michigan State University

To follow through on this communication, the setter must make sure to compliment the passer if he or she gives the setter what was wanted. Everyone remembers the exciting kill, but it was the great pass that made it possible. A setter who learns to connect and communicate with passers will build positive relationships that create a positive cycle of focus and effort. Passers perform better if they know they'll get some praise and be appreciated, and the connection before and after the pass is what strengthens the bond between the two.

## Communicating Physically

Some communications must be nonverbal in order to prevent your opponent from knowing your plans. One example involves the setter giving hand signals to hitters between plays. Whether used on offense or defense, hand signals can be an effective way to communicate information and clarify the game plan to all the members of the team. The more advanced teams get, the more they need a way to convey information between players.

In most offenses, the setter will look to each hitter and give a hand signal. Coaches need to come up with a variety of good hand signals that symbolize each set in their system. Here are some examples:

- Index finger: quick-set 1 ball
- Two fingers: a 2 ball in front of the setter
- Three fingers: a 31
- Four fingers: an outside 4 ball
- Fist: a 32 or a gap (i.e., a loop set landing between the middle and right-side block)
- Flat hand: a slide behind the setter to the antenna
- Hang loose (thumb and pinky extended, other fingers tucked to palm): a quick slide in front of the setter

Between plays, the hitters should look at the setter for their signals. If a hitter is distracted or forgets to look, the setter must get his or her attention in order to call the play. A smart opponent will look across the net to try to steal signals and learn the plays, so the setter should hide the signal from the other team's view. One way to do that is for the setter to turn his or her back to the net to shield the signal from view. If needed, the setter can also put his or her jersey forward with one hand to block the view while the other hand gives the signal.

Once the first play takes place, the hitters must stay with the called sets or audible to the setter if they want to change the play. The audible system (discussed in chapter 5) is an important form of communication if the play continues on after the initial attack. The hitters must be loud in order to overcome crowd noise and any other talk on the court that could confuse the setter. If the setter sets to one spot while the hitter goes to another, that's usually a clear sign of miscommunication between the two. Either the setter didn't hear what the hitter was calling, or one of them simply forgot what was called.

Blockers use the same type of hand signals to tell back-row players how many hitters there are and where they are going to set up the block. First, the blockers will hold one or both hands above head height with two or three fingers showing to correspond with how many hitters are front-row. If the blockers hold up two fingers, the defenders know that the setter is front-row and that they have to be alert for a dump. If the blockers hold up three fingers, there are three hitters and the setter is back-row, which generally tells the defenders they can start back a little deeper and don't have to worry as much about the setter. Some setters will still throw the ball over on the second contact, but it will be a little slower since it has to start from below the top of the net before it goes over.

Blockers might next signal the direction in which they'll be moving or blocking. In the two-person sand game, the blocker will tell the defender if he or she plans to block the crosscourt shot or the line shot or straight on the body or ball. Before the serve, the blocker at the net will put both hands behind his or her back and get ready to signal. The blocker will then indicate to his or her partner what he or she will do as a blocker if the opponent moves to the blocker's left to attack (signal with the left hand), and what he or she will do if the opponent moves to the blocker's right to attack (signal with the right hand). The blocker shows the index finger to say that he or she will be blocking line, whereas showing two fingers means the blocker will be blocking crosscourt and showing a fist means he or she will be blocking on the ball. In the indoor six-person game, the middle blocker might tell the defenders if he or she is kicking out early to the right or the left; this is called a two-and-one or a one-and-two (2-1 or 1-2). Some coaches will try to put a double block on the opponent's top hitter whenever possible to slow him or her down. By scouting an opponent, coaches can learn, for example, that player A gets 70 percent of the sets in a specific rotation and that players B and C combine for 30 percent. By putting two blockers on player A, then, the coach hopes to stress that attacker enough that the opponent must go to its weaker options. In that case, of course, the coach is hoping to stop hitters B and C with a single block and the defenders.

## Maintaining Positive Communication Under Stress

Confidence is a key to winning, and players must continue to communicate even under the most stressful situations. Most players find it easy to be upbeat and communicate with their teammates when things are going well, but how does a team behave when mistakes are being made and points are being lost? When coaches talk about breakdowns in communication, they're usually related to a team's inability to play well under duress. The goal of most good coaches is to get the opponent out of its comfort zone and into stressful situations, thus increasing the chance that the opponent will break down in terms of skill execution and communication. To prevent that from happening to your own team, it's important to train your players in ways to avoid lapses in confidence and communication. Put players in difficult situations during practice so that they learn how to react positively and continue communicating effectively in matches.

One form of stress derives from poor conditioning. Giving the team hard, exhausting drills challenges them to push each other through the tough times and stand strong. Putting big blocks up against the hitters or placing extra defenders on the court forces them to handle stress. Given the opportunity to work through these situations, players will learn to continue using good communication skills during the toughest of matches.

Another way to make a point about the importance of communication is to disallow it. Initiate a scrimmage where no one is allowed to speak or even make sounds during a 15-point set. It will be very strange to have a totally quiet gym, but the players will begin to understand the importance of talking. After the first set, play again and allow the players to make sounds. Players will start to grunt or clap their hands to get their teammates' attention. This may get a little silly, so you might want to establish a consequence (e.g., push-ups, sit-ups, or sprints) for the losing team in order to keep things serious. In the next set, allow only one player on each side to talk—and make it the quietest person. This will force the quiet players to step up and be the ones to call balls and hitters, as well as encourage their teammates. If one team is stronger than the other, you can start the set by giving the weaker team a 5- to 7-point lead in order to put the first team under the kind of stress they will find themselves facing during a match. Finally, play one more set, this time to 25 points, in which everyone is allowed to communicate. The team will probably communicate better both verbally and physically. Sometimes coaches need to take something away from a team in order to show them how important it really is to winning. If they can do it under duress, they will know how to stay composed and be mentally stronger.

## Creating Team Ownership Through Communication

As team members improve their communication skills, they will become more engaged with each other and take more ownership of the mental side of the game. Volleyball is very much like a game of chess that is played at a much higher speed. Every play is countered by the opponent, and the match is a constant strategic battle. Every volleyball team has its pawns, bishops, rooks, kings, and queens, because each player is strong in some ways but limited in others. On some volleyball teams, the coaches shuffle the players around and dictate every move. Those teams feature very little thought by the players, who constantly rely on the coach to tell them what to do. In contrast, players who communicate well have the ability to take ownership of winning strategy by learning to create situations on the court that enable them to win more rallies. Once they start thinking more for themselves, they play with more confidence, more hunger, and more aggressiveness.

One great way to teach communication, ownership, and independence is a game called Xontro (pronounced Zontro). I developed this game several years ago as a way to work on skills and plays in which we were weak. My goal was to give the players a way to compete against each other while using problem-solving skills, communication, and teamwork. This game helped them to think outside the box, trying new strategies and skills, even as it allowed them to make mistakes without penalties. Having the freedom to try new things releases the pressure they feel from coaches who often expect them to be perfect.

Here's how the game is played (and you can create your own form of it very easily). First, create a scorecard that consists of 8 to 10 categories in which players on two separate teams will compete. Make each category something that your players need to work on and include skills or plays that they're not always comfortable making. Here are some sample categories:

| Category | Number Needed | Points Earned |
| --- | --- | --- |
| Kills off nonsetters | 3 | 10 |
| Deflection blocks | 3 | 10 |
| Slide kills | 5 | 10 |
| Setter kills | 5 | 10 |
| Aces | 5 | 20 |
| Tip or roll kills | 5 | 20 |
| Hand digs | 5 | 20 |
| Coverage plays off the block | 5 | 25 |
| Quick-set kills | 5 | 25 |
| Digs by defensive specialist or libero | 5 | 30 |

Once the team understands how to play the game, the coach can come up with other categories. It would be even better to ask the players what areas they need to improve in and use those as goals for the next game. Other category possibilities include line kills off the block, jump-float aces, X-play kills, middle blocker making the coverage play, and kills off bump sets. If a coach wants a little less going on, he or she can narrow the focus and have players really zero in on, say, five categories.

For each category, assign a number as a goal to earn the "big" points of the category—for instance, 5 coverage plays to earn 25 points. If they get 10 coverage plays, they earn 50 points. As you can see from the list, the team will start to figure out how they can score the most points.

Each game is played for 30 minutes, and automatic time-outs (2 minutes long) are taken at 10 minutes and 20 minutes. During the time-outs, teams get together with their scorer (the scorer should not be a coach, but a teammate who is not playing at the time) to determine which categories they want to redeem next. It is suggested that each team meets separately during the time-outs so that the other team doesn't know what the opponent needs to achieve. The players on the sidelines will become the coaches, and they'll be sharing information with their teammates. As coaches observe the teams, they'll see the players develop leadership skills and find ways to earn points from multiple categories in the same rally. For example, they can make a coverage play, then run a slide with a tip kill. Their scorer will be able to put a mark next to those three categories, and they'll be eager to do it again.

This game can be expanded when the team is ready, and it will pose a new challenge every time. One variation is to give team A one set of categories and team B a different set. If the two teams aren't told the opponent's categories, they'll have to figure out what their opponent is trying to earn. As soon as someone picks up on that, he or she will communicate it to teammates so they can work together to prevent the other side from scoring points. They'll try to avoid getting aced or letting the setter score on them, and they'll be communicating and thinking between every play. Once they figure out the opposing players, they will work even harder to keep them from scoring. They start using their brains, they become more creative, and they work together as a team. It's really a coach's dream to see everyone on the roster talking and making plans together.

The game of Xontro can be adapted for novice-level teams as well. Simply make the categories easier and lower the number of points needed to redeem a category. Examples include serving to zone 1 five times, having everyone yell "Cover!" and get in position before the hit, scoring five times with a pass-set-kill sequence, and digging five balls to the target area. Again, with teammates keeping score, the players will all learn quickly to think and speak up. As subs rotate onto the court, they bring the knowledge of the score sheet to their teammates and really get energized to earn points. Xontro gives players the skills they need to have when they play regular matches that really count. I've seen this drill work wonders for high school and college teams in just a short period of time. Skills, problem solving, teamwork, and communication become second nature, and teams play more aggressively and with more confidence.

## Communication Between Coaches and Players

When most people think of communication in volleyball, they automatically picture teammates needing to talk to each other and share information. We usually think of communicating during matches, but the most important communication connection must be formed between player and coach.

One main part of a coach's job is to pass on his or her knowledge of the sport to the players. While doing that, the coach must be aware of the fine line between teaching and being critical. When teaching, coaches give information to players. It might concern hand positioning on the block or an approach pattern. Players usually react well to teaching and are willing to try to make changes in their game. The difficulties arise as the season moves on. Coaches can teach the same skill only so many times before it comes to seem redundant. At a certain point, the coach will have to critique players in order for them to take their game to the next level, and this is when players may take the coach's intended help as criticism and often feel offended by the comments. As with all areas of communication in life, it's always best to start with a compliment or two before critiquing. Before the season even starts, it helps if the coaches make sure that players understand how to listen to what is being said and not take offense at it. Especially during heated matches, players must try to listen to what is said rather than *how* it is said. At the same time, coaches must be careful with negative criticism and try to be constructive whenever possible. One of the worst things to do is to call a player out after a loss and place blame for what happened. I'm not saying that it should never be done, but be aware of the long-term risks to the relationship between player and coach. Coaches are often accused of playing mind games with their players when they try to push players' emotional buttons to get a reaction. Yes, it happens. If it works, the coach is a genius. If it doesn't, long-term problems can arise.

While giving information, it's important that the coach observe the player's reaction. Some players look coaches in the eye and nod to indicate that they understand. Other players might give an excuse right back to the coach before he or she even finishes the sentence. Still others drop their eyes, look to the floor, and act like they're being beaten down. If a coach senses anything but a positive reaction to the advice, he or she should talk with the player about improving his or her learning skills. Some players really need time to absorb what is said, and they may react initially with a defiant attitude. Some players are very resistant to trying new skills, and they put up a bit of a wall. That wall can be frustrating to coaches and eventually may cause the coach to no longer want to work with the player. Unfortunately, the player is hurting his or her own progress by doing this. Whether or not my players agree with what I say, all I ask them to do is look me in the eye and nod. The nod doesn't necessarily mean that they agree with me; it means that they are hearing what I am saying. The coach and the player may have to come to an understanding about how they can best communicate with each other. If one gets mad at the other and stops listening, the impasse is likely to grow into bigger problems that come to a head during matches. Some players are easy to communicate with; others are much more challenging. One of my favorite sayings is, "She's (or he's) a tough nut to crack." Some shells are thicker and stronger, but if you find the right spot to tap, you have a good chance of getting it to open up for you. Players are the same way. Find the right way to communicate with them, and you can both move on to bigger and better things.

Just as coaches ask players to go out of their way or out of their comfort zone to connect to teammates, coaches need to do the same thing. Being named the coach doesn't necessarily mean that you were born with extra-special communication talents or that you're comfortable in one-on-one relationships. In order to make sure that players and coaches are on the same page, it's important for the adult in the situation to find ways to communicate better. One way coaches can do this is to give every player a high five before practice begins in order to establish a positive connection to start the session. Even in that brief moment, the coach can tell what kind of mood the players are in and intervene if he or she senses a problem. Some coaches schedule weekly or biweekly meetings with their players, and others do it as they think each player needs it. I'd suggest being proactive rather than waiting until something explodes and catches everyone off guard. Coaches should make a point of spending one-on-one time with each player whenever they can. The best places to do it are often out of the office in a nonthreatening environment—talking before or after practice, on the bus, or while walking around school grounds can create a relaxed situation for the player. If the talk is done in the office, it's best to meet on a regular basis so the players don't think they're coming in just because they are in trouble. Coaches should try to get the player–coach relationship to a point where players are comfortable with coming in on their own if they ever want to talk. Building these relationships off the court often improves communication and trust on the court.

Coaches can also use technology to connect and create bonds with players. Any players brought up since the mid-1990s have probably spent a great deal of time using their phones and computers, and motivational messages can be sent as text messages or e-mails to allow players to express themselves in a medium with which they are comfortable. Just as some coaches post inspirational messages on the locker-room wall, they can also send weekly inspirational e-mails or texts. Such messages can be sent to individual players or to the entire team. A coach can also show that he or she cares about a player by sending a text on the player's birthday or after the player has submitted a good paper or exam. After a good match—or a bad match—an encouraging message can help the player keep a positive mind-set as he or she moves ahead. And in some cases, electronic messaging gives players the courage to ask the coach a question or make a comment about a situation. At the same time, coaches must be aware of how things are said. Some comments can be misinterpreted in written form since the player receiving them can't hear or see how the words are being said.

Another form of electronic communication includes social networking Web sites, which are extremely popular these days. In fact, players often look at their accounts on these sites before they check their e-mail. Some coaches use these sites to send group messages to the team or to post announcements, but I would warn against using them to send personal messages. The coaching staff should maintain the line between being a coach and being friends and keep some level of separation. Facebook and MySpace are used basically as friend sites, and messages are often more public when they are posted. Texting and sending e-mails can be more private, and the player will appreciate the one-on-one time. For older coaches, it's important to be familiar with current technology and find ways to use it to communicate better with the team. Again, this is a building block of the trust that is needed on the court when coaches will be asking their players to step outside their comfort zone and believe that what the coaches are saying will work.

When communicating with players on the court, it's best if coaches keep emotion out of it. If the coach gets stressed during practices and matches, players are likely to tighten up when they see him or her reacting that way. A coach who brings drama to the court can hardly expect his or her team to stay calm and composed during high-intensity matches. At times, coaches need to be like actors and display the type of emotion they want to see from their team. If the team is overexcited and making errors, the coach should help the players relax and calm down. If the team is flat and not communicating, the coach may need to step in and bring the energy to get the team going. When the team looks particularly stressed, the best thing the coach can do is smile and laugh. The coach might feel just as stressed, but piling on more anxiety could cause the whole team to crumble. One metaphor I've always liked captures the need to stay calm even when you're working as hard as you can. It compares the individual to a duck—smooth and calm on the surface but paddling like hell underwater.

Courtesy of University of Wisconsin Athletic Communications

Coaches can affect the outcome of the match by how they guide their team through each obstacle that arises.

It is instructive to watch coaches from all different sports when they get in the huddle with their team. Some are calm and encouraging, while others are screaming at their players and getting in their faces. The coaches who scream are hoping that it motivates their players and gets them fired up. Sometimes it does, and in these cases the players take on the personality of the coach and play with renewed energy and confidence. Players who play under coaches who yell all the time often become immune to it, and it doesn't phase them much. Some psychologists say that those players perform well under stress because the coach is constantly putting them under stressful conditions.

I believe the best coaches find what works for them in light of their own personality but are also willing to break through their personal barriers to try emotions that they're not usually comfortable with. Consistency from the coaching staff is always appreciated by players, but it's also the coaches' job to find a way to get the team on track when players are out of sorts. Playing volleyball aggressively means that aggression is involved. *Aggression* is a word that evokes emotion and calls for toughness from everyone in the program. Wanting to play at the highest level means that everyone is willing to experiment and improve their communication skills in order to raise the bar for the team. The overriding mind-set has to be this: One team, one goal, and we're doing this together. That's why this chapter on learning to communicate better is as important as any other in this book.

# Communication Drills

## DEFEND OFF-SPEED

**Purpose**    To teach players to read and pursue off-speed shots effectively, communicate well with each other, and transition into their offense.

**Goal**    In part 1, to earn 10 good run-downs; in part 2, to earn 10 good transitions (subtract 1 for each error made).

**Equipment Needed**    Balls; coaching box.

**Explanation**

- Part 1: Coach self-tosses and tips or rolls shots from across the net to players by position. Each group needs 10 passes to the setting target to get out; use six or seven players in each group. The coach should hit to spots that the defenders would typically need to cover (e.g., center court, up the line, corner). Make sure to include the drop-off diggers on the left and right sides. Challenge the off blocker by forcing him or her to come across the court to play a ball behind the block.

- Part 2: Remove the coach and the box from the court. Put one player in each position, including a middle blocker to defend live hitters. Have a player self-toss and hit, tip, roll, or throw the ball anywhere. The defense needs 10 good transitions to get out; each error subtracts 1 from its total.

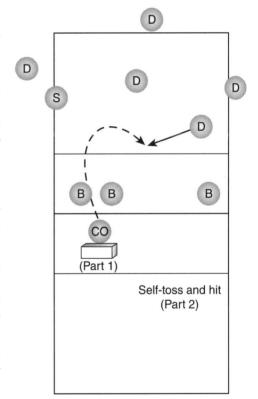

(Part 1)

Self-toss and hit
(Part 2)

## DOWN BALL VERSUS DOWN BALL

**Purpose**    To teach passers to communicate well with each other and to have players in all positions learn to make good down-ball plays.

**Goal**    To earn 30 points as a team; subtract 1 point for an overpass and 5 for an ace (unplayable).

**Equipment Needed**    Balls.

**Explanation**

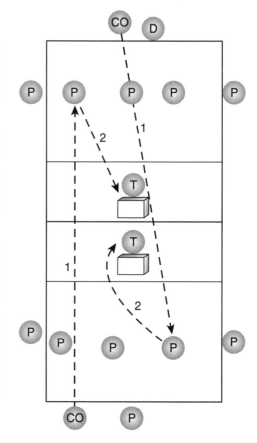

- This drill mimics passing and digging three-quarter-speed hits or hard topspin serves. The three passers on each side must communicate well in order to avoid giving up points for being aced.

- Coaches hit at the same time and go at a rapid pace. The targets should be on a box just off the net at center court. The players or managers who are on the boxes will keep track of the points for their passers.

- If a passer or digger passes a ball on target for a point, then he or she gets to stay in the drill. This condition should encourage multiple good passes in a row. If a player does not pass for a point, he or she steps off the court and a new player enters. Coaches can hit the next ball to the same spot to encourage the new player to hustle in and focus right away. Players will communicate better in order to win.

## HITTER COVERAGE

**Purpose**   To teach players how to intentionally hit into a block so their teammates can cover the ball. The intent is for players to communicate about who will be in charge of setting the ball after the coverage play and deciding where to go with it.

**Goal**   To cover the hitter, then transition immediately and score. Rotate each time these goals are accomplished.

**Equipment Needed**   Balls; Blockette (a padded board measuring at least 2 by 4 feet [0.6 by 1.2 meters]) held at the blocking spot.

**Explanation**

- Play starts with the serve, and the set goes out to the hitter in front of the Blockette. That hitter must hit a flat shot into the block (tap it in) so that the coverage team has a chance to play it up. (The diagram shows the players covering after they have passed the serve.) Once the ball is played up after coverage, the entire group shifts into transition mode and communicates who will set (if the setter covered the ball) and which plays the hitters want to run. The set can then go to any hitter, including the one at the Blockette. They all attempt to score, but if blocked, they can transition to score again. If dug by the defense, the play ends; do not play it out.

- This drill teaches hitters to be comfortable when hitting into the block on bad sets, then attacking aggressively to score. Players must talk and flow together to form a good coverage team.

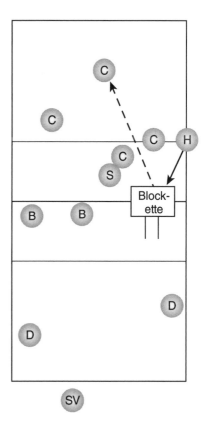

## NARROW-COURT DOUBLES

**Purpose**    To teach ball control within a confined area and improve communication between teammates; to help servers use control and try long and short serves; to help defenders read shots around and off the block; and to promote attacking off the block since the hitter doesn't have much room to go around it.

**Goal**    To win a game played to 7 points. An alternative goal is to win a timed game of 5 or 10 minutes (this approach helps players create an urgency to win).

**Equipment Needed**    Balls; antennae; floor tape or discs to designate the sideline.

### Explanation

- This is a 2v2 game played on a full-length court narrowed to a width of 10 feet (3 meters). Use extra antennae to mark the width; tape or hash-marks can be used to mark the sideline within the court.
- Participants play to 7 points, or for the designated length in a timed game.
- This drill can also be done with triples teams. Rotate winning teams to the top court and losing teams in the opposite direction.

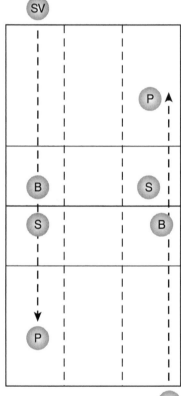

## PASSING LANES

**Purpose**    To teach players what the passing lanes are and how to communicate better as a passing unit.

**Goal**    To pass five perfect balls on target before being aced and to do so before the opponent does.

**Equipment Needed**    Balls; floor tape or discs to designate player channels.

### Explanation

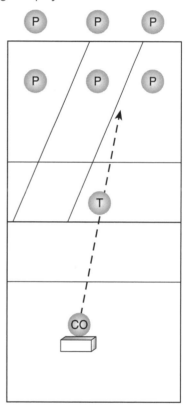

- A coach is positioned on a box past midcourt, serving balls at the seams between passers. Being higher up and closer to the net, the coach can simulate jump floaters and jump topspin serves. The ball arrives at the passers sooner than if the coach were serving from the ground, so they will improve their reaction time. You can tape lines on the floor as shown so that passers know which channel they are responsible for. When possible, players should attempt to play only those balls within their lines.

- Two groups, each with three passers, alternate on the court. If the group makes a 2- or 3-point pass, it can stay on the court; if it makes a 1-point pass or gets aced (0), it rotates off.

- Each team tries to be the first to make five on-target, 3-point passes. If a team gets aced, it rotates off and goes back to zero. This drill helps players learn to communicate when faced with serves into their seams.

## SHORT-COURT TRIPLES

**Purpose**    To teach ball control within a confined area and improve communication between teammates.

**Goal**    To win a game played to 7 points. An alternative goal is to play timed games of 5 or 10 minutes (this approach helps players create an urgency to win).

**Equipment Needed**    Balls.

## Explanation

- Figure *a* shows a server initiating play. Once play has started, all normal rules apply, but the boundaries are the sidelines and the 3-meter (10 foot) line.

- Figure *b* shows the setter on the right with a middle and outside hitter attacking. The outside hitter gets the set, so the defenders prepare to block, dig, and pick up tips.

- Figure *c* shows the team deciding to put the setter in the middle and use two outside hitters. The setter is shown attacking on the second contact in an attempt to score.

- Hitters should try to take strong swings to learn angle shots and tools off the block.

- Communication is important since each team must flow together in a small area.

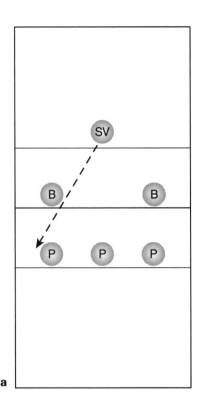

**a**

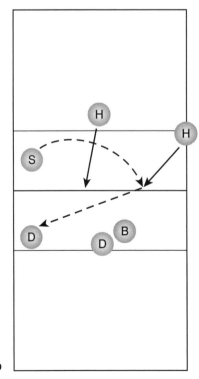

**b**

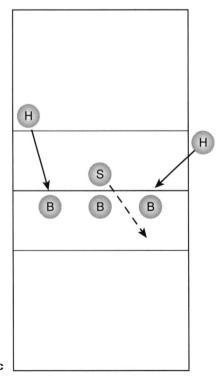

**c**

# 8

# Coaching Matches Aggressively

The number one goal for any team playing in a competitive league is to win the match. Everything you do in practice should focus on what you want to happen come game time. Although a majority of the work done by coaches takes place in practice situations, it's the coach's ability to help the team alter the course of a match and win competitions that makes him or her an excellent teacher. A coach makes dozens of decisions on game day, and every one of them takes the team closer to or farther from victory. To help coaches develop their ability to make the right decisions, this chapter discusses scouting the opponent and addresses what coaches need to be doing before, during, and after a match. This information is important because the coach dictates so much of what happens with every team. By making wrong decisions, the coach can hurt the team's chances of winning; with the right moves, the coach can be the one who ultimately puts the team in position to win on a regular basis.

## Coaching Before the Match

People may disagree about exactly when you begin coaching a match. Is it when your team first steps on the bus, or when players have their pregame meal together? What a coach does, or has the team do, during these parts of the process can make a difference in the outcome. Actual coaching, however, generally doesn't begin until the players get in uniform and meet with the staff before the match. Whether it's a 5- or 15-minute talk, it's a good idea to gather the team together to help players begin to focus on the task ahead of them. This is a chance to help players become mentally prepared for the match and create the right level of energy. If the coach combines some good motivation with the right game plan and warm-up, the team will be ready to take on anyone. This section gives you some thoughts on motivating players, planning a game strategy, and warming up for a match.

### Motivating Players

When most people think about a prematch speech, they picture a Knute Rockne motivational pitch. Plenty of movies depict the football coach pumping up his players and getting them ready to storm the field, and there is generally a lot of locker slamming and helmet banging to raise the team's intensity level. In a contact sport like football, it's probably important to prepare players for the physical battle about to take place. The entire game is made up of short bursts of high-velocity hitting with about 30 seconds between plays. Volleyball, on the other hand, involves hundreds of short plays with only 10 to 12 seconds in between, and since it involves no body-to-body contact with opponents, we'd like to think that the whole team has to be more level-headed over the entire length of the match.

So, how should a coach mentally prepare a team just prior to a match? Every coach has his or her own style, but there are generally two ways to approach it. One option is a motivational speech that grabs players' attention and attaches meaning to the effort they are about to make. Reading a quote from a great leader can inspire players to conquer great heights as past competitors have done before them. Another option is to ask a different player each match to share a motivational saying with the team. This approach often helps players take the ritual more seriously because they are giving their heartfelt thoughts about the match and what it means to themselves and the team.

Some coaches are good at finding a theme to motivate the team for each match. It may be a story about the rivalry with this opponent or about a local child who is ill but gets fired up to see his or her heroes play. When a team faces an opponent who is leading the standings, coaches can use the David and Goliath theme. I recall a season when one school had been dominating the conference, and it seemed that no one could slow them down. Most teams were intimidated by their physical play and would fight for a while before folding and giving away an easy win. This team came to us undefeated (21-0) and ranked in the top four nationally. My strategy in the pregame talk was to compare them to bullies who would push people around and make them cower. I told the team that the only way to beat a bully was to punch him or her right in the nose at the start of the fight and just keep pounding away. Hit 'em in the nose so their eyes start to water, then give 'em everything you have. That was one talk that I think really worked. Our team went out that night and won in three straight games. We played with great confidence and intensity, and I'd like to think that my talk gave the players some of the focus they needed in order to win. Every team has to believe it has a chance, no matter what the odds. If players have the skills and the determination, they can overcome teams who may be more physical or experienced.

The important thing for the coach to know is whether the team needs to be energized or calmed down. Against a very strong opponent or a heated rival, it's usually unnecessary to get the players more riled up. In fact, if they get too high, they could step on the court and be so wired that they make more errors than usual. In matches like that, it often takes a few rallies for a team to settle down and begin to play the way it really can. The job of the coach is to get the players to play well from the first whistle, and in some situations revving them up can be the worst thing for them. This is especially true in the college game. Right after the talk in the locker room, the team usually has about 45 minutes to an hour of warm-up time. During that physical activity, the pump-up speech usually wears off and is forgotten.

Whatever approach a coach decides to take in motivating players for a match, the overriding theme should be to prepare them to play aggressively and with confidence. The coach should use words that are strong and powerful so that the players head to the court thinking, *"We can do this!"* If the coach is a talented motivational speaker, he or she might infuse the right amount of energy into a group by being physically demonstrative and aggressive during the talk. Stern facial expressions and a louder tone can help give the players the tougher attitude they need. The game of volleyball requires a fine balance between being ultra aggressive and maintaining a calm mind. Too much aggression can distract the mind from performing the skills that are crucial to winning, but with too little aggression the team may lack the confidence and toughness that it needs to sustain throughout the match.

## Developing a Game Strategy

Some of my pregame talks have worked well, and others have not. There have been nights when I thought I gave a great talk with all kinds of inspirational messages, but the team played like we hadn't practiced in a week. What I've learned is that the motivational speech can work on certain days, but it's more important that the team be prepared for the match with important information.

For each of our pregame meetings, one player from each position is assigned to go over the responsibilities for that position. I'll call out a position, and the designated person will talk about goals for the game and say how she will stop the tendencies of the opponent. We may start with the middles, then go to the setters, the outsides, and finally the defenders (defensive specialists and liberos). Sometimes I've called out the positions in random order so that the players are all on their toes, but even so, I've been impressed with how prepared they are. This method gives the players ownership in the outcome of the match, and over the course of time it helps the quiet players feel more confident about talking to the group. Once they know that this is the system, they will listen better during the week's practice sessions and during any video work or review of shot charts. Our players have even taken it upon themselves to rotate the people who talk before each match. Now I'll just say, "Who wants to go first?" and someone will begin giving her report. When she's done, a player from another position starts up. Even those who don't play still take turns in this process, and it really helps prepare them for being called on to go into the game. Sometimes players have added motivational messages to their informational segment. You can almost feel the electricity building as they all buy into the plan. When players take the preparation and motivation seriously and do it themselves, they become far more invested in the outcome. They often motivate each other more than any coach could, and the result is that they play harder *for* each other when they go to battle.

When a strong team meets a weak opponent, it pays off to have a talk about goals for the match. The team can focus on statistical goals, such as striving for a certain number of digs per game or a certain overall hitting percentage. Strong teams sometimes play down to the level of a lesser opponent because they don't feel threatened and they think they can crank it up enough to get the win when they want to. This situation drives coaches nuts, and there will be days when the team can't get out of its lethargic play. Meanwhile, the underdog will often play above its normal level because its players know that giving their all is their only hope of winning. In these cases, the higher-ranked team needs to learn how to play with an urgency to win. Players must be used to training in that way so they know how to do it in a match, even if they aren't being threatened by the opponent or excited by the environment. If the stronger of the two teams allows players on the weaker team to *believe* they have a shot, then anything can happen. Suddenly, the two teams can be in a dogfight, and there's no way of knowing who will come out on top.

In almost every match, one of the teams is perceived to be the stronger of the two. How does the underdog come out with the win? You see it in all sports; there are major upsets every sporting weekend, yet on paper the underdog didn't have a chance. A number of factors come into play here. One is that the stronger team overlooks the weaker team and can't raise its level of play when the match gets tight. If the stronger team doesn't feel threatened by the weaker team, it may not bring its A-game to the match. Players don't mean to do it, but they unintentionally lower their level of play, thus giving the underdog the chance to gain confidence. Psychologically, the underdog has nothing to lose, so its players may play above their heads. The goal of the weaker team has to be to find a way to disrupt what the opponent prefers to do on the court and sustain a high-level, low-error game. Low-error is the key. The best teams keep their unforced errors down to 12 to 15 percent for the match, while lower-level teams typically have an error rate of 18 to 25 percent. As they say, the cream usually rises to the top, and the best team usually outlasts the weaker team. Underdogs have to be able to sustain a high level of play for longer than they usually do in order to earn the upset. Consistency is what makes teams great, and inconsistency is the roller coaster of losing teams. If the underdogs can stay organized long enough to get the opponent out of its normal rhythm, they have a great shot at the upset.

As with everything in life, people absorb information in different ways. Some benefit from hearing it, and others do better if they can see a visual example of what they'll be dealing with. Some coaches draw shot charts or defenses on the whiteboard for the team to see. Others hand out sheets containing the same kind of information or require players to bring a scouting binder to the meeting. All of these methods are good for making sure the team has a good plan of attack for defeating any given opponent. Whatever method is selected, it's important to give players just enough information that they understand but not so much that they overthink the game. If a scouting session takes the coach longer than 30 minutes, the team may start losing focus. In a pregame talk, 10 to 15 minutes should be enough for any review of key information, such as the opponent's defensive bases and offensive patterns per rotation, as well as keys to focus on for the match. Coaches should avoid providing too much information and giving long-winded talks, which tend to confuse players and hinder them from flowing naturally on the court.

Sometimes the opponent comes onto the court and does something very different from what was projected in the scouting report. That's when a coach realizes that the preparation done during the week has to teach players to be flexible and ready to go with plan B. Some of the best coaches don't use motivational speeches but do a great job of preparing their teams to play with confidence and solve whatever the opponent throws at them. This kind of flexibility has to be emphasized to the players during training so they don't get flustered during the match. They should try to *solve* every drill and find the most efficient way to reach the goal. If they learn to enjoy solving the opponent's game plan and play with an urgency to win, they will find themselves in the upper echelon of the conference at the end of the season.

## Warming Up

The next stage of a match is the warm-up sequence. The coach's main focus during this time is to prepare the team physically for the match. Given the allotted amount of time, the goal is to get the blood flowing and get the players' minds sharp. Most teams develop a ritual that includes a variety of drills to simulate movements in the game, and touching briefly on ball handling, defense, serving, blocking, and attacking gets all of the body parts warmed up. Some teams start with a light stretch, or ball-handle first and then stretch. Some combination of movement and stretching is recommended by most strength and conditioning coaches and athletic trainers. They call it "active stretching," and it may involve moving across the court while stretching separate body parts. It's a great way to get the blood flowing and to be ready for a really active warm-up with the balls.

Coaches should select at least one good defensive drill during warm-ups to get the players in an aggressive mind-set. Some choose positional digging lines; others play variations of coach-on-three. If coaches are hitting at the players, they need to hit hard but with control, since warm-up is an opportunity for players to gain confidence and get in the right mind-set—not a time for coaches to show that they can make their players look bad. Getting the team into a good rhythm helps players start the match feeling like they can beat anyone.

Be careful to not let players use all of their energy during this period. Many universities currently allow an hour and 15 minutes to warm up, but going that long can tire the team out and take the edge off. It's important to remember that it's called a *warm-up*. Some players bring so much energy and intensity to warm-ups that they may not have enough gas left in the tank at the end of a long match. There's something to be said for still having a feeling of nervous excitement when the first whistle blows instead of already being flat and tired. In addition, players who are nursing injuries need to be reminded to limit their swings and jumps as they get ready. Shaving 10 or 15 minutes off the warm-up time can really add up over the course of a long season. You get no bonus points for winning warm-ups. What's most important is feeling good physically and emotionally when the game begins.

## Setting the Lineup

Coaches usually decide on the lineup during practice on the day before the match. This helps players prepare for the match knowing what role they will be playing. Most coaches consider any changes during the match based on players' execution, consistency, effort level, and injuries. If a coach is lucky enough to have a team with depth and variety, he or she may be able to select the starters according to the type of team featured by the opponent. If the opponent is bigger and strong offensively, the coach may want to go with a taller blocking lineup. If the opposition is smaller and good at ball handling, the coach may want to match up with the smaller lineup, since the big lineup might not work if the opponent's shorter players are great at banging off the big block and digging the attacks.

Besides matching up physically, coaches must consider strategic matchups that can give their team the advantage. Each different starting rotation creates specific situations on the court. Here are some matchups that can stress your opponents and slowly wear them down:

- Put your best servers against their weakest passers. Your hope is to get aces or keep the opponent out of its quick offense.

- Put your best blocker(s) against their strongest hitter. If you can stress this player out and slow him or her down, his or her teammates will be forced to pick up the slack.

- Put your best slide hitter against their worst left-side blocker. If this is in the rotation when the setter is front-row, the left-side blocker will be forced to start in on the setter and chase the slide hitter out. You may get easy points or at least keep the opponent out of its quick offense.

- Match up your top left-side hitter against their front-row setter. If the setter is not a great blocker, this move will create great scoring opportunities, or, if the ball is dug off the net, it will cause the setter to chase the ball into center court. Bringing the setter off the net keeps him or her from attacking and often eliminates his or her ability to run anything with the middle attacker.

- Put your best defender opposite their best attacker. The plan may not be to stuff the ball at the block but to channel it to a great defender. Some phenomenal liberos and defensive specialists have shown the ability to wear hitters down by picking up their best shots. Once a hitter's favorite shot is dug a number of times, the hitter may start trying shots to other zones that he or she isn't as comfortable with.

Some coaches always start in the same rotation. This decision may be made for a variety of reasons, most of them related to the strengths and weaknesses of the team. When a team has a small setter who doesn't block well, the coach may start the setter in the first rotation (right back) to hide his or her blocking flaws for the first three rotations. If a team has one dominant hitter, the coach may want to start that hitter in the left front position in order to get him or her coming across the front row right away. The same would be said for the fifth and deciding game of a match: Since it is shorter, most coaches start with their strongest rotation. Many college teams use statistical programs to track the scoring percentages of each rotation, and if you view these numbers after each match, you can easily see where your team is scoring points and where you need to improve your percentages.

One final consideration in deciding your starting lineup is knowing which players can sustain the high level of play to complete the match. Some players are good in short bursts but if left in too long may do more harm than good. It's important to know who can come off the bench and give the team a boost when it's needed. In fact, this knowledge is just as important as knowing who to start. When a coach goes to the bench to make a sub, it's usually because the group on the court is faltering. I prefer to keep someone on the bench who can go in and raise our level of play when we need it. The real challenge is to convince that player that this role is vital to the success of the team. The player must be unselfish and willing to wait until his or her number is called. Fresh arms, fresh legs, and a fresh attitude can provide the lift the team needs at the end of any game or match, and a good sub can influence the course of the match and be the hero who comes in and saves the day. Just like some pitchers in baseball, he or she can be the closer who has just what it takes to win the match.

The decision about whether to change the starting rotation between games often depends on the success of the previous game. If a team loses badly in game one or loses the first two games, it's usually a good idea to try starting with a different rotation. This is when coaching decisions become a bit like a chess match. Whatever lineup you choose depends in part on what rotation you think the opposing coach will use. If you're facing a familiar opponent, it's possible to keep track of its tendencies from match to match, and looking at past lineup sheets can show you when a coach likes to flip the starting rotation and even which spots he or she prefers. Most teams will start in only two or three different rotations, so it is possible to counter their move with your preferred rotation to seize the advantage.

In selecting which players to put in the lineup, there is no golden rule to follow. It really comes down to knowing your own players and paying attention to what is working. If it's working, stay with it and ride the momentum as long as possible. If it's not, be patient yet willing to change if you're falling too far behind. The more experienced a coach is, the more readily he or she will recognize when it's time to go with plan B.

Every once in a while, you'll be watching the start of a game and you'll see the down official take an extralong time looking at the lineup sheet. Suddenly you realize that the coach made a mistake with the lineup sheet and either forgot to tell the team the right rotation or forgot to tell a certain player he or she was being subbed out of the match. Every coach does his or her best to make it right every time, but coaches have a lot of things going through their mind at that moment and it's easy to see how a mistake can be made. Even veteran coaches with decades of experience will tell you that they have occasionally made the same mistake. There are two ways to try to prevent this from happening. The first is to have your usual lineup typed up as it would be in each of the six starting rotations; this approach allows you to look at the sheet between games and decide which lineup will work best, then copy it right onto the official's lineup card. If you think you might make drastic changes, you could even print up two different lineups and lay out what each of the six rotations would look like. The other way to prevent errors is to have an assistant coach check the lineup before you put it in; the assistant might catch a mistake before it gets written into the scorebook. If these two safeguards fail, you can start the match by making a substitution to correct a personnel error—if, for example, you accidentally put a middle blocker (who doesn't play in the back row) in the backcourt in the lineup sheet. On the other hand, if you mistakenly flipped the middles or outsides, just get the team to go with it as it stands, since you don't really have a choice. Your only option would be to sub new players in from the bench, and you'll want to play with your top players out there. If you're lucky, they'll play well in that rotation and win the game. Sometimes this kind of mistake will shake players up just enough to get them to focus even better. Every coach would love to get it right every time, but this sort of mistake pops up occasionally to prove that coaches are human too.

## Coaching During the Match

All coaches wear two different hats—one for who they are in practice, where they do most of their teaching, and the other for who they are during matches, when they hope to be coaching. The hope is that teams are well taught, so coaches can focus on coaching rather than teaching during matches. While the two are interrelated, coaching well during a match can help keep the momentum on your side of the net. This section of the chapter provides information about communicating with players, making adjustments and substitutions, using time-outs correctly, and dealing with officials and fans. None of these skills will get a team very far unless it's playing aggressively and giving the coach an opportunity to help out. A team that plays passively or plays high-error ball forces the coach to search for answers and plug the holes in the dike. Coaches who can take the team to a higher level by means of what they say or do are the very definition of a good coach.

### Communicating With Players

How much information should a coach give the team from the bench, and what kind of information should it be? Every coach has a style that he or she is comfortable with, and it's usually connected to his or her off-court personality. Some sit on the bench and give only occasional feedback; others stand constantly and push information out to the team after every play. It's important for a coach to know what works for him or her and what doesn't. Overcoaching is a common problem during matches. If a team is looking to the sideline before and after every play, players can get very distracted. That's when a coach should know that he or she is giving too much information. Some information is good, but too much can cause an overload. Players should be taught in practice to think for themselves, and whatever information the staff gives during the match should enhance the players' understanding of each situation.

From the sideline, coaches can relay information about what defense or blocking scheme the opponent is using. That kind of information can help the setter or hitters know where to attack in order to improve their odds. On the court, players often get wrapped up in the game as it spins around them at a high speed. Being off the court, coaches can think with a clearer head as they help their team work through each situation. They can also alert players to the opponent's hitting tendencies so they can block or defend from better positions. During time-outs, coaches can be more thorough and grab everyone's attention at once. When the coach is yelling to the team from the sideline, it's important that players pass the word among themselves if the information relates to all of them. For example, if a coach changes the defense and everyone isn't on the same page, the resulting confusion can lead to lost points.

Yelling at players after every play causes them to flinch each time they make an error, and if the practice continues from match to match, they will become so concerned about getting yelled at that they won't be able to play as loose as the coach would like. Coaching during a match can be informative, instructive, and encouraging. Just be sure that what you are doing benefits the players and doesn't hinder them in playing their best. Sometimes coaches just have to bite their tongues and be patient while the players work things out.

Courtesy of University of Wisconsin Athletic Communications

Specific information from the staff is important so the players can make the adjustments needed to win the points.

## Making Adjustments

There are very few matches in which a coach should just leave the team as it is and make no adjustments. Oftentimes, a slight adjustment can give the team what it needs in order to run on all cylinders; at other times, making a major change can spark a struggling group to life. In general, if it ain't broke, don't fix it. When a team is playing well, the coach should keep changes to a minimum. If things are not going well, however, a good coach will work hard to find ways to help out. Statistics can play a major role in helping coaches identify trends taking place right at that moment. Tendencies can be found within the charts, and such information can be extremely helpful when trying to outwit your opponent.

Coaches, players, and managers can take a variety of statistics from the bench during games in order to help the team understand what is taking place while the ball is in play; statistics can also help break down an opponent to gain an advantage. The number of statistical charts kept by a team is often dictated by its number of coaches, managers, and players. The coach must decide which charts are most beneficial for the team at any given time, and trying a variety of charts can help a coach figure out which ones to use on a regular basis. Some might be used only for certain matches, but they can all play vital roles in earning more wins. Here are some possibilities:

**Passing Chart**   Keeping track of your passers will tell you who should be covering more of the court and who you should be covering up more. The chart uses a 3-point passing system based on how many options the pass gives the setter (figure 8.1). The marks range from a perfect 3 (the setter can set a quick set, high outside, or high back), to a 2 (high outside or high back), to a 1 (forced to set one place), to a 0 (ace or setter can't set the ball). Depending on whether it is at the high school or college level, a good passer rates between a 2.2 and a 2.5. Anything above that is exceptional, and anything below is hurting the offense. Since liberos and defensive specialists don't have kill stats to look at, it's important for them to see their passing stats each week so they can set goals and improve. You can also keep this chart on the opponent to see who is struggling that day.

Date _____   Opponent _____

| Player | Game 1 | | | | Game 2 | | | | Game 3 | | | | Game 4 | | | | Game 5 | | | | Total |
|---|---|---|---|---|---|---|---|---|---|---|---|---|---|---|---|---|---|---|---|---|---|
|  | 3 | 2 | 1 | 0 | 3 | 2 | 1 | 0 | 3 | 2 | 1 | 0 | 3 | 2 | 1 | 0 | 3 | 2 | 1 | 0 |  |
| #4 | III | IIII | I |  | IIII | THL |  |  | II | IIII | I |  |  |  |  |  |  |  |  |  | 2.29 |
| #19 | I | III | I |  | I | THL III | I |  | II | I | III |  |  |  |  |  |  |  |  |  | 1.95 |
| #15 |  | II |  |  |  | IIII |  |  | I | I | I |  |  |  |  |  |  |  |  |  | 1.66 |
| #21 | IIII | III | I |  | I | THL |  |  | IIII |  |  |  |  |  |  |  |  |  |  |  | 2.22 |
| #5 |  | I |  |  |  |  |  |  | I |  |  |  |  |  |  |  |  |  |  |  | 2.0 |
| #7 |  |  |  |  |  |  |  |  | I |  |  |  |  |  |  |  |  |  |  |  | 2.0 |
|  |  |  |  |  |  |  |  |  |  |  |  |  |  |  |  |  |  |  |  |  |  |
|  |  |  |  |  |  |  |  |  |  |  |  |  |  |  |  |  |  |  |  |  |  |
|  |  |  |  |  |  |  |  |  |  |  |  |  |  |  |  |  |  |  |  |  |  |
|  |  |  |  |  |  |  |  |  |  |  |  |  |  |  |  |  |  |  |  |  |  |
|  |  |  |  |  |  |  |  |  |  |  |  |  |  |  |  |  |  |  |  |  |  |
|  |  |  |  |  |  |  |  |  |  |  |  |  |  |  |  |  |  |  |  |  |  |

**FIGURE 8.1**   Sample passing chart.

**Shot Chart**   On a shot chart (figure 8.2), each opposing attacker has a court diagram and every swing is identified and located (including the setter). A line is drawn from the point of attack (left, middle, right, back row) to where the ball ended up. The end of the line is left open if the ball was dug, and a dot is put at the end of the line if the hitter got a kill. Roll shots can be shown as curved lines, and hits off the block can go off at a diagonal. Soon, it will be very clear which hitter is

#10 (setter)　　　　　#6　　　　　　#3

#7　　　　　　#9　　　　　　#12

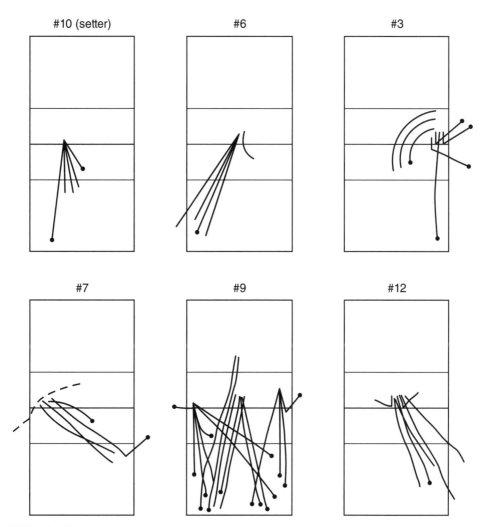

**FIGURE 8.2**  Sample shot chart.

getting the most sets, which spots the hitter likes to hit from, and which area of the court he or she is hitting to. Attackers who have only one shot (cross or line) can be blocked or dug in those spots and virtually taken out of the game. Great players can make shots from anywhere to everywhere, but strategies can still be used to serve or block them in certain ways that may slow them down. This is a good chart for the players on the bench to do so they will learn how to stop the opponent when they get in the game.

**Serving Chart**    This chart can be taken on your team or on the opponents. It is much like a hitting chart in that lines are drawn to where the serve goes (figure 8.3, page 180). Alternately, numbers could be put in those spots; the numbers would correlate to the 3-2-1-0 passing system, and you could learn where serves are going and how tough they are. The scoring system is reversed, though, so a

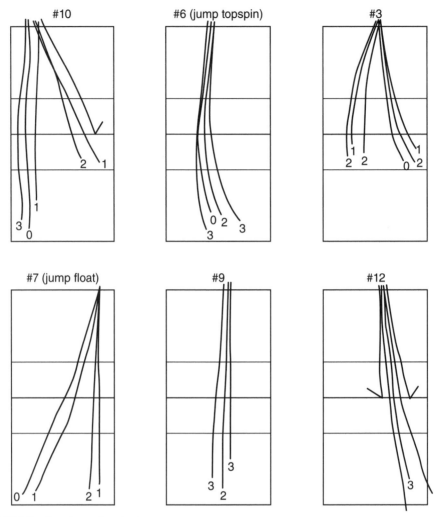

**FIGURE 8.3**   Sample serving chart.

3 means they're serving too easily and a 1 or 0 means they're serving well. If a player is always serving to zone 6 (center of the court) and the number 3 (perfect pass) is written all over that zone, then that player clearly isn't serving aggressively enough. In contrast, if a player is serving 2s, 1s, and 0s, then he or she is doing well. Numbers can be averaged, and a good server will average between 1 and 2 points. That kind of number shows that a tough serve is keeping the opponent from running a quick offense.

**Offensive Routes Chart**   Charting the opponent's offensive patterns in each rotation can tell you what plays they like to run (figure 8.4). Using one blank court diagram for each rotation, you can write down where the player begins, where he or she makes the hit, and where the ball goes. If a left-side hitter passes in middle back, then swings to hit on the right side behind the setter, the block

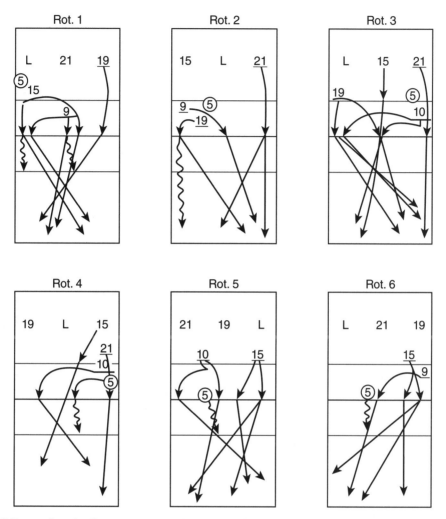

**FIGURE 8.4**   Sample offensive routes chart.

can anticipate the movement and be there waiting for it. As each game goes on, it will be easier to see when specific patterns repeat themselves. Many times, one of the hitters is a "ghost" (i.e., hardly ever gets the set), and the block can virtually ignore that player and focus on the others. Separate serve-receive and transition charts can be used to see how the opponent changes routes when rallies continue. Most teams stay in the same general serve-receive formation, and this chart can also be used to see if they are illegally overlapping. Over the course of a season, some teams will unknowingly shift into an illegal formation and be off by a few feet. Often, they look so comfortable doing it that even the down official doesn't notice unless he or she is very observant, and alerting the official to the overlap between plays can help your team earn a point and keep the opponent from gaining an advantage.

**Plus-or-Minus Chart**   It's a very simple process, but it can clearly define who is playing well and who is not. First, list every player on the roster on the left side of the sheet. Then, every time a player touches the ball, assign either a plus or a minus on the chart depending on whether the player made a positive play or a mistake. A good pass, dig, serve, or attack gets a plus, whereas a shanked pass or a serving or hitting error gets a minus. An average play can be logged as a W (wash), so that you can still tell how many times this player is touching the ball. This kind of chart can be very helpful in working with teams or individual players who are making so many mistakes that they are beating themselves. Once players see their charts, they'll know that if they just bring down the number of minuses, they will give the opposition fewer points and the coach will be willing to play them more. This is especially important since we've gone to rally scoring, where every error is an automatic point for the other team. With regular scoring, you could make an error and give the team the serve, but you could also get the ball right back without allowing the opponent to score a point.

**Computerized Statistical Program**   Various computer programs are available to help coaches get a clear understanding of how their team is performing. At the collegiate level, sports information departments usually take game-time stats for both teams and compile final box scores for the coaches and media. In the past, stat sheets were given to each coach after every game. Now, technology allows us to position a monitor next to each coach during the game so they can watch the numbers point by point. It's a great way to keep track of stats such as hitting percentages, blocks, and digs as the match takes place. In addition, many college and international volleyball staffs now use statistical programs synced with video of the match to facilitate postmatch analysis. These systems can be used to break down almost every part of the sport. The only two downsides are cost and maintenance. Some schools may not have the money to purchase the systems, and even if you do have one, you may need a good amount of technical support to keep it up and running. If necessary, you can still gain a lot of information by using the old-school methods of taking statistics.

Information gained through statistical analysis should be combined with a coach's subjective evaluation of each player. With that combined knowledge, the coach must make decisions during the match to give the team its best opportunity to win. Knowing the players' strengths and weaknesses allows the coach to make adjustments from one point to the next. Sometimes the moves are made to hide weak or struggling players while making use of stronger or more consistent teammates.

Here's an example involving serve-receive formations. Whether a team is in a three- or four-person serve-receive pattern, there comes a time when a passer will struggle and the coach will have to answer this question: How long do I wait before making a change? With rally scoring, every passing error is a point for the other team, and you have to earn those lost points back soon. If a player is aced, my answer would be to shift the passing formation toward that player to give him or her less area to pass. Make the shift right away so that not even one more point is lost. If at first the player was in charge of a 10-foot (3 meter) width, trim it down to 4 or 5 feet (1.2 to 1.5 meters) so the player can get the ball more easily if it comes that way again. It's possible that the server will then see that another area of the court is more open but won't feature quite as tough a serve going to that new zone. In addition, if the passer being pinched over is at the sideline, the server may make an error if he or she tries to go back to the player who was just aced. Making a shift after an ace is a good idea because a passer without confidence can really struggle, and this problem can trigger a long run for the other team. If 3 or 4 points in a row are lost because of poor passing, the next step is to make a sub in hopes that the new passer will do better or that the time it takes to make the sub will take the server out of his or her rhythm. A time-out can do the same thing. It's amazing how many servers miss the serve right after a time-out. They know it's one of the cardinal sins of the sport, but it happens more than anyone would imagine.

Coaches can also influence the game in their decisions about which defenses to run and when to change them. If you're not able to stop the opposing team with what you're using, it is vital to make a change to keep the opponent from scoring more points. If your team always runs a perimeter defense, many opponents will realize that they can score with shots to the center of the court. If the defenders just aren't good enough to move and pick up those shots, it's important for the coach to know when it's time to switch defenses to stop the bleeding. Going to a rotation defense or even a roaming defense (one player is assigned the center of the court) can enable your team to start making plays. The same goes for a team being beat in the two corners (zones 1 and 5). A roaming defense can put people in those spots without having to move much at all. Once defenders start making some digs, their energy and enthusiasm will pick up, and the opponent's offensive players may get flustered and start making mistakes when they try different shots. Volleyball can be like a chess match for a coach if he or she plans a few moves ahead of the opponent. Some teams don't react well to seeing a change in the defense (just as a basketball team may struggle when facing a man-to-man defense and then a zone). Coaches shouldn't change defenses too often because it could confuse their own team, but if a change is made at the right time in the middle of a game, it can change the momentum dramatically.

## Making Substitutions

Some of the most important decisions a coach makes during a match involve substitutions. They should be used to change the momentum, not just the bodies. Here are some reasons to make substitutions:

• Adding energy. If the team's confidence is slipping, an energetic player can come into the game and lift everyone's spirits. A couple of great digs or blocks can turn the game around.

• Stopping the opponent's momentum. Sometimes a player gets pulled when he or she wasn't really doing anything wrong. It's important to tell that player that you're just trying to stop the momentum and that he or she should be ready to go back in soon.

• Stopping a server's run. Servers can get in a groove, and slowing the game down can change their rhythm and cause an error. If possible, wait until just before the official blows the whistle for serve and then call a time-out. This is similar to football coaches calling a time-out to ice the field-goal kicker. Also, teach the players that they don't have to sprint in when subbing. Just changing the tempo of the game slightly can make a difference. There's a good chance that if you make the server wait for the substitution to be made, it'll be just enough to alter the serve.

• Seeing from the sideline. Sometimes it helps a player to come out for a short time and see the game from the sideline. If the game isn't going well, some players get flustered, and their field of vision gets very narrow. This is especially true for setters, since they have so much to think about. A coach can take a setter out, sit down beside him or her, and explain what needs to be done. Don't all coaches think the game looks so easy from the sideline? Well, that's because the coach is on the outside looking in. Given the chance to come out and see things from the sideline, many players can go back in with a calmer and more confident outlook on the game.

• Taking a small setter out and putting a big block in. There are times when a coach wants to take a calculated risk for one play in hopes of getting a point with a stuff block. A small setter is an attack point that opponents plan to take advantage of. In order to prevent this, a coach will sub out a small setter and bring in a bigger blocker. If the team is running a 5-1 offense, it means that if the setter goes out, the team is hoping to end the play at the net. If it works, the coach is a genius. If not, the setter has to sub right back in to set the team.

• Introducing a new serving style. Over the course of a match, passers get used to the types of serves that have been coming at them, and it can really throw them off if you make a substitution to bring in a player with a totally different style or tempo. A short serve or a deep, bombing serve can give passers fits and disrupt the entire offense.

Coaches should think ahead so they know who they might put in for each rotation, and every team member on the bench should be tuned in to the match in order to be ready when called upon. Players should watch a teammate who is on the court playing in the same position in order to see what they will be up against. They have to know what defense both teams are playing and be ready to enter the game in a split second. Subbing in off the bench can be challenging, and subs have to either stabilize or raise the level of their team. Too often, players are watching the game like spectators rather than watching to learn and be prepared.

It's important for teammates on the court to help the new player ease into the game if possible. If a passer comes in, the other passers can shift over a bit to give the new one less responsibility right away, because most coaches will intentionally serve the new player on the court. Setters may also want to avoid setting the new hitter because the player may be cold coming off the bench; in addition, the opponent may be anticipating that set.

The right substitution can spark a team to grab the momentum.

Making substitutions should be a way for a coach to make a positive contribution to the match. Both the staff and the players need to be on the same page and understand the reasoning behind each move. Subbing a player out shouldn't be based merely on the fact that he or she has made one or two mistakes; if that happens on a regular basis, players will start looking to the sideline after each mistake, thinking that they will be pulled. Watch for how a player handles being subbed out. It may help to ask the player if he or she understands why; if not, explain it to them. Though the reason may be clear to the coach, the player may have an entirely different opinion of what happened leading up to the substitution. Knowing in your own mind why you make substitutions is one thing; making sure the players understand the process is another. Unfortunately, it's hard to explain every sub over the course of a long season, but I promise you that many players will harbor negative thoughts if they don't understand the reason. It may be a sign of the times when players these days want to be given a good reason for being subbed out rather than trusting that the coach is trying to find a way to help the team win.

One of the many difficult decisions a coach faces is how to get court time for players who don't usually start or contribute. If a coach is lucky, the schedule includes a few weaker opponents and liberal substitutions can be made in these matches. As the season moves on, however, each match becomes more important for regular-season standings or seeding purposes in the playoffs. By midseason, the lineup is usually established, and there always seem to be a couple of players who just never get in. At times, a coach may feel that a substantial lead affords a chance to get such a player into the game for some experience or to reward him or her for hard work during practice. If it works, then great—the coach just made the player and his or her parents happy. Unfortunately, putting in that weaker player sometimes changes the mentality on the court. It's not always that player's fault, but other players tend to let up a little because they feel the coach wouldn't make the sub if the game wasn't in the bag. It's an unfortunate scene when a coach tries to be nice by subbing in a player who doesn't usually play, then has to take that player back out when the opponent goes on a run and gains the momentum.

Thus, before the sub is made, the coach should emphasize to all players the importance of sustaining a high level of play when any substitution is made. The team should work harder at that moment to provide a good environment for the entering player. The other players should make a great effort to thank that player for all of the hours he or she puts in on the scout team so that they have a positive experience in the match. Volleyball is not like basketball, where coaches can make a mass substitution in the last minute of the game to let the starters get a hand as they come off the court. Volleyball has no clock, and there is no guarantee that the opponent won't stage a comeback, so coaches should be sure they have a lock on the game before making this type of sub. Another tough decision comes on senior night if the team includes seniors who don't usually play. The bottom line is that the coach is there to help the team win and therefore should put the strongest team on the court. I learned some lessons the hard way when I tried to be nice and it came back to bite me. I'll still do what I can to reward players, but I'm very cautious when it's an important match.

## Using Time-Outs

Coaches get two time-outs per game, and it's important to know how and when to use them. When momentum needs to be regained, a coach will usually make a substitution or two, but if that doesn't work, then a time-out is the next step. In rally scoring, if the opposition jumps out to an early 5- or 6-point lead, you may need to call a time-out. The longest you might want to wait is 7 or 8 points, but that's with a team that you trust to stage a comeback. If possible, save a time-out for later in the game. In a 25-point game, don't let the opponent get more than a 4-point lead after the 15-point mark. In a 30-point game, the same thing goes after the 20-point mark. Here are some dos and don'ts for using time-outs (I've seen coaches at all levels do all of these things):

- Don't wait to call a time-out until the opponent is at game point and leading by 5 or more. Take it sooner.

- Don't call a time-out when your team has the momentum just to tell the players they're doing great.

- Don't forget how many time-outs you've called. If you take an extra one, the official can penalize you with a delay of game and you can lose a point or a sideout.

- Don't spend the whole time-out dwelling on the past. Make sure you plant something positive in your players' heads as they take the court.

- Do use all of your time-outs if you're behind. You have to do everything you can to help your team.

- Do tell your players something helpful, and say it with confidence. Yelling at them during the whole time-out gives them no plan of action when they walk back on the floor.

- Do your best to include everyone, and make sure they are all listening.

- Do make good eye contact with both the starters and the subs. Coaches can use more than words to convey their message. A smile or a laugh can loosen up your players, and a stern or intense look can help them refocus and gain energy.

Every team should have a specific way of gathering for a time-out. Some coaches prefer to have their team stand in a circle with their arms around each other. The benefit is that they are all facing inward and paying attention; they are connected and tight as a group. Other coaches have the players who came from the court sit while the others circle around or stand behind the chairs. Whatever approach a coach chooses, it should facilitate a group dynamic where individuals don't wander off on their own. If even a single player isn't paying attention, it could mean a lost point when the game begins again. Use the time-out to provide information to the players and give them a strategy to take back onto the court. Sometimes you can show them shot charts or draw a diagram on a whiteboard; some players understand and remember information much better when it's presented visually.

Coaches have all kinds of information and opinions for their players, and it can't all be relayed to them during and between plays. In the college game, coaches are allowed to step up to the sideline to give their team information. At the high school and international level, however, coaches are not always allowed to approach the court. Whatever the rules may be, coaches should get information to the team during play as allowed if it can help win some points. Coaches have to decide on the right amount of information so that players aren't distracted or overwhelmed on the court. During time-outs, coaches have a little more time to explain things to the whole group and even provide statistics. Whatever the information, the overriding message should be one promoting confidence and aggressive play. Momentum shifts in volleyball on a regular basis, and the team must play with an urgency to win each point throughout the set and the match. When calling a play during a time-out, it's a good idea to tell each hitter what he or she is running, then tell the setter and the team who the primary hitter will be. The primary hitter is whichever one the coach wants the setter to set on the first ball. Here's an example: "We're

---

# A Tip From the Top

Our team played against Penn State on January 14, 2006. The match was extremely well played, and the margin of victory in each game was just two points (32-30, 30-28, and 30-28). Thus, every point was vital. The match was particularly intense because our team was the underdog (we were ranked 14th, Penn State 6th) and we were playing in Penn State's gym. After winning the first two games, we found ourselves trailing in the late stages of game 3. Following a kill by Penn State's middle (Nate Meerstein), the score stood at 27-28 in favor of Penn State. After we won two rallies on a kill by Pat Durbin and an attack error by Penn State's Alex Gutor, the momentum turned in our favor and we stood at match point. My assistant coach, Kevin Furnish, reminded our players that Penn State likes to run combination plays and had done so many times in this rotation throughout the match. Our team's starting setter, Dave Carlson, watched Penn State's bench, followed the eyes of their coach, Mark Pavlik, and saw him give instructions to one of their outside attackers (Gutor) and to the team's setter (Dan O'Dell). Dave then knew that Coach Furnish's instructions to watch for a combination play were on the nose, and he immediately communicated with our other two front-row players, middle Zoran Grabovac and outside Evan Berg, that Penn State was going to run a combination play in the middle of the court. As the play developed, Penn State's Gutor ran to the middle of the court to attack a 2 ball inside of their middle, who was hitting a 31. Dave fronted Penn State's middle attacker, but, seeing the set go to Gutor, he joined with Grabovac and Berg to triple-block Gutor for set and match point.

This experience illustrates how players and staff can attend to details and use the information they gain to be successful. In an environment where many teams become passive, we stayed aggressive and thus earned a significant victory in our program's history. We went on an 11-match winning streak and climbed to 9th in the country. A month later, following a victory over Loyola, Ball State stood as the lone unbeaten team in the country.

—Joel Walton, Head Men's Coach, Ball State University

---

running a 4-31-5, and the 5 to Pat is the primary." By identifying the person to go to, the coach takes the pressure off the setter to make the decision. It also gives the hitter (in this case, Pat) more confidence because the coach believes he or she can put the ball away. This is a great way to get players to be more aggressive coming out of a time-out.

Occasionally, it's important to change the place where you meet or the energy you give the players. Far too often, it's only the coaches spewing their opinions to the team as the players are asked just to listen. Every once in a while, the players should be asked what they think ought to be done; better yet, the coach can step aside and let players do all of the talking. Once they are given the chance, leaders will step forward and take ownership of the situation. They will realize that they are the ones who ultimately determine the outcome of the match, and they will likely rally together and fight harder than ever.

## Dealing With Officials and Fans

Officials are meant to help a match run smoothly, and if they are doing a good job, they should hardly be noticed. However, officials are human beings, and they don't always see things the way the coaches do. It's important for coaches to know how to work with officials—and not just always work them over. Constantly complaining about calls can also distract your own team, and eventually your players will begin to whine every time the official makes a call that doesn't go their way. Coaches need to learn to pick their battles so that the team can eventually benefit from their efforts. All coaches should read the rulebooks so they can argue points effectively. If an official isn't doing a good job, or doesn't know the rules well, the coach should stand up for the team. I've watched high school matches where officials didn't really know that a back-row setter can't attack the ball (dump) when it's above the plane of the net. Worse than that, I've seen coaches just sit there after a missed back-row attack and not say anything. That's a point that they lost for their team because they didn't stand up and make the officials do their job. To coach matches effectively, everyone on the staff should know the rulebook inside and out; doing so might help the team gain a point or two over the course of each match, and we all know that can make the difference between winning and losing. A coach can't suit up and play, but he or she can certainly get points for the team by knowing the rules.

Anytime you play a match, you're up against an opposing team that wants to stress your team out and defeat you. On top of that, teams have to deal with distractions coming from fans in the stands and still find a way to win. When your team is on the road, of course, you will face a major distraction in the form of the opposing fans. They love to say and do things to get in your players' heads in the hope of throwing them off their game. A good home-court advantage not only throws off the visiting team but also gives the home team more energy when it's needed. As a coach, it's important to teach your players how to deal with fans and still play well. One of the best methods is to make sure the players enjoy the environment and even find a way to laugh with the fans doing the harassing. It'll keep your players more relaxed and able to stay focused. A great goal for the team is to quiet the opposing crowd by making great plays and staying on top in the points column. Your players may also face another distraction from the bleachers in the form of their own parents. They mean well, but the really boisterous ones can draw the attention of their own daughter or son to the point that the player's game goes downhill. Coaches need to watch for this and address it with the parents if it's hurting the play of the team. The first step would be to have the player talk to his or her parents, but if it continues, the coach will have to take care of it. If this type of distraction is allowed to continue, it can send some players into a downward spiral from which they may not recover.

# Coaching After the Match

What coaches say after a match is just as critical as what they say before or during. Most people tend to be positive after a win and negative after a loss. If a coach does talk to the team after a match, he or she should try to pull as many positives from the experience as possible. Teams can learn from winning, but they can learn even more from a loss. Losing merely means that the opponent exposed your weaknesses. If a coach can pinpoint those areas, then they should be the points of emphasis for the following week's practice. If only negatives are discussed, players will begin to focus on them and can easily begin to lose confidence; then, over the course of the season, they will fall back into their losing ways very easily.

Some coaches meet with the team immediately after every match to focus on the goals they met and the goals they are still striving for. If a coach meets with the team only after losses, he or she must be careful not to bring the players down further than they already are. Everyone is emotional after a loss, and calling specific players out runs the risk of making them feel blamed. Teams should be taught ahead of time to keep the emotions out of the equation as much as possible. A certain amount of critiquing must be done in order to make corrections and improve, and players have to understand that coaches are evaluating the performance, not the performer.

On away trips, we may meet briefly and then allow players to visit with family members or fans who have traveled to see them. At home, we rarely leave the court and meet. I'd rather the players spend time meeting the young fans and families who have come to see them. Doing this can really help improve match attendance, because it helps fans feel a real connection to the players. Making sure the team is accessible makes more people want to come back and get to know them. This has worked well for my programs, and we've seen fan support grow every year. Fans want to get to know the team, whether it's a college or a high school program, and administrators will support volleyball programs that show they can win and show they can build a good, solid fan base. Volleyball is still growing as a sport because coaches are learning how to coach matches effectively. The best coaches have learned that coaching teams to victory is important but creating a strong fan base is the key to truly having a successful program.

There are occasions, though, that warrant holding a team meeting right after the match. Sometimes there is no better time than the present to address major issues that are blocking the progress of the team. If goals were set for the match, then reviewing which goals were met can keep the players striving for more. Coaches must learn, however, when the time is right for these meetings, because doing them constantly will wear the team down. I'm more of a results-oriented coach. I've seen teams win a match despite losing almost all the statistical categories. Most everything can be handled at the next practice when everyone has had a chance to cool off so they can think straight.

## Wrap Up

When a match concludes, players and coaches look back at it to see what they can take from the experience. When a book ends, you always feel a sense of accomplishment, and your mind reviews what you just absorbed. I hope that you'll feel that the time you took to read this book was well spent and that you can use some of the information or ideas for your program. Bringing something new to your team can take your players to higher levels and raise their passion for the game. Best of luck as you create an exciting vision for your team. *See you in the gym!*

# Index

*Note:* The italicized *f* following page numbers refers to figures.

# About the Author

Pete Waite has led his Wisconsin Badgers to a record of 228-67 (.773). Qualifying for the NCAA championship tournament in each of Waite's nine seasons, Wisconsin was national runner-up in 2000; finished in the top eight in 2004 and 2005; advanced to the Sweet 16 in 2001 and 2006; and saw second-round action in 1999, 2002, 2003, and 2007. In the Big Ten, the Badgers won league titles in 2000 and 2001 and were runners-up in 1999, 2002, 2005, and 2007.

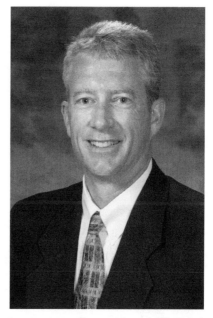

At 494-169 (.745) in 20 years overall, including 11 years at Northern Illinois, Waite ranks 13th among active Division I head coaches in winning percentage. He has been conference coach of the year seven times in four different conferences, winning 10 conference championships. Statistically, Waite's teams consistently rank high nationally in the major categories (hitting percentage, assists, kills, and blocks), indicating not only a skilled team but also an aggressive style of play.

Pete lives in Madison, Wisconsin.